BEING INDIAN

Inside the Real India

PAVAN K. VARMA

For Carol –
with all good wishes

14/3/05

WILLIAM HEINEMANN : LONDON

Published in the United Kingdom in 2005 by William Heinemann

1 3 5 7 9 10 8 6 4 2

First published in India by Viking, a division of The Penguin Group (India)

William Heinemann
The Random House Group Limited
20 Vauxhall Bridge Road, London, SW1V 2SA

Random House Australia (Pty) Limited
20 Alfred Street, Milsons Point, Sydney
New South Wales 2061, Australia

Random House New Zealand Limited
18 Poland Road, Glenfield
Auckland 10, New Zealand

Random House (Pty) Limited
Endulini, 5a Jubilee Road, Parktown 2193, South Africa

The Random House Group Limited Reg. No. 954009

www.randomhouse.co.uk

A CIP catalogue record for this book
is available from the British Library

Papers used by Random House
are natural, recyclable products made from wood grown in
sustainable forests. The manufacturing processes conform to
the environmental regulations of the country of origin

ISBN 0 434 01391 9

Typeset by SX Composing DTP, Rayleigh, Essex
Printed and bound in Great Britain by
Mackays of Chatham plc, Chatham, Kent

BEING INDIAN

A member of the Indian Foreign Service, Pavan K. Varma has served in Moscow, in New York at the Indian Mission to the UN, and as High Commissioner in Cyprus. He has been Press Secretary to the President of India, official spokesman for the Foreign Office, and is currently director of the Nehru Centre in London. His other books include translations of Hindi poetry, a study of Krishna, and the widely acclaimed *The Great Indian Middle Class*.

'Pavan Varma is one of India's most admired and widely-read writers of non-fiction, and in *Being Indian* he has excelled himself. The book is a brilliant exercise in mythocide. Witty, perceptive, clear-sighted and highly literate, Varma shows how India's self-image has been distorted by simplistic myth-making, and sets out to find instead what it really means to be Indian at the beginning of a new century which is likely to see India grow into a major world power. Varma asks all the right questions and *Being Indian* contains striking insights on almost every page. It should be essential reading for all Indophiles.'   William Dalrymple

'[Varma is] one of the country's most perceptive writers.' *Guardian*

'Varma uses a clever mix of history, religion and personal examples to give his book depth and clarity. India shining could well end up as India whining, but Varma gives enough reason to believe in the ascendancy of the former.'   *India Today*

Also by Pavan K. Varma

The Book of Krishna
Ghalib: The Man, The Times
Yudishtar and Draupadi: A Tale Of Love, Passions and the Riddles of Existence
Krishna: The Playful Divine
The Great Indian Middle Class

With Renuka Khandekar

Maximize your Life

Mushquilen mujh par padin itni
Ke aasaan ho gayeen

So many hardships came my way
That they were all resolved

Mirza Ghalib

Contents

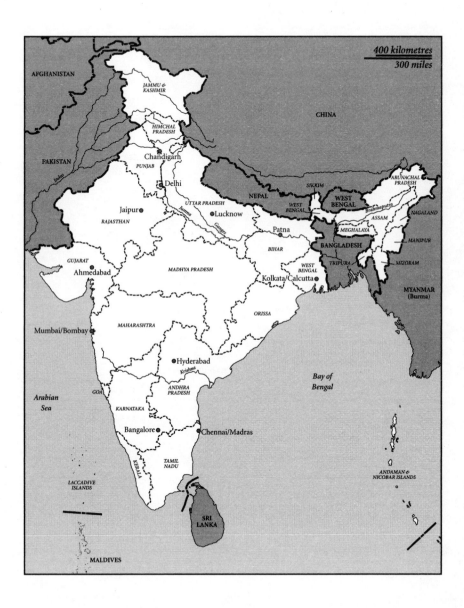

Preface

Haridwar, where the Ganga descends from the Himalayas and enters the plains on its long journey to the sea, is a holy city for Hindus. Thousands of pilgrims visit it everyday. Amidst the hustle and bustle of piety and prayer, a few men can be seen standing even in winter on bare feet in the shallows of the icy river. They have a transparent glass pane in their hands, and spend the day looking through it at the fast-flowing waters. Their unblinking eyes speak of a concentration perhaps greater than that of the throngs of devotees nearby. But their purpose is different: not prayer, not moksha, not salvation for a departed soul. Their attention is focused on the coins on the river bed, which they trace and scoop out expertly with their feet.

India is a difficult country to characterize, and Indians not easy to define, especially today when they are in transition, emerging from the shadows of history into the glare of a globalizing world. This book is an attempt to try and understand who we really are, in the context of the past, and the framework of the future. The task is fraught with dangers. India is too big and too diverse to allow for convenient cover-all labels. To every generalization there is a notable exception. For every similarity there is a significant difference. I would like, therefore, to apologize in advance for anything in this book which hurts the sentiments of some, or appears to be contrary to their perception about themselves. My only consideration has been to paint as truthful a portrait as possible, but I accept that truth is not universal and could have notable exceptions. I must mention too that I have on occasion used the word Hindu and India interchangeably. This is not motivated by any chauvinism, but only because such a large majority of Indians are Hindus. In any case, there are traits which are decidedly Indian, and are applicable to all Indians, irrespective of their religious beliefs.

India appears to be on the threshold of take-off today, but the reasons for this have to go beyond the euphoria of the current 'feel good' wave. In analysing a people who have been in the crucible of history for millennia, no picture can be starkly black or white. Not everything can be right and not everything wrong. The challenge is to draw a balance sheet calculated on the foundational strengths of a people, and to essay the argument that in spite of the obvious weaknesses, the strengths will prevail. Culture, history, and the structure of society play a vital role in this calculation. So does the innate resilience of a people, and their aspirations and ambitions. In our case we must also take into account our inexplicable talent to muddle through, the ability to convert weakness to strength, and, of course, luck.

This book has been researched for several years, but I wrote it mostly when in Cyprus on diplomatic assignment. The beautiful island provided both the setting and the distance to write on a subject so close to my heart. I must express my deep gratitude to David Davidar, now with Penguin Canada, for having first suggested the idea of this book. I am greatly indebted to my agents Malcolm Imrie and Martina Dervis who kept faith in this book, and to Ravi Mirchandani, my editor, the best any author could hope to have. A word of thanks is due too to Cassie Chadderton at Random House. I am also very grateful to William Dalrymple for his friendship and support, and to Bhiku Parekh, Usha Parasher, Rohit Khattar and Salman Mahdi, for theirs. My family is practised now in bearing up stoically with my writing preoccupations. My late mother, with her deep knowledge of Indian culture, was a very willing point of reference. My son Vedanta, and my daughters Manvi and Batasha, often doubled as research assistants, as did their friends, of whom I cannot but mention Rishabh Patel. I am, as always, especially grateful to my wife Renuka for her patience and emotional support, and her views on so many aspects of this book.

Chapter One

INTRODUCTION
Image versus Reality

The purpose of this book is to attempt a new and dramatically different inquiry into what it is to be an Indian. Such an inquiry is especially relevant today, not only for India, but also to the world as a whole. In the twenty-first century every sixth human being will be an Indian. India is likely to emerge as the second largest consumer market in the world, with a buying middle class numbering over half a billion. The Indian economy is already the fourth largest in terms of purchasing power parity. It is in the top ten in overall gross national product. The world's largest democracy is a nuclear power, convinced of its right to become one of the permanent members of the UN Security Council.

Moreover, significant changes are sweeping across the sub-continent. With more degree holders than the entire population of France, India is finding new recognition in the field of information technology. Software exports are expected to top US $50 billion in a few years. The Indian diaspora is, after China's, the second largest in the world. Indians have emerged as the richest immigrant community in the USA, and are a growing and increasingly affluent presence in many other countries, including the UK and the Gulf states. Whether the world wants to or not, it will be difficult not to interact in many more ways with Indians in the new millennium. It is important, therefore, to understand, with much greater clarity and honesty than before, what it is to be an Indian.

Such inquiries in the past have been greatly handicapped by two factors. The first is the stereotypes through which foreigners see India. The second is the self-image that Indians seek to project about themselves. Foreigners usually gape or gulp when in India. The sheer variety of the auditory and visual experience overwhelms them. Many examples can be given of their reaction, but one will suffice to illustrate its slightly hysterical tone. Mark Twain wrote this after his visit to India at the end of the nineteenth century: 'This is indeed India! The land of dreams and romance, of fabulous wealth and fabulous poverty—of genii and giants and Alladin lamps, of tigers and elephants—the country of a hundred nations and a hundred tongues, of a thousand religions and two million gods, cradle of the human race, birthplace of human speech, mother of history, grand-mother of legend, great grandmother of tradition . . .'[1]

During the colonial period perceptions were distorted by what Edward Said has referred to as the 'Orientalism' of the West. The Orient was the unfamiliar 'other', its people a strange 'them' set against the known 'us'. For most Englishmen, India provoked either broad-brush euphoria or condemnation. The country was seen as irrevocably fragmented or spiritually transcendent, hugely ungovern-able or simplistically self-reliant, venal beyond redemption or bliss-fully unmaterialistic, impossibly opaque or wonderfully ancient and revealing. In tandem, Indians were incorrigibly lazy or surprisingly diligent, horribly superstitious or remarkably evolved, disgustingly servile or always rebellious, amazingly talented or transparently imitative, greatly cultured or despairingly poor and, basically, just far too many. British scholarship was good on specifics, such as the description of flora and fauna, and the writing of gazetteers. But specifics were often effortlessly stretched into less well-researched generalities. The German Sanskritist F. Max Müller, who spent a lifetime studying Hindu philosophy, argued with great intensity that Indians were also very honest.[2]

Mahatma Gandhi's leadership of the freedom struggle, his personal commitment to communal harmony, and his choice of *ahimsa* or non-violence as the strategy to defeat the British, created a new image of Indians as a tolerant and non-violent people. The long innings of Jawaharlal Nehru as the first Prime Minister of India conjured up another vision of millions of democratic Indians struggling to make the transition from tradition to modernity. Yet the visible diversity of the land, and the complexity of its cultural traditions, continued to bedevil accurate or deeper understanding. The noted economist John Kenneth Galbraith, who lived in India and was a friend of Nehru's, once famously described India as a 'functioning anarchy'. Decades later he was to admit that he had said it only to 'attract attention'.[3]

The economic reforms of 1991 and the testing of a nuclear weapon in 1998 gave a little more substance to the Indian dot on the radar screens of geopolitical strategists and economic analysts, especially in the West. The *Economist* invoked the image of an awakened elephant, finally lumbering to its tryst with the marketplace. Stephen P. Cohen wrote a well-documented work wondering whether India would one day emerge as a major power or remain forever 'arriving'. But such existential doubts are hardly preponderant in the minds of less 'scholarly' visitors who, alas, do not come in the numbers the Indian tourist department would like them to. Those who do, mostly come to discover an ancient culture and find it in the extraordinary monuments that are strewn carelessly across the land. They have read about spiritual India, and see it in the soaring pinnacles of the temples of South India and in the devotees taking a dip in the Ganga in Varanasi. The diversity of food and dress devours the reels in their cameras. They buy handicrafts at cheap prices as evidence of the incredible exotica they have been promised. They find modern India in the English-speaking Indian and the high-rise buildings in the metropolises. The tout who cheats them is proof of the essential corruption of underdeveloped economies. The filth and poverty is nauseating but is hazily attributed to the timeless other-worldliness of spiritual India. Some time is spent in arguing how a nation which professes to be non-violent can explode a nuclear bomb. But soon the visit is over. The visitors return home, wondering how such a vast country has held together, and how its poor and ill-clad hordes have succeeded for so long in remaining a democracy.

None of these impressions is entirely off the mark. The Indian reality is transparent and opaque simultaneously. What is visible is as much a part of the truth as what remains unseen. Foreigners see what is overt, and conflate it with their preconceived notions of 'the great Indian civilization'. In the process many assumptions evade critical scrutiny, and a great many inferences are either incorrect or only partially true. But foreigners can be forgiven their errors. Not so the Indians. Over the years the Indian leadership, and the educated Indian, have deliberately projected and embellished an image about Indians that they know to be untrue, and have wilfully encouraged the well-meaning but credulous foreign observer (and even more the foreign scholar) to accept it. What is worse, they have fallen in love with this image, and can no longer accept that it is untrue.

The image has been created by a quantum leap of logic, an ideological sleight of hand that derives an untenable *ought* from an undeniable *is*. India has been a parliamentary democracy since Independence in 1947; therefore, Indians are undeniably democratic by temperament. Several important religions were born and flourish in India; therefore, Indians are essentially spiritual in their outlook. People of different faiths have found a home in India; therefore, Indians are basically tolerant by nature. Mahatma Gandhi defeated the British by relying on *ahimsa*; therefore, Indians are peaceful and non-violent in temperament. Hindu philosophy considers the real world as transient and ephemeral; therefore, Hindus are 'other-worldly' and un- materialistic in their thinking. India has nurtured a great deal of diversity; therefore, Indians are of an eclectic and catholic disposition.

India is much too important today, and its potential far too significant in the coming decades, to be held hostage to this simplistic myth-making. There was reason, perhaps, in 1947 to encourage such myths. Serious doubts about the survivability of the newly-independent nation hung ominously on the horizon like August monsoon clouds. The polity was fragile. Partition had severely bruised the hope of communal harmony. The unity of the country could not be taken for granted. In such situations, all nations indulge in myth-making to bind their people together, and India's need was, if anything, greater than most. But what was expedient for a fledgling polity soon became the conscious—and enduring—deceit of an entire nation. Since myths often contain a kernel of truth; it took some time for even the astute observer to notice the disjoint between the embroidery and the fabric. But the issue is far more serious than merely criticizing the pretensions of professional image-makers. The imperative today is to understand that this deliberate distortion has been—and is—detrimental to India's long-term interests in at least two very important ways: one, the choice of appropriate policies and programmes to tap the real genius and strengths of the Indian people, especially in view of the new challenges ahead; and, two, the projection of a more accurate appraisal of India, and the Indian people, for a global community poised to become more involved with both.

To effectively demolish the untruths of the past requires courage, because it is tantamount to questioning the dogmas of the modern state. Too much, however, is at stake for the task to be postponed, or pursued in a perfunctory or less than rigorous manner. The situation demands an intellectual solvent that cuts through the woolly-headed posturing of our make-believe world, and compels us to ask some foundational questions. Why was the Indian elite, the end product of 5,000 years of civilizational continuity, colonized so easily by the British, to become the model children of Macaulay? Was it our non-violent nature that allowed invaders to conquer us repeatedly, or was it our willingness to accept, and even collude with, the more powerful? Why do Indians prostrate themselves so abjectly before the rich and the mighty, and why are they so indifferent to the suffering of the weak and the poor?

In spite of the glaring inequities of its socio-economic system, India has not had a violent revolution either in the lead up to Independence or later. Is this also evidence of our intrinsically non-violent nature, or does the answer lie elsewhere? Why has a nation, which had Mahatma Gandhi as its towering role model of rectitude, become so unbelievably corrupt so quickly? Do we really devalue the end in favour of the right means, or are we only concerned with the end result, whatever the means employed?

The Hindus practised untouchability against the largest numbers of their own faith, and were (and are) practitioners, as part of the caste system, of one of the world's most rigid systems of exclusion. Do they then really have a claim to be called tolerant? If not, why has secularism survived in India, and why can we expect it to strengthen in the years ahead? Can a people who are so cannily attuned to the validity of hierarchy and 'status', and the ordained inegalitarian order of things, be considered democratic by temperament? If not, why has parliamentary democracy survived, and even flourished, in India? Can a people, whose educated members may beat a domestic servant to near death, blind undertrials to extract a confession, or burn wives for larger dowry, be considered essentially non-violent in their make-up? If not, then why did Gandhi's strategy of *ahimsa* succeed, and why did the revolutionary fervour of such independence leaders as Subhash Chandra Bose or Bhagat Singh find so few followers?

The first requirement of any attempt at reappraisal is honesty. A nation which calls a trader 'mahajan' or great soul, which pervasively worships Lakshmi, the goddess of wealth, and exalts the pursuit of material well-being, *artha*, as a principal goal of life, is also widely regarded as spiritual and 'other-worldly'. In what manner, then, are we spiritual, and what role does this much vaunted spirituality play in our lives? A country with so much diversity—ethnic, cultural and linguistic—has nevertheless managed to remain united. Is this due to the oneness of an Indian 'soul' or 'spirit', or is the growing sense of pan-Indianness the result of something less exalted, and more congruent with our real selves?

These questions need to be answered calmly. They have not been posed to provoke criticism or invite appreciation. They are value-neutral, meant only to compel reappraisal. The answers that we propose constitute a significant premise of this book, and can be beneficially summed up here. Indians are extraordinarily sensitive to the calculus of power. They consider the pursuit of power a legitimate end in itself, and display great astuteness in adjusting to, and discovering, the focus of power. They respect the powerful, and will happily cooperate or collude with them for personal gain. In the game of power they take to factionalism and intrigue like a fish takes to water. Those who renounce the lure of power are worshipped, not because their example is capable of emulation, but in sheer awe at their ability to transcend the irresistible.

In spite of recent changes, which we shall discuss later, Indians are exceptionally hierarchical in outlook, bending more than might be thought to be required before those who are perceived to be 'superior', and dismissive or contemptuous of those accepted as 'inferior'. Understandably, notions of self-esteem and personal image, in conformity with perceived 'status', are of great consequence to them. They are not democratic by instinct or temperament. Democracy has survived and flourished in India because it was very quickly seen to be one of the most effective systems for upward mobility, and for the acquisition of personal power and wealth.

Indians have never been, and will never be, 'other-worldly'. They hanker for the material goods that this world has to offer, and look up to the wealthy. They pursue profit more tenaciously than most. They make shrewd traders and resourceful, even ingenious, entrepreneurs. Their feet are firmly on the ground, and their eyes fixed on the balance sheet. As in the case of temporal power, they are concerned more with the successful result, and less with the means. Their spiritualism, although lofty in its metaphysics, is in religious practice mostly a means to harness divine support for power and pelf. It does help, however, to weather periods of adversity, and thus reinforces resilience. Most Indians are 'other-worldly' only in their indifference to anything in the external milieu that is not of *direct* benefit to their immediate and personal world.

This complete self-absorption is truly in evidence in their remarkable tolerance of inequity, filth and human suffering. They are a pragmatic people, naturally amoral in their outlook. There is no notion of ultimate sin in Hinduism. Any action is justified in certain contexts, and gods are routinely bribed. Corruption has grown endemically because it is not really considered wrong, so long as it yields the desired result. If discovered, it provokes great moral outrage, in inverse proportion to the degree to which it is accepted. The concept of morality, and of high-minded principle, is dear to Indians as a theoretical construct, but largely ignored in real life as impractical.

'Modernity', in the Nehruvian or Western sense of being able to react to issues 'rationally', without prejudice or subjectivity, is a professed goal for many educated Indians, but in reality only a garb to hide the continued hold of tradition; and modernity and tradition continue to coexist within them in ways which are truly unique. Finally, Hindus are not so much non-violent as they are practical in understanding the limits of violence. They are willing to eschew violence for the more important goal of ensuring survival. They are hesitant to be violent against a superior force, preferring coexistence to suicidal annihilation. Their historical 'tolerance' of other religions, especially those backed by superior military strength, is understandable in this context. Incidents of communal violence do occur in India, but contrary to what is often projected, they are not the norm. In general, Indians are opposed to violence if it creates a degree of instability or disorder that threatens the social system. However, in a controlled milieu, such as the enforcement of caste hierarchy or purity, when violence has social sanction or is backed by numerical strength, they can be as violent as any other race.

The above is a description of some dominant traits, not a comprehensive enumeration. Every rule has exceptions. The human personality allows for infinite nuances, and character can always have specific variations. Nor is this portrayal intended to be a critique. Undoubtedly, it is at variance with our conventional self-image. But nations are not good or bad, or strong or weak, in accordance with some absolute moral yardstick. A depiction is not uncharitable merely because it does not conform to a preconceived notion of what we think we are, or would *like* to be. On the contrary, the real strength and resilience of a nation is often due to precisely those traits that are a derogation from the romanticized perception it has of itself. Equally, no one trait can be seen in isolation. The rampant corruption in India would appear to be negative in an absolute sense. But perhaps if Indians did not set so much store by material wealth, they would not be such resourceful entrepreneurs; if they were less pragmatic and more 'other-worldly', and were less concerned with success at any cost, they would also be less corrupt.

The essential truth is that the personality of a people is complex and interconnected. It cannot be dissected in preferred segments. In fact, this book will make the argument that some so-called 'uncomplimentary' Indian attributes may have helped India in the past. For instance, if Indians actually thought parliamentary democracy to be a magic wand to create an egalitarian society (as some Anglicized members of the Constituent Assembly genuinely believed), they might have been disillusioned far too quickly, and could have followed much of the developing world in opting for more totalitarian systems. This unlikely political transplant from

Britain survived its fledgling probation precisely because most Indians perceived it to be, in practical terms, a welcome and effective means for personal aggrandizement—a fortuitous occurrence indeed, for over time the butterfly looks all set to escape its flawed chrysalis. The intrinsic attraction of a quick ticket to personal power gave an increasing number of influential Indians (and their camp followers) the incentive to participate in the democratic process. The inherent fear of uncontrolled instability prevented the established polity, for all its flaws, from being violently overthrown. The amoral respect for profit, and for the material rewards life can offer, kept a trading class solvent, and nurtured entrepreneurship, even in such alien and hostile locales as Ouagadougou, the capital of Burkina Faso in Africa, where the only department store is owned by an Indian who arrived penniless but a few years ago. The propensity to compromise and coexist when survival is at stake, rather than heroically fight and die to the last man, allowed Hindu culture and civilization to outlive (and even be enriched by) the relentless conquests of proselytizing invaders.

This book will also touch upon three new developments that are likely significantly to influence Indians in the coming years. The first is the emergence of a new pan-Indianness. The civilizational unity of India has been much written about, and not without reason. But such writings have been largely an attempt to identify continuities of culture in a people separated, at the micro level, by fairly impenetrable diversities. History, culture and tradition had forged an identity recognizable as Indian, with definitive elements of a common psyche, but the sum of this unity did not as yet have an all-Indian personality. An Indian in Varanasi and an Indian in Trichur may have read the same text in Sanskrit, or celebrated the same festivals, but they knew very little about each other, and shared very little in terms of a common exposure to the overarching Indian experience. This has changed gradually in the decades after 1947, and more dramatically in recent years.

A second development is the slow but perceptible erosion of social hierarchies, earlier considered sacrosanct. Indians continue to be very conscious of hierarchy, and the influence of caste loyalties is still pervasive, but the formerly quiescent downtrodden, at the lowest end of the social spectrum, are restive as never before. Their aspirations to have a bigger piece of the national pie can no longer be suppressed or camouflaged. Democratic politics may not have been intended by the elite to have such undesirable consequences, but incremental political empowerment and economic trickle-down has by now fuelled ambitions and aspirations in more Indians than in any period of their history. How will these newly empowered, upwardly mobile Indians transform India in the twenty-first century? What will be the energy unleashed when social certainties, centuries old, are interrogated in actual practice, and not only in the rhetoric of politicians? Will the structures of the past, and the attitudes they breed, be overturned by the iconoclastic fervour of the newly resurgent? Or, will they emulate their erstwhile 'oppressors', seeking merely a bigger piece of the pie, not a change of recipe?

A third factor is the emergence of India as a world power in information technology. It may sound paradoxical for a country with the largest number of illiterates in the world, but education has always been valued by the Indian elite, and in particular the Brahmins, as a means of perpetuating their supremacy. Not surprisingly, after Independence, the ruling class invested consistently in the creation of institutes of higher learning, even while paying lip service to the greater need of primary education. Over five decades, this duplicity had the predictable result of giving India one of the world's largest pools of technically proficient manpower, and some very good training institutes in engineering, medicine and computer sciences. The right educational degree, like a career in politics, is now recognized as a passport to fast-track upward mobility. The involvement of young Indians in the infotech revolution must be seen in this context. Indian software professionals are in demand globally. Software exports from India have come to be compared to what oil exports have meant to the Arab world. India is being labelled a call centre superpower. Over 40 per cent of the world's 500 largest corporations now do some of their back office processing in India. Will this rising curve last? Do Indians somehow have a natural talent in this field? How many of them are participating in, or benefitting from, this 'revolution'? Will the innovative example of the new Indian millionaires in Silicon Valley be replicated? Or will most Indians be willing to remain software coolies? Above all, how will this trend influence the image of Indians overseas? In Cyprus, for instance, maids and servants come from Sri Lanka and the Philippines; software experts come from India. Will Indians change in response to this global expectation? And in what ways will they still remain the same?

Societies change, but there are limits to change. Certain traits, which are the products of centuries of conditioning, do not easily change, and it is these that provide the distinctive cultural labels of a people. Others can be diluted or modified. Some new ones can, perhaps, be added, but they are mostly scaffolding on a largely unalterable edifice. It is this combination of (mostly) the old, and something of the new, that people carry as their cultural baggage in the journey towards the future.

For Francis Fukuyama, author of the best-selling *The End of History and the Last Man*, the future has already arrived with the end of the Cold War and the triumph of Western capitalism. But even if the universality of his assumption is accepted, history will continue to be made by how ancient cultures like India reach that destination. The manner and degree in which Indians differ from the Americans, or from the Japanese, the Chinese or the Germans, will be of critical importance in an increasingly interconnected world. Fukuyama himself concedes this in his later, and far more perceptive work, *Trust: The Social Virtues and the Creation of Prosperity*. The ability of nations to create social and economic prosperity will depend, he argues, on their culture. Culture is 'inherited ethical habit', a compound of images, habits, and social opinions that are arational, and 'incapable of being systematized into universal laws'.[4] The functioning of societies is conditioned by 'certain premodern cultural habits'. There can be no immutable economic law applicable uniformly to all peoples, because, as Fukuyama points out, economics itself is rooted in social life, and cannot be comprehended in isolation from the broader issue of how modern societies structure themselves.[5] On this premise, Fukuyama concluded that only societies with a high degree of social trust, which he defines as a community's mutually shared norms of what they hold to be honest and cooperative practices,[6] will be able to create the flexible, large-scale business organizations that are needed to compete in the new global economy.

Fukuyama observes American society, and the failure of Americans to perceive their own society accurately. He also offers observations on the societies of China, France, Italy, South Korea, Japan and Germany. He did not study India. Nor has Samuel P. Huntington in his much-debated *The Clash of Civilizations and the Remaking of World Order*. Like Fukuyama, Huntington argues that culture and cultural identity are crucial to most people's identities. In the post-Cold War world, he asserts, the most important distinctions among peoples are cultural, and not political, economic or ideological; and ancestry, religion, language, history, values, customs and institutions are the attributes by which people define themselves.[7] The differences in the political and economic development of civilizations are, Huntington suggests, ascribable to their cultures.[8] Attacking the 'universalist pretensions' of the West, he warns of an impending clash with other civilizations, most seriously with Islam and China, that could pose a grave threat to world peace.

Huntington's generalizations about peoples and civilizations are well researched, if occasionally just that. But what is of significance to us is his confession that discussions of his thesis '*exposed me to all the major civilizations except Hinduism*' (emphasis mine). Is there a reason why both Fukuyama and Huntington, in arguing theses that purport to encompass the globe, have omitted India from their research? Perhaps Indians are a sui generis people. They cannot be colour-coded for convenience into white, black or yellow. They do not belong to the Christian world. They cannot be included in the Islamic. Hindus, who constitute the overwhelming majority in India, live (in such large numbers) only in India and the Himalayan kingdom of Nepal. They cannot be so easily fitted into a mould. They are not post-communist, nor are they pre-democratic. They are not theocrats, nor are they irreligious. They are too many to be ignored, but somehow too *different* to be included in convenient generalizations. Moreover, for all their complexity, they are not entirely unfamiliar. They practise parliamentary democracy, and their elites can often speak very good English.

But as we have argued in the very beginning, it may no longer be in anybody's interest to ignore or blur over what Indians are really about, and where they are likely to take India in the twenty-first century. In *The Protestant Ethic and the Spirit of Capitalism*, Max Weber linked the growth of capitalism in Western Europe to the frugality, thrift and materialism of the early Puritans. Do Indians too have a USP, and if so, what is it? Fukuyama's great virtue of social trust may be deficient in Indian society, but does that mean Indians will never be able to create a viable capitalist future for themselves? Will their natural amorality consign their society to terminal corruption, or will their materialistic pragmatism ensure sustainable economic growth in spite of this vice? Will their propensity to focus on ends (giving little thought to means) mire them in unproductive shortcuts, or will this very 'weakness' strengthen, too, the ability to win, whatever the hurdles?

Will their excessive love for the perks of power fatally debase their political institutions or will this susceptibility foster also the accommodation and restraint necessary for the polity to survive? Will they regress towards sectarian extremism, or will common sense and their aversion to disorder reinforce the practicality of co-existence? Will some of their leaders contrive to threaten the secular fabric of the country, or will they realize that successful politics in India has no option but to transcend religious lines? Will regional sensitivities increase, resulting in the balkanization of India, or will the growing sense of pan-Indianness prevail? Will the desire of the Indian elite to see their country as a global power fan military adventurism, or will the inherent Indian traits of compromise and self-preservation make for a responsible nuclear nation? Finally, will recent successes in information technology enduringly transform the self-image of Indians, or will the 'dream' last only until the next global recession?

These are also some of the questions this book will seek to answer. Not all the answers can be categorical, or unquestionable. But they will perhaps show pointers to the likely destiny of India, *on the basis of who Indians really are*. Six years before the end of the last millennium, Henry Kissinger predicted that the twenty-first century will be dominated by at least six major powers—the United States, Europe, Russia, Japan, China *'and probably India'*.[9] (emphasis mine) Will this note of uncertainty always define the future of India? Perhaps not, but quite clearly any serious assessment of her future needs to go beyond a mechanical tally of visible assets and obvious liabilities, to an analysis of the Indian *personality* and the culture that created it.

Only such an approach can give outsiders appropriate insights into the strengths and weaknesses of India, and help them interact with Indians in more effective ways. Most importantly, it could help the Indian leadership to formulate policies that are congruent with the Indian psyche. Policies based on false assumptions about the character and traits of a people are likely to be subverted in practice, and fail to achieve desired national goals. A basic mistake by early policy makers in India was to assume an underlying idealism in the people, a commitment to some larger 'public good'. Lawmakers sought to construct, and act upon, a transcendent set of desired goals, without focusing on the intricate web of narrow *personal* interests that actually motivate Indian society. The result is one of the world's largest corpuses of high-minded laws, and one of its poorest records of implementation. A more honest self-estimation would have directed policy making to laws that rewarded ingenuity rather than equity, resourcefulness rather than compassion, profit rather than welfare, and the private rather than the public sector. For instance, it is only now being somewhat understood that measures for distributive justice in India tend to be successfully defeated by the haves and wastefully underutilized by the have-nots. Given the nature of Indians, only an increase in the size of the pie can genuinely hope to benefit the millions who are poor.

Two other Indian traits will also be highlighted in the course of this book. The first is the often amazing ability of Indians to retain hope. A person living in the most appalling slum in Mumbai will still nurture the hope that one day he will make it big, or at least bigger, and that his children will lead a better life. The trickle-down from the top to the bottom has certainly been inadequate, but it has probably been just enough to keep alive the intrinsic Indian propensity for not losing hope. The second is the resilience that comes from being continuously exposed to adversity. Even a middle class Indian struggles for such basics as electricity, clean water, transport and medical care. The very poor, of course, survive in the absence of all of these. This relentless grappling with adversity has bred by now an inventiveness and *a will to survive* that can only be described as remarkable.

Finally, a word about methodology. A portrait of a people cannot be drawn only through theoretical paradigms. Individuals are complex, and cultures far too deep, to submit to dry hypotheses without illuminating surmise by example, inference by anecdote, and deduction by personal experience. Economists can believe in universal constructs applicable to all societies. But those who study people in the context of their unique cultural habitats must rely on what has been called 'thick description'[10], which fleshes out the manner in which people actually react and respond, and behave and conduct themselves in everyday life. This book, therefore, is not intended to read like an academic discourse, nor does it pretend to be one. It will tell a story, recall an incident, describe an event and cite a fact from the everyday lives of Indians, in order to portray the Indian for what he or she is. Any failings in terms of 'scholarly' technique will, it is hoped, be compensated for by greater readability for the average reader.

Chapter Two

POWER
The Unexpected Triumph of Democracy

The departure zone of the Indira Gandhi International Airport in New Delhi is crowded with the usual gaggle of friends and relatives milling around the entrance gate, which for security reasons only passengers may cross. It is a hot and steamy monsoon morning in the first year of the new millennium. Suddenly a convoy of cars comes screeching to a halt. The lead car is a white Ambassador, with a blue light on its roof. A policeman in the front seat, machine gun slung around his shoulder, leaps to open the back door. A young police officer steps out. Uniformed minions, walkie-talkies in hand, spring to clear the way. The official guarding the entrance falls back with a deferential salaam. Gun-toting escorts guide the officer to the VIP lounge.

Security is strict for the rest of the passengers: X-ray machines, manual check of hand baggage, checked-in baggage identified by its owners before boarding the plane. A smartly dressed middle-aged lady walks out of the terminal to identify her baggage. She has her handbag with her which, according to the rules, should have been left inside. A security official calls out: 'Madam, please leave your handbag inside.' She pays no attention, not even looking back to acknowledge the request. He raises his voice. No response. He runs towards her. Just as he reaches her, she turns around, and says in a voice like a whiplash: 'Don't you know I am a Member of Parliament?' The official crumples, retreating with mumbled apologies.

The junior police officer sipping tea in the VIP lounge genuinely believes that the manner of his entering the airport is legitimate, a visible perk of the power he wields. The MP is equally convinced that her status entitles her to be above the rules for ordinary mortals. Both are well-educated Indians, and could speak eloquently, if required, on the sacrosanct equality of all of India's citizens.

In the Indian tradition the powerful are not expected to be reticent or modest in the projection of their power. In the eighteenth century Lord Wellesley told the East India Company in London that to rule the 'natives' it was essential to build palaces to *awe* them into submission. The Company was persuaded to accept his logic, and the massive Governor's Residence came into being in Calcutta. More than fifty years after the British left, this imposing palace fulfils more or less its original purpose. The Governor of West Bengal lives in isolated splendour in a sprawling estate, maintained by 168 underlings.

The departure of the British effected a transfer of power. A transfer of the *paraphernalia* of power accompanied the transfer of power. This was not an uncommon occurrence. Colonized elites all over the world emulate the pomp and ceremony of their oppressors, once rid of them. But the Indian elite could have been different. The man who inspired their struggle for independence, and whom they chose to call the Father of the Nation, shunned the trappings of power. He did not live in government palaces. He travelled in the lowest class in trains. He celebrated his austerity, wearing little more than a loincloth. He wanted the massive Viceregal Palace in New Delhi to be converted into a hospital. He exhorted the members of the new Indian government to live, and rule, with humility. Undoubtedly, Gandhi's example was very difficult to follow. Even those who believed in him could hardly be expected to be as austere, or as utopian, or as self-denying as he. But, considering the massive following he commanded, why were his values betrayed so easily and almost immediately?

As an independent nation India chose to be a democracy, and has remained one, almost without interruption. Jawaharlal Nehru, India's first Prime Minister, genuinely believed in the egalitarian goals of a republic. The first President, Dr Rajendra Prasad, was a committed and prominent devotee of Gandhi. Yet, soon after the Union Jack went down and the Indian tricolour first fluttered proudly in the breeze in August 1947, Nehru moved into Flagstaff

House, the palatial residence of the British Commander-in-Chief. The residence of the Viceroy, arguably the world's largest palace, became the home of President Prasad.

Given their ideological beliefs, and the tutelage of Gandhi, it is not unlikely that the two leaders moved into their new homes with a slight twinge of guilt. But they were probably aware that the average Indian would have been disappointed, perplexed and even dis-approving, if they had renounced the opportunity to *project* power. Power, in the Indian way of thinking, is a legitimate pursuit, and the powerful are entitled to display their success. Those who wield power are nothing if they cannot convey to others the visible symbols of their acquisition. Ideologies take root in the psyche of a people refracted through the prism of their own traditions and inherited ways of life. The twentieth century spawned the myth of universal constructs, applicable to all people, irrespective of cultural and historical differences. The clarion call of Rousseau in the eighteenth century for the creation of an equal society was assumed to be powerful enough to overwhelm the tonal variations of people every-where. Certain ideals were taken as given, and certain institutions considered sacrosanct. Colonized societies were particularly vulner-able to swallowing the idealized prescriptions given to them 'for their own good' by their former rulers. But, as the last several decades have shown, the efficacy of the prescriptions have been greatly dependent on the intrinsic metabolism of the patient. Broad-spectrum anti-biotics may work in the field of medicine, but they do not work in societies, especially those with traditions of resistance and immunity going back centuries.

The manner in which political theory congeals into practice is conditioned by individual variations in tradition and historical experience. This is evident even in those societies that have been democracies for the longest period of time. For instance, the pursuit of an egalitarian order led to the abolition of monarchy in France. It did not do so in Britain. Both are democracies, committed to equal opportunity, but Britain has preserved a royal family based on the accident of birth, and preserves many of the inherited privileges of a feudal elite. Again, democracy is a vibrant part of the American way of life, but its continuous practice for over 200 years has not yet enabled a woman to become President, or for anyone not a white Anglo-Saxon Protestant (with the exception of John F. Kennedy) to reach the highest rung of the political ladder. Nations respond to accepted goals in different ways, and the manner in which they do so provides clues to the nature of their societies. Distortions occur when an idea is exalted as a universal goal, without an appropriate appreciation of the milieu in which it is to grow and mature.

The Indian response to the ideal of an equal society must, therefore, be seen in the specific and unique context of its own culture and tradition. If Jawaharlal Nehru and Rajendra Prasad were uncomfortable about deviating from the spartan austerity of Gandhi, they would be appalled today to see the effortless progression of what they began. In a provincial capital such as Lucknow in the northern state of Uttar Pradesh even a deputy director of a minor department flaunts an official car, with outlandish plaques in the front and at the back proclaiming his 'exalted' position in the bureaucratic hierarchy. The plaques are in bold red, the lettering in brass. This is not all. A red or blue light on the top and on the bonnet is a must. A siren to clear the way is not unusual. A minister's importance is judged not only by the patronage he distributes but also by the size of his office and residence, the number of sub-ordinates he controls, the quality of his car (white Ambassador, several antennae, red light, spotless white upholstery) and the number of security personnel detailed to protect him. A senior bureaucrat will be offended if the telephones on his desk are reduced in number, or the lettering announcing his designation not large enough. The minion, his superior, and the minister know that these accessories will determine their importance in the eyes of others.

Such behaviour is probably more in evidence within the bureaucracy and government, but the obsession with hierarchy, and the symbols that project it, is not a monopoly of officialdom. The caste system began several thousand years ago as a functional categorization, but over the years it degenerated to become one of the most inflexible and institutionalized tyrannies of any society. Today it is officially frowned upon, and democratic empowerment has, as we shall discuss later, loosened its asphyxiating stranglehold. *But the mentality of a stratified society remains very much in evidence in everyday life.* The structure of hierarchies may be changing, but 'for an Indian, superior and subordinate relationships have the character of eternal verity and moral imperative—(and the) automatic reverence for superiors is a nearly universal psycho-social fact.'[1] This acceptance of the hierarchy of power gives a particularly Indian colouring to the meaning and operation of modern concepts like democracy and equality.

To an Indian the projection of power and the recognition of status are intimately related. When a person's entire worth is dependent on the position he occupies on a hierarchical scale, the assertion of status (and its recognition by others) becomes of crucial importance. In order to preserve status one has to be seen to be above those below, and below those above. There can be no ambivalence in these equations. Under the caste system transgression was impermissible. Old rigidities are blurring today, but the preoccupation with the notion of hierarchy very much persists, and in some respects has become even more frenetic. In the past, status was prescriptive, a consequence of one's birth. Today it can be acquired by other means, including greater avenues of upward mobility. This has not made Indians more egalitarian in their outlook. On the contrary, the new uncertainties—and opportunities—have only heightened sensitivities about who stands where in the pecking order, and only accentuated the obsession with status and power. Even corruption is not necessarily about only material gain: 'In a society like ours, where the equal moral worth of individuals is rarely affirmed, one of the ways in which people affirm their own worth is by being able to exercise discretionary power over others. Corruption is as much about the allure of power as it is about money, and the intensity of competitive frenzy for power in this society is largely due to the fact that without power, your moral worth will not be affirmed. Corruption is a form of exercising that power.'[2]

Societies reveal how they actually think and behave in the smallest things. Behavioural patterns are best discovered not in the considered stance before an observer, but in the insignificant reflex preceding or following it. The behaviour and body language of an Indian in the presence of someone hierarchically superior is usually most revealing. A civil servant, say a diplomat or a senior administrator, well educated and otherwise quite urbane, will consider it blasphemy to call his minister by his first name; he will not even address him as 'Mr'; a minister will always be addressed as 'sir'; sometimes a sentence will both begin and end with 'sir'; if the minister is seen approaching, the underling will move to one side with alacrity; in conversation he will avoid direct eye contact; when the boss speaks he will keep his head deferentially bowed; he will rarely question or contradict him; he will always keep a certain physical distance, as if his 'junior' presence could be defiling; and if the boss cracks a joke he will laugh with exaggerated pleasure, as if it were the best joke he has ever heard.

The subordinate will expect comparable behaviour from his own subordinate. Some companies in the corporate sector, which encourage a more professional atmosphere, could witness a lesser display of deference. But even in the private sector such organizations are rare. 'The principle of a hierarchical ordering of social dependencies extends beyond its home base in the extended family to every other institution in Indian life, from the *jajmani* system to corporate business, from the *guru-chela* relationship in religious education to department staffing in an Indian university, from village *panchayat* politics to the highest reaches of government bureaucracy.'[3] The essential choreography, where the hierarchy of power acutely influences every move and step of an individual, is effectively universal in practice, and Indians have finely developed skills to locate a person's exact standing on the ladder. When two Indians meet as strangers, the encounter is often a duel to ascertain the *auqat* of the other. *Auqat* is a difficult word to translate accurately into English. It means 'status', but not only. If a person has to be asked what his *auqat* is, the question is already an insult. People need to have some *auqat*, but they are not expected to exceed it. If they do, and fail, the resultant fall will elicit little sympathy. It will be seen as just punishment for ignoring the limitations of their *auqat*. The concern with *auqat* is pervasive. It is not uncommon to see this legend on trucks on the highway: '*Apni auqat mat bhool!*: Don't forget where you belong!'

In earlier times a person's caste was the surest way to determine *auqat*. This is still a factor, but not entirely. Today, other means have to be employed to home in on status. This is a task of the utmost priority. To meet someone without knowing the coordinates of his status is like entering a pool without knowing its depth. Everything— response, behaviour, body language, social niceties, form of address, receptivity—depends on an assessment of where the other person stands on the scale of power and influence. In some cases, such as those of very senior functionaries in government, or people in media or sports or business who are known nationally, hierarchical pre- eminence is transparent. But where it is not obvious, Indians have a knack of ferreting out details by asking a series of increasingly intrusive questions: What did (does) your father do? Where do you live? Where did you study? Who are you related to? Who do you know who is powerful? The questions are asked without any inhibition. They are understood by both parties as a necessary prelude to establish the right equation between themselves, so that the accepted lines of deference, distance and familiarity are not crossed. To the uninitiated, such questions may seem innocuous enough, but the answers they seek are pregnant with significance. What a person's father does reveals important details of social background. Where a person stays is proof not only of affluence, or the lack of it, but much more. For instance, Vasant Vihar in New Delhi is an upmarket residential suburb. If you live there, it is reasonable to infer that you are relatively well off. But Vasant Vihar began as a housing cooperative society of senior government officers. The fact that you live there can then also indicate that your father was a senior government functionary. Similarly, spacious bungalows line the roads of Lutyens's Delhi. Those who live in them do not own them, but their tenancy is sure proof of a stake in the hierarchy of power. The examples can be multiplied. Cities in India are shaded in conformity with an invisible index of power. The ramparts of premier educational institutions have been somewhat breached by the policy of reservations (an official policy of affirmative action) and the system of open entrance examinations. But graduation from elite schools and colleges still conveys as much a message of merit as of *auqat*. There are other variables in getting a fix on status. For instance, the accent and fluency with which a person speaks English is a sure indicator of social background, for only the 'elite' have such proficiency. The result is that even those who do not speak English well often choose to speak only in English. It is for this reason too that many successful and powerful politicians, who do not know English, denigrate the language in public while sending their children to English-medium schools.

Indians show little reticence about the importance of having the 'right contacts'. If a person knows someone important, or is related to one, he must reveal this as soon as possible, in the secure and accurate knowledge that it will influence the behaviour of his interlocutor. The psychoanalyst Alan Roland has remarked that Indians possess a radar-like sensitivity to the relative importance of a person. This sensitivity 'makes them say things that are appropriate to person and context . . . In such a world, systems of meanings are elicited by contexts, by the nature (and substance) of the listener'.[4] A person claiming to be immune to, or independent of, a web of connections is not likely to be believed. Even today, the first reaction of an Indian when introduced to a person who claims to have done well only on merit, is very likely to be: who is his godfather, who does he know, what contacts does he have?

Nothing reveals the obsession with status more dramatically than the matrimonial ads in Indian newspapers. The front pages may churn with political twists and turns in the functioning of the world's largest democracy, but the true story lies buried in the densely-packed columns of the matrimonial pages. The smallest part of the matrimonial section is titled 'Cosmopolitan'; the rest of the fourteen-page insert lists ads strictly by caste or religion. A few mention that caste is no bar; some others emphasize that the merits of the boy or girl are the only consideration. But the overwhelming majority seek an alliance only with a family of 'high status'. In a random survey of the matrimonial section of a leading daily, the *Times of India* (Sunday, 26 January 2003), the expression 'high status' occurs in as many as 1,532 advertisements. A great many others have labels like 'well respected', 'highly reputed family', etc. This overriding pre-occupation with status determines the information the ads carry. The father's status is often spelt out in greater detail than the bride's or groom's. Every nugget of information that can profile the status of the family is crammed in. Even if caste is stated to be not a consideration, a great deal of collateral information is offered, so that the 'high status' of the bride or the groom remains clear, as the wording of this rather interesting advertisement in the *Hindustan Times* of 15 September 2000 testifies:

> Wanted FAIRY LOOKS Slim, Very Tall Educated MODERN Extremely Beautiful Bride from Industrial Family For 27/187, Slim Very Fair Handsome Only Son of Affluent, High Caste Hindu, Presently Most Liked, Senior **Cabinet Minister of India.** Boy is Vegetarian Having Clean Habits And Well Settled **In London** in his Own Business. Caste No Bar. If YOU are Ready to Give Your **Particulars** first, Please Reply -

It is interesting to note that the father of the prospective groom needs to clarify that as a cabinet minister he is 'Presently Most Liked'. The motivation appears to be to reassure prospective brides, and their parents, that he is not a minister on his way out, an important consideration in an era of coalition politics, where governments can be very short-lived. A 'popular' minister could also be expected to return to power, should the term in office end prematurely. Of course, the minister need not have bothered so much about his likeability, except in the context of retaining the proximity to power. To Indians what is important is the *existence of status in the hierarchy of power*. The status should be both recognized and *recognizable*. It should be efficacious in yielding dividends that matter: power, patronage, contacts, influence, favours and money. Other considerations, of morality or popularity, or the *means* by which such status has been acquired, are of secondary or no importance.

Mahatma Gandhi believed that the means are as important as the end. His creed quite spectacularly failed to attract followers because the concept was alien to Indian tradition. India's most well-known treatise on statecraft, the *Arthashastra*, written by Kautilya almost two thousand years ago, wastes little time on the moral under-pinnings of power. On the contrary, it advocates a compellingly unsentimental recipe on how to seize power through means fair or foul. Power can be acquired or enhanced, Kautilya argues, by four principal methods or *upayas*. These are: *sama* (conciliation by negotiation), *dama* (gift or blandishment), *bheda* (sowing dissension in the enemy's camp), and *danda* (punishment or use of superior force). Of other expedients, especially useful is *asana* (sitting on the fence). Kautilya's essential thesis, which he states with clinical detachment, is that expediency is far more important than conventional morality in conducting affairs of state.

One of the most lovable gods in the Hindu pantheon, Krishna, pursued precisely such an approach during the Great War between the Pandava and the Kaurava clans, fought several hundred years before the birth of Christ. The epic recounting of the war, the *Mahabharata*, one of India's most important literary texts, narrates several incidents, crucial to the final outcome, where the ethicality of Krishna's role—in terms of the prevailing code of fair play—comes into question.[5] Krishna, who is allied with the Pandavas, wants to wean away the mighty warrior Karna from the Kauravas. This he does, not by appealing to Karna's sense of rectitude, nor by persuading him to see the legitimacy of the Pandava claim. His strategy instead is to use a crucial nugget of information about Karna's personal life to break his pledge of unshakeable loyalty to his childhood friend and benefactor, the eldest of the Kaurava brothers, Duryodhana. Karna is in reality the firstborn of Kunti (the mother of the five Pandavas, Yudhishtira, Bhima, Arjuna, Nakul and Sahdev), from an unintended liaison before her marriage with Surya, the Sun God. Krishna is aware of this and chooses the right moment to reveal the truth to Karna. The news has a traumatic impact on the young warrior. The ground is thus prepared for him to concede a boon to Kunti that at all times at least five of her sons will remain alive.

During the war, the Pandavas, at the explicit urging of Krishna, manage to kill the leading Kaurava warriors by means which are at best expedient. Drona, the towering guru of the Kauravas, and a formidable warrior, is killed when Yudhishtira, the eldest of the Pandava brothers, who is renowned for always speaking the truth, is persuaded by Krishna to knowingly tell a lie. Drona is extremely fond of his son Ashwathamma. If he were told that Ashwathamma had died, Drona would, Krishna knows, lose all desire to fight. While it is true that an elephant called Ashwathamma has indeed died in battle, and Yudhishtira does not utter a complete lie when he says in Drona's hearing that Ashwathamma has died. But Yudhishtira is aware of his deceit. Drona, on hearing Yudhishtira's words, lays down his arms.

Karna is killed when during his fight with Arjuna, he descends from his chariot to lift its wheel, which has sunk into the ground. It is against the rules of war to attack a man when he is unarmed, and Karna asks Arjuna to respect this code of conduct. But Krishna is quick to intervene. Fair play in war has no application to those who have scant respect for it themselves, he argues. 'Kill Karna now, before he returns to his chariot', Krishna presses Arjuna, and the next moment, Karna, his head severed from his body, lies dead on the battlefield.

Jayadratha, the ruler of Sindhu, has killed Abhimanyu, the son of Arjuna. Arjuna has sworn to avenge his son's death by killing Jayadratha before sunset the next day, or else immolating himself. Jayadratha emerges triumphantly from hiding only after he is entirely sure the sun has set. But just as he does so, Krishna's divine manipulation ensures that the sun peeps out of the darkness again, enabling Arjuna to kill Jayadratha.

Duryodhana is killed in a duel with Bhima. Duryodhana is much the more agile and skilled warrior. Krishna, who is watching the duel intently, confides to Arjuna that Bhima would never be able to win in a fair fight. He can only be defeated by unfair means. It is then that Krishna draws Bhima's attention to Duryodhana's vulnerable spot— his thighs. It is against the rules of war to hit below the navel. Duryodhana is not expecting to be hit on his thighs, but Bhima breaks the rules of war at Krishna's unambiguous and emphatic urging.

Krishna's response to accusations of unfair play is most interesting. First, he *admits* that he has resorted to unfair means. The Kauravas, who are great warriors, could not have been defeated by fair means. Deception, Krishna argues, is acceptable when the enemy is stronger. 'The gods themselves are not above it; we have only followed their example', he says. The Kauravas symbolize *adharma* (evil). They have to be defeated. In such a situation, the end justifies the means. In the prevailing times, 'unsullied righteousness' cannot be practised.

The fourth quarter of time, the Kalyug, has begun. In this age (which continues today), absolute morality is at a discount. The workings of fate and destiny do not allow right and wrong to retain their sharply distinctive focus. 'It is the rule of time. You must not try and change the course of destiny. She will have her way. She is unrighteous too, and she fulfils herself in many ways, mostly unrighteous.'[6]

In the late 80s the *Mahabharata* was adapted for television. It was a hugely popular serial, evidence of the continuing hold of tradition and mythology. The actor who played the role of Krishna went on to win a parliamentary election. Undoubtedly, the personality of Krishna is too complex and versatile to be defined only by his dubious role in the Great War. His other roles, particularly as the mischievous child-god, Balgopal, and the irresistible lover, Kanha, account greatly for his divine popularity. But his actions in ensuring the victory of the Pandavas echo the Machiavellian message of the *Arthashastra*. Nor is the *Arthashastra* unique. The *Shantiparva*, a section of the *Mahabharata* devoted to the elaboration of statecraft, can have few rivals in the history of political theory for its hardbitten pragmatism. There is no binding or universal code of conduct in Hinduism that gives unequivocal primacy to the moral dimensions of power. 'India has no developed indigenous ethical system—it has concentrated more on the mystical apprehension of an ultimate reality which transcends good and evil than on differentiating between good and evil acts.'[7] *Dharma* is an undefined and ephemeral ideal, too subtle (*sukshma*) to be etched in stone—as Yudhishtira, the very symbol of rectitude, himself says in the *Mahabharata*. In everyday life, it is in fact noteworthy for the exemptions it grants to correct behaviour as normally understood. A man can do no wrong if he acts to protect his *svadharma*, conduct that is right for one's *jati* or station. He cannot be held accountable for actions that are a part of his *ashramadharma*, conduct that is appropriate to one's stage in life. He cannot be penalized for transgressions made in the interests of *kuladharma*, conduct that is right for one's family. And finally, almost anything he does would be justified in a situation of distress or emergency, when he would be guided by his *appadharma*, conduct that is called for in moments of crisis.

The essential point is that Hindu tradition has always allowed for a conveniently fractured response to the moral imperative. There are no uncontested definitions of right and wrong. The only consistent concern is the end result. In the pursuit of the desired goal, morality is not so much disowned as it is pragmatically devalued. 'Hindu ethics has its public face—*Dharma*, or normative rules—and its private wisdom, or pragmatic rules, to distinguish between the principles men espouse and the tactics they adopt.'[8] The consequence is a down-to-earth relativism, a flexibility of approach, a willingness to prune absolutisms in the interests of a larger purpose. Success, visible in terms of status, power and money, matters. It subsumes moral niceties. But failure attracts great moral opprobrium, for it symbolizes *wasted* action, an unpardonable sterility, a lack of ingenuity, a shortage of resourcefulness, and a deficiency of worldly wisdom.

As a child I remember hearing a popular story about a king and his *wazir*, or prime minister. The king was tired of eating aubergine. One day he mentioned to his *wazir* that the aubergine was an absolutely useless vegetable. The *wazir* agreed wholeheartedly with the king, and went on to decry the poor vegetable so emphatically that the king was left in no doubt as to how right he was. A few days later the *raj vaid*, the king's personal physician, met the king and spoke about the excellent health benefits of eating aubergines. Now the king recommended the vegetable to his *wazir*. The *wazir* couldn't agree more. The aubergine was truly the king of vegetables, he said, and even as he continued to speak eloquently about its many qualities, the king suddenly remembered how on a previous occasion this very man had so roundly condemned it. With anger he asked how the *wazir* could maintain two absolutely contradictory points of view. The *wazir*'s answer came from generations of distilled wisdom. He said: 'My Lord, I work for you, not for the aubergine. What good would it do *me* if I disagree with you and agree with the aubergine?'

Sometimes folk tales can reveal the truth far more effectively than carefully-worded theories. The *wazir* did not think he was doing anything morally wrong by changing his views to accord with the king's. His amorality was based on the pragmatic perception that the power of his position was more important than the strength of his convictions. This clarity makes sense in an Indian context because to most Indians private beliefs are never expected to come in the way of personal benefit. In the absence of absolute moral commandments, only *avidya*, an error of perceptions, is culpable. And failing to cultivate a manifest focus of power, such as the king, would be *avidya* of a very high order.

Significantly, most Hindus genuinely believe that regardless of their expedient behaviour, they belong eternally, by the very nature of their being, to the moral sphere. They see no contradiction between this vague sense of moral superiority and the obvious immorality of their actions. This explains why Indians moralize so effortlessly. In any case, in traditional Hinduism, almost any wrong can be washed away by ritual expiation. The Hindu gods are benevolent, infinitely forgiving, easily mollified, and eminently bribable. In fact, traditional Hindu society had no real concept of moral problems. Any action considered wrong in a certain context can be condoned and even lauded in a different context. It is this cheerful acceptance of a morally flexible world that saves Hindus from the dreariness of a soulless cynicism. Even in their worst actions they are never overwhelmed by their lack of morality, nor do they lose faith in their ultimate virtue; for after all, in an ephemeral and transient world, can anything ever be eternally right or wrong?

On such moral foundations, any edifice of power finds Indians willing to prostrate themselves before it. The edifice must be visible. The power it radiates must be manifest. The benefits it can bestow must be self-evident. If these conditions are met, an Indian will acquiesce in power. The powerful have hierarchic pre-eminence. They have status, and can help others to retain or advance theirs. There is no element of doubt in Kautilya's declaration: 'It is power and power alone which . . . maintains both this world and the next.' Morality, scruple, compunction or ideology must be invoked, if required, in the public arena. The need to invoke them is as universally accepted as the general belief in their irrelevance. Society sanctions, or at least fully understands, the requirement for an external and internal persona: the first is for public consumption, the second for the interests that really matter. The powerful must always profess to act upon, and have knowledge of, *dharma*. This is not a facetious or optional requirement. It fulfils a deep-seated need for

Indians to belong to the moral and the moral-less world simultaneously. An Indian finds it very difficult to accept an open or
blatant severance from the moral. The cosmos has a moral principle.
People are born, and reborn, in accordance with their *karmas*, the
moral quality of their deeds. A world without some kind of moral
order would be much too stark, sorely lacking the subtleties that
nourish the complexities of the Indian psyche. Morality is thus an
assurance of ultimate redemption. It has its ontological value,
provided it does not interfere with the imperatives of the present.

The British, and before them the Mughals and the Turks, must
have wondered why it was so relatively easy to vanquish and rule a
people who belonged to a culture and civilization of such strength
and antiquity. Hindu culture was not, as is widely believed, benevolent towards interactions with outsiders. It regarded all foreigners
as *mleccha*, unclean, perennially beyond the pale. It was based on the
most inflexible insularities within, and the most unforgiving barriers
without. Even travel to a foreign land across the seas sent one beyond
the pale. Why then were so many Indians willing to work with
'unclean' and socially unacceptable foreign conquerors? The answer
is quite simple. The conquerors were more powerful. The pragmatic
Indian was willing to collude with a stronger power. Personal
aversion, socially prescribed ostracisms, the stigma of capitulation,
and all the sophistication and sophistry of an ancient civilization
were not sufficient to outweigh the essential wisdom that it is futile
to fight the powerful. Once the reality of the new power became
evident beyond reasonable doubt, acceptance made a smooth
transition to cooperation, and cooperation to collusion.

The uniquely non-violent nature of the independence movement
under the leadership of Mahatma Gandhi has blinded both Indians
and outsiders to the spectacular collusion of most of the Indian elite
with British rule. Those with the greatest knowledge of their own
culture and tradition bent over backwards to publicly disown their
inheritance and acquire that of the British: in speech, in dress, in
mannerisms, in the style of living. Of course, all colonizing powers
seek to colonize the minds of their subjects. But the degree to which
the British succeeded must surely be unprecedented even among the
history of the colonized. Their success was due not so much to their

own ingenuity, or their undoubted military superiority, as to the essential *absence of opposition* to such attempts among their Indian subjects. Accommodation with the power of the moment held the promise of visible benefits in the here and now: a toehold in the new hierarchy of power, status, upward mobility, enhanced income. Such seductions convincingly overruled personal doubts about the morality of the partnership, including very strong and socially prescribed taboos relating to contacts with foreigners. The knowledge that this compact was humiliating—and the educated Indian was never in doubt about this—could not outweigh the willingness to accept the powerful, for as the ancient *Chandogya Upanishad* puts it with telling brevity: 'Power is superior to knowledge.'

The pursuit of a place in the hierarchy of power is a socially acceptable goal unfettered by notions of rectitude. The powerful are entitled to receive loyalty, but the very absence of morality in the transaction ensures that the transfer of loyalty can be expedient, not absolute. Foreigners often take time to realize this, but to Indians such pragmatism is routine. Tulsidasa says in the *Ramayana*: '*Sur nara muni sab ki yeha riti, svaratha lagi karahin sab priti*: Gods, men and saints, the practice is the same, self-interest is behind their display of loyalty.' Give unto the powerful what circumstances and practicality demand, but not everything, because the powerful can be replaced by others, and one must have enough reason to convince the next incumbent of one's neutrality. In actual fact an Indian is being neither deceitful or duplicitous, in his own estimation, when he believes that his loyalties must be agile. How can there be a betrayal when the trust was never meant to be absolute? But, so long as the next incumbent is nowhere in sight, and the power base of the current one is beyond doubt, the practical Indian will serve with complete devotion, even servility. The outsider sometimes errs in thinking that this dedication is personal; the Indian remains consistent in his detachment. Nirad Chaudhuri comments on this in analysing the manner in which the Indian served the British. 'The more thoroughgoing his external and interested servility, the more complete was also his emotional disaffection . . . The Hindu clung desperately to his disloyalty but gave service to the foreigner.'[9] This detachment, this ability to collude without ever being subsumed, probably explains why historically Indians were easily defeated, but never fully subjugated. Their personal world, their culture and civilization, may have been mauled, but could not be destroyed. With the exception of the British, who were themselves more influenced than they were willing to accept, it was ultimately the foreigner who was assimilated, even if the Indian willingly served him while he ruled.

This proclivity to venerate power and the powerful has given rise to distinctive behavioural patterns. Sycophancy was and is one of them. In India there is social acceptance of the fact that the powerful need to have their egos massaged, and that supplicants must fulfil this vital need. M.N. Srinivas, in his path-breaking anthropological study of a village in Karnataka, noted that 'individuals who were economically and socially inferior seemed only too ready to agree with their superior, and flatter him when an opportunity presented itself. *Agreeing with a superior and flattering him were approved if not prescribed ways of getting on,* and every patron attracted one or more flatterers.'[10] Those who seek to benefit by enhancing their proximity to power must outdo competitors in their ability to say the right thing, at the right time, with the right degree of exaggeration and deference, so as to leave no doubt about their abject loyalty and the unquestioned primacy of the benefactor. When Prakash Singh Badal, the previous chief minister of Punjab, had a grandson in October 2001, his followers, some of them ministers in his Cabinet, took out full-page advertisements in local papers to felicitate him. Here is a sample of how they expressed their ecstasy in banner headlines: 'We extend lakhs and lakhs of congratulations to the Badal family at the son, who is like a shining moon!'[11] Flattery is not expected to be subtle. It must be obvious, and excessive. The benefactor will not be embarrassed to hear it. The supplicant will not be uncomfortable in voicing it. Observers will understand it to be the fulfilment of a well-defined and necessary social ritual, for according to the Vedic poets, even the gods cannot resist praise.

The words *chamcha* or sycophant and *maska* or flattery are understood all over India. A person may be accused of being a *chamcha*, but the pejorative meaning of the word is no bar to the acceptance of the importance of *chamchagiri*, the art of flattery. A patron can pretend to be annoyed by a subordinate's *maskabazi*, but the subordinate knows that it is only pretence, and knows further that the expected response is to protest that the praise is absolutely true, and will be voiced whether the patron welcomes it or not. The body language of the *chamcha*, and that of the patron, are all part of a carefully choreographed and extensively practised code of behaviour that reinforces the differences in the status of people within the hierarchical order. In the past, the ability of a subordinate to say the apt thing in acknowledgement of a difference in status was influenced by the courtly traditions of the Muslim courts. My father was fond of recounting the story of a particularly clever peon in his office when he was the chief of a district in the Central Provinces in the years before 1947. One day a photograph suddenly fell from the wall. The peon, who was in the room, exclaimed spontaneously: '*Hazoor ki dahshat se!*: Out of fear of your Lordship!' Today courtiers may not have this poetic presence of mind, but one has only to observe the behaviour of most bureaucrats in the presence of a minister, or senior executives in the private sector with their proprietor, or Indians in general in 'superior-subordinate' relationships, to realize how flattery continues to flourish in a relentlessly hierarchical system.

Flattery fulfils a social need, but both the flatterer and the flattered know it for what it is. The consistent focus is power. The individual who wields it is important, but his power may be transient. The courtier has a role in bolstering self-esteem, but is replaceable. This is well understood by both parties. The bedrock of the relationship is therefore distrust. No one can be taken at face value. Everyone is suspect. Benevolence can never be presumed. Motivations must be doubted. A person's external professions of goodwill could well be camouflaging ill-will. It is accepted as axiomatic that people will be envious, and will cast an evil eye. Srinivas is quick to observe this in the behaviour of the villagers: 'Envy was a familiar phenomenon . . . A well-to-do person expected others to envy him and feared such envy . . . The eye was an important locus of envy . . . The phenomenon of envy loomed large in the minds of villagers . . . All this resulted in an ambivalent attitude towards intimates and equals— there was need for wariness.'[12] A common legend on Indian trucks reads: '*Buri nazar wale tera muh kala*: May the face be blackened of the person who casts an evil eye.' One of the country's largest producers of television sets sold its product very successfully by simply saying: 'Owner's pride, neighbour's envy.' Kapila Vatsyayana, who has spent a lifetime studying India's cultural traditions, told me once in all seriousness that the only enduring emotion (*sthayi bhava*) among Indians is envy (*irshya*). Even educated families routinely succumb to the need to '*utaro nazar*', to remove the effects of the malign eye. A handful of chillies sprinkled with salt are waved around the victim of the ubiquitous evil eye. The chillies are then thrown into a fire. If the smoke does not get into the eyes or cause coughing, it is proof, if proof is needed, of the need to ward off the evil eye.

An instinctive suspicion pervades Indian society. The *Mahabharata* is a labyrinthine epic of human deceit and betrayal, but even India's other great epic, the *Ramayana*, which narrates a more simple and straightforward theme of the triumph of good over evil, 'is full of suspicion and doubts—every character and virtue, even the chastity of [Rama's wife] Sita and the fidelity of [his brother] Laxman, are tested in the crucible of doubt.'[13] Altruism, the ability of an individual to act in the public good without a self-serving ulterior motive, is deeply suspect. This ambience of distrust creates two opposed but coexisting worlds, one of deference, the other of hostility. Deference exhibits itself when the gravitational pull of the centre of power is strong; hostility surfaces when this pull weakens; both coexist when the situation is in balance.

The dialectic of deference and hostility explains why a person whose power is ascendant will always find enough Indians to salute him. Conversely, a person who falls on bad times will be deserted without much ado by those who happily fawned on him. This is not an uncommon trait in other societies as well, but in Indians such behaviour is vivid and extreme. A rising star is greeted with disproportionate adulation, a fallen hero condemned with unjustified vehemence. When I once commented on this trait to an old man, he said in a matter-of-fact way: '*Chadhte sooraj ko sab salaam karte hain*: Everyone salutes the rising sun.' If hierarchies are secure and unchallenged, the person at the top, and those who are perceived to be within his orbit, receive unquestioned loyalty. Once again Tulsidasa puts his finger on the pulse: '*Samaratha kar nahin dosha gusain, ravi pavak sursari ki nahin*: The powerful can have no faults; they remain as pure as the sun, the fire and the Ganga.' But when the hierarchy unravels, there is unmistakable glee at the discomfiture of the fallen. Political leaders are keenly aware of this phenomenon, which causes not the slightest sense of guilt or embarrassment. The deference of the past is forgotten through an amnesia that has social sanction. The future is immediately animated by speculation about the next focus of power. This too has social sanction. When Rajiv Gandhi came to power in 1984 with the largest majority in the history of the Indian Parliament, he may have been surprised, as a new entrant in the world of politics, by the tumultuous adulation he received. Nothing he did could be wrong. So long as his power seemed unshakeable, there was hardly a critical cloud on the horizon. Those close to him, many of them as new in politics as he was, could be forgiven for believing that his reign, and their status within it, was eternal. However, when things began to go wrong, he (and they) may have been taken aback by the speed with which the ranks of his critics grew. Nothing he did now could be right. His mother, Indira Gandhi, whom he succeeded as Prime Minister, could have warned him, from personal experience, of the inevitability of such behaviour. So could Narasimha Rao, who succeeded him, but Rajiv was by that time no longer alive to witness history repeating itself. In India, the pendulum swings naturally to two extremes: adulation or rejection, and the journey between them is littered with factionalism, intrigue and division.

Indians take to factions as naturally as a fish to water. It is a cliché that if there are two Indians there will be two parties. Swami Vivekananda had once observed that 'three Indians cannot act together for five minutes. Each one struggles for power and in the long run the whole organisation comes to grief.' A strong centre of power can keep factions in abeyance. But not for long. In a sustained atmosphere of distrust, where loyalties are expected to be agile, people constantly seek new equations to jockey closer to power. Stories of betrayal and treachery, of sellouts and breaches of faith, find a gullible audience. People are ready to believe that other players will be unprincipled. This conviction fuels equally unprincipled actions in response. The *Arthashastra* says that miraculous results can be achieved by practising the methods of subversion. The king is required to set up an elaborate network of spies. The integrity of ministers and of high officials is to be constantly tested. Individuals are never to be overestimated for their morality nor underestimated for their craftiness.[14]

There is also the feeling that constant mobility in finding new relationships of support is the only antidote to isolation. Isolation threatens Indians. Their conditioning from birth is to belong to a group: caste, kin or extended family. The desire to have a scaffolding of support against other groups that only have their own narrow interests at heart, predisposes Indians to view all associations as a collection of factions in a state of constant hostility towards each other. Unity as a concept is valued, but as something transcendental, even remote: the cosmos is a seamless continuity, the Absolute is indivisible, mankind is an undivided fraternity (*vasudhaiva kutumbakam*). Such theoretical notions attract precisely because they contrast so greatly with affairs in real life. In real life division is taken for granted. Like amoebae, group interests are expected to mutate and coalesce and further mutate endlessly. The notion of 'objectivity' in social interactions is quite alien to Indians. They cannot believe that anyone can transcend the loyalties of their immediate environment. Their approach to foreigners, who are outside their milieu, oscillates between unceasing distrust, because they will always remain 'the other' outside the impenetrable walls of acceptance, and inexplicable trust, precisely because being outside the known milieu, they are unlikely to be influenced by it. Under the often deceptive calm of a deeply stratified society, factions lead a secret life of unending energy in the Indian way of life, fuelled by a subterranean world of personal rivalries and jealousies that are taken for granted.

When status is not only dependent on merit but on the shifting equations of power, any change in the degree of deference accorded by others is a matter of the most acute concern. Indians have hidden antennae to detect any variation in power signals. As we have discussed, they seem to possess a special talent to locate where exactly a person stands in the hierarchy of power, and their behaviour changes in direct response to such perceptions. People are therefore extremely sensitive to fluctuations in the 'esteem' accorded to them. If the level of esteem falls, it is a slight to their status (*maan-hani*); if it remains as it was, it indicates status is secure; if it increases it could indicate a rising position in the hierarchy. The manner in which esteem is extended or denied is thus a language that quite accurately conveys the position of a person in the calculus of power. Indians are very insulted if denied the esteem that they believe is their due. A deficiency in *izzat* or 'respect' can provoke an irrational response totally disproportionate to the level of the slight. 'In the indigenous Indian self-psychology there are three categories of experience that deserve special attention. They are esteem (*maan*), insult (*apmaan*) and pride (*abhimaan*) . . . Interpersonal transactions in India reveal an acute awareness of the need to accord and to receive appropriate esteem.'[15]

The paradox is that this exaggerated notion of self-esteem can be renounced as easily as it is invoked. A person who swears that he will never countenance an insult to his *izzat* will compromise it the very next day if the benefits are verifiable. The enormous contradiction between the two stances will be apparent but, ultimately, irrelevant. Critics who vehemently criticize such hypocrisy will nevertheless privately understand the need for such pragmatism. If the negation of self-esteem is efficacious, and delivers enhanced status and power even in the short term, the betrayal will be forgotten. It will be highlighted again only when the person's fortunes decline. A well-known Congress Party politician in the 1970s, who was both a cabinet minister in New Delhi and the chief minister of an important state, said publicly that he would be willing to give his very skin to make *chappals* or slippers for Prime Minister Indira Gandhi, whose power then seemed unassailable. His self-debasement stood in stark contrast to the respect and deference he demanded from his subordinates and his own peer group. Such incidents, where personal esteem is considered indispensable and yet is easily dispensed for larger personal benefit, occur quite routinely. They rarely cause comment because Indians *understand* the motivation that prompts them. I recall an incident in New York some years ago, when the wife of a minister had arrived at JFK airport, and the private secretary to the minister, a senior civil servant very conscious of his own esteem, was five minutes late in receiving her. When he met her, she exploded: '*Ullu ke patthe, ye time hai aane ka!*: Bloody fool, is this the time to show up!' The officer quietly swallowed the insult and continued to occupy the coveted post of PS to the minister.

This tendency to demand esteem, and the ability to negate it when required, can lead on occasion to hilarious consequences. When I joined the diplomatic service in 1976, I was sent for a short stint of grass-roots civil service training to Anantpur district in the state of Andhra Pradesh. The atmosphere at the district level was very feudal: the Collector, who headed the administrative hierarchy, was akin to God, and I, as the Assistant Collector, was a demigod in training. Anantpur gets very little rainfall. The World Bank was funding a drought assistance programme, and a motorcycle bought out of these funds was, quite against the rules, handed over to me for personal use. One day, on my way home I hit a man on a bicycle that had turned without warning. The man fell, but was not injured. However, his anger was quite uncontrollable because he was a policeman. In that area his power was unquestioned, and nobody was going to get away with knocking him down even if the fault was his own. There was nothing to indicate in either my bike or my demeanour that I was the Assistant Collector, and the policeman unleashed a vituperative barrage of abuse in Telugu, the local language. I did not understand Telugu, but abuse in any language sounds like abuse. A crowd had collected by now, and the policeman was in full swing. Just then, by sheer chance, my *chaprasi* (peon) came cycling down the road, and swiftly informed the policeman who I was. A particularly choice insult was already on the policeman's lips. He could not prevent its articulation. But even as he abused me, his right hand flew into a salute!

This incident took place many years ago, but the situation in the districts and, indeed, in much of the bureaucracy has not changed, and is perhaps even worse now. There was a brief period after Independence when a handful of senior civil servants, influenced by British norms, strove to give free and fearless advice to their political masters. Their valiant effort was soon asphyxiated by the resurgence of the tradition demanding capitulation before hierarchy. Politicians, who have their finger on the real traditions of the country, were probably the first to seek its return. But bureaucrats, who otherwise love to blame politicians, were not themselves blameless. In fact, in all likelihood, it was not the politician who first compromised the bureaucrat, but the bureaucrat who first conveyed to the politician his willingness to be compromised.

The rules that govern a modern democratic society are well drafted in India. They usually serve as a useful reference point to measure the extent of their breach in actual conduct. Indians have the greatest appreciation for the manner in which rules are respected in other countries. When British Prime Minister Tony Blair's 16-year-old son was arrested for being drunk, educated Indians were full of admiration that Blair and his wife were present at the police station when their son was 'cautioned'. But this admiration easily co-existed with the acknowledgement that a similar incident in India involving the child of a high-up would be 'suitably' hushed up. Any attempt at egalitarianism or accountability flounders against an earlier and more powerful tradition that runs directly against it. The pervasiveness of this tradition shows up in the most unlikely places and in the most unexpected manners. I once went to see the Permanent Secretary of the Department of Telecommunications in New Delhi. The distinguished gentleman came personally to see me off to the lift. As is usual with senior officials in government offices, his peon ran ahead of him to call the lift. He pressed the button repeatedly, but to no avail. In the putative nerve centre of India's celebrated communications revolution, he then took recourse to traditional methods. With his open palm he gave the closed doors three loud thwacks. The message was instantly conveyed to the idling lift operator: the person waiting was a VIP. The elevator opened before us in a second.

An Indian will always seek to give expediency the appearance of principle. His 'self-image' of his essential morality compels him to try and camouflage his unprincipled behaviour. Just as an immoral world needs to conjure the protective awning of a higher moral order, principle is used to provide an omnipresent fig leaf to the unethical pursuit of power. No Indian will ever admit to wrongdoing for the advancement of his personal interests. There is always a larger purpose, a larger goal, a nobler reason, a higher justification to explain his conduct to himself, and to an audience that sees through the charade, but would behave in exactly the same way in a similar situation. Ideologies proliferate in the barren moral landscape of India. Politicians spout them endlessly, people dispute them ceaselessly. Tradition is invoked, and tradition is condemned, in their support. The legacies of leaders are interpreted and reinterpreted to justify any course of action. Political parties are born, and reborn, on the basis of 'ideological differences'. Indians need always to prove to themselves, and to others, that their relationship with power is 'honourable'. They like to suggest that they seek power not for itself, but for a cause distinct from themselves. Ideology is the perennially available midwife to deliver 'respectability' to the jockeying for power. Ironically, the ability to renounce power is a goal all Indians accept as laudable. It is part of a philosophical tradition that looks to spiritual salvation beyond the finite world. Indians will often cite this tradition to prove their 'detachment' from the lure of power. They do not expect to be taken seriously, except perhaps by foreigners excessively taken with India's 'spirituality', and increasingly not even by them. A few, like Mahatma Gandhi or to a lesser extent Jayaprakash Narain, who actually did transcend conventional notions of status and hierarchy, were promptly all but deified, for only 'great souls' could be expected to have the strength to resist the lure of power.

The working of democracy in India provides the widest possible canvas to witness the Indian response to power, status and hierarchy. The absence of idealism and the rank display of opportunism that very quickly became the hallmark of Indian politics were not accidental; they cannot be explained away by the distortions that inevitably accompany fledgling institutions; they cannot be attributed to one leader or one party; *they were the result of a societal consensus on the primacy of ends over means.* The end was power, and the rewards it could yield in terms of personal benefit and access to the resources of the state. All the rest were instrumentalities, of importance only in reaching that end.

Only a total clarity about this priority enables most Indian politicians to consistently pay lip service to principles and ideologies they have no intention of following. Indeed, the effort India's one million or so practising politicians invest in embellishing the empty shell of idealism is nothing short of remarkable. Manifestos are carefully and elaborately drafted; political parties compete to spell out their high-minded concerns; every grouping endlessly reiterates concern for the weakest and the poorest; the supremacy of precept over power is proclaimed by all leaders. However, in actual practice, the blatant use of money power, the incitement of sectarian prejudices, the cold-blooded calculation of caste equations, the forging of the most unprincipled alliances, and the recourse to a kind of populism that would invite criminal proceedings in any other system, are the norm.

I need to emphasize that my intention is to identify a trend, not to tar the honest exception. But the question needs to be asked. Why, after all, has behaviour of this kind become par for the course in a country which prides itself on its 'moral' heritage, and would like to be seen by others as belonging firmly to the 'moral sphere'? The answer is that, whatever the protestations to the contrary in public, such unethical conduct is not considered to be wrong in an absolute sense. There is, in the sheer verve and pervasiveness with which it is practised, the unmistakable resonance of both tradition and sanction. I recall a meeting in the summer of 2001 with a well-known politician, let us call him Z, whose flamboyance and political savvy were creating waves across the country. We were meeting at his home, over a relaxed lunch, with no one else present. Z was explaining to me how he won a crucial by-election for his party against difficult odds. The opposing camp had to be divided by the blandishment of money. Caste affiliations had to be trumped up to sow dissension. The local toughs had to be instructed to use force where necessary. Promises had to be made which could not be fulfilled. Z spoke in a self-congratulatory tone; without the slightest trace of remorse or guilt. He took pride in his ability to devise a strategy that yielded the desired results. His narration was pragmatic; it assumed a similar lack of rectitude in his opponents, and empha-sized the need to deal with the realities of the world as they exist, not as they should be. Winning the by-election was the only priority; no other consideration could, or needed to, distract from this goal. Any notion of ethics or legality would have seemed completely out of context and irrelevant in this power game.

In India, the working of democracy has effortlessly adapted to the undemocratic social structures of the past. Obviously, the two are mutually opposed and in other societies the contradiction would have asphyxiated the institution. Yet in India the older tradition *co-opted* the younger institution. People flocked to polling booths but voted mostly according to caste affiliations. Numerical majorities prevailed, but candidates continued to represent segments of the established hierarchic structure. In the 1990s, the largely agrarian intermediate castes—the OBCs or the Other Backward Castes— sought to convert their steadily growing economic clout into political power. Their leaders asked for—and got—reservations of government jobs in the name of the downtrodden. But the OBCs remained firmly inimical to those lower down the traditional social hierarchy, the Dalits and minority tribes, earlier beneficiaries of affirmative action as the so-called Scheduled Castes and Scheduled Tribes. The opportunity for democratic empowerment did nothing to obliterate the preoccupation with hierarchy, and in many ways only heightened such concerns.

Irrespective of their social background, the elected are acutely conscious of their status. The privileges and immunities that proclaim their superior status have grown, not lessened, in democratic India. The process unconsciously mimics the special privileges accorded to the higher castes. The democratic idea has blended too with the felt need to project power. Elected representatives show no reticence in flaunting their visible symbols of authority: bungalows, minions, official cars (bearing big plaques announcing their owners' positions), gunmen (both those provided by the state and personal ones), ministerial retinues, durbars—in short, an entire lifestyle that is more reminiscent the hubris of chieftains than the effacement of democrats. The chief ministers of impoverished states celebrate weddings and birthdays on a scale that would leave erstwhile maharajas asleep at the post. In the years just after 1947 there was a conscious attempt, probably under the short-lived influence of Gandhi, to curb the proclivities of the earlier tradition. It was a losing battle. The mentalities of the past very soon got the upper hand over the fledgling new values enshrined in the democratic experiment. In fact, over the years, as the very functioning of the democratic process enhanced the 'legitimacy' of those who emerged victorious, their behaviour has acquired a blatancy that openly mocks notions of democratic restraint or rectitude.

When parliamentary democracy was introduced, most Indian politicians were attracted by the potential rewards of the democratic process, not by the democratic ideal. Under the 'warrant of precedence', an elected member of even a provincial legislature was ranked higher than the highest bureaucrat of the state. More importantly, at the local level an elected representative was suddenly catapulted above the district administrative chief and the superintendent of police who, following the practice of the colonial regime, had previously been all powerful and quite unapproachable. Success in democratic politics therefore ensured rapid upward mobility, and the possibility of this sudden accretion of power sent a surge of anticipation through the stagnant waters of Indian society. The entrenched classes, especially in the countryside, saw democracy as a means to enhance their status, and reinforce existing patterns of dominance and hierarchy.

It is no surprise then that the phenomenal growth in the *infrastructure* of democracy—the size of the electorate, the number of polling booths, the thousands of counting machines, the length of ballot papers, the reach of the Election Commission—has happily coexisted with undemocratic trends in political behaviour. Political parties are rarely democratic internally. The word of the leader is law. Political dynasties proliferate, irrespective of individual merit. Dissent is neither encouraged nor tolerated. Sycophancy abounds, and has conventional sanction. Strong leaders are venerated for the power they exude, not always for their democratic credentials. A leading magazine recently did a survey on which leader Indians trusted the most. The not unsurprising choice was Indira Gandhi, the prime minister who suspended democracy to impose dictatorial powers under the Emergency in 1975. Her imperious style, and the unemotional way she dealt with her political opponents and those who fell from her favour, answered a subconscious predisposition in the Indian psyche to look up to and accept a 'strong' leader. The leading Indian psychoanalyst Sudhir Kakar ascribes this to 'an unconscious tendency to "submit" to an idealized omnipotent figure, both in the inner world of fantasy and in the outside world of making a living; the lifelong search for someone, a charismatic leader or a guru, who will provide mentorship and a guiding world-view, thereby restoring intimacy and authority to individual life.'[16]

Indira Gandhi continues to be widely respected for the dexterity and confidence with which she played the power game, and the ruthlessness with which she moved to achieve her political goals. A concern for democracy was, in any case, conspicuously absent in most educated Indians when she imposed the Emergency. There was not even a semblance of credible protest anywhere in the country when almost the entire opposition was put in jail. The bureaucracy quietly accepted the new regimen. The corporate world welcomed it. The most spectacular capitulation was among the so-called guardians of the right of free dissent and free expression—the media. They crawled when they had only been asked to bend, with many top editors assuming the 'traditional Indian posture of respectful sub-servience, (in which) they remained—not looking particularly dignified until the Emergency was over.'[17] A dominant image of that time was a much publicized painting of Mrs Gandhi, a triptych in oils painted by the colourful artist M.F. Husain, representing her as the goddess Durga triumphantly vanquishing her foes. The poor bore the brunt of the excesses of the Emergency, and ultimately, when elections were called, it was their hostility that defeated Mrs Gandhi. But what is most significant is the extent to which most Indians—poor and rich alike—were willing to quietly acquiesce in the abuse of power when in the first instance it seemed undefeatable.

A strong and charismatic leader commands exceptional displays of loyalty, which have few parallels in any other democracy, and recall the fanatical personality cults of communist regimes. When in September 2001, Jayalalithaa, the charismatic leader of the southern state of Tamil Nadu, was indicted by the Supreme Court on corruption charges, eleven of her followers killed themselves in grief, and two died of shock. Jayalalithaa listed the names of the 'loyal and loving brothers and sisters' who had become 'martyrs', and gave details of how they died: six committed self-immolation, three hanged themselves, two consumed poison, and two died of shock.[18] Her rival in Tamil politics, M. Karunanidhi, could claim that sixty of his party workers had committed suicide or died of heart attacks when he was arrested in June of that same year. Tamil Nadu's greatest public icon was the actor-turned-politician M.G. Ramachandran who, as chief minister from 1977 to 1987, was literally worshipped by millions of fans. This in a state that had in the 1950s witnessed a significant movement against personality cults! Such extreme forms of 'devotion' are neither firmly discouraged by leaders, nor disapproved of by their followers. For leaders 'lacking stable internal supplies in the maintenance of self-esteem . . . and dependent on external sources of admiration'[19], such 'martyrs' are trophies for display. Among followers, such 'martyrdom' is driven by a craving to be somehow *noticed* by the leader. The modern arena of politics continues to reflect the cloistered world of the ashram, where the guru is supreme and devotees are judged by their absolute surrender to his will. Powerful political leaders routinely present themselves ceremonially to their followers; and followers seek to be noticed by newer and more bizarre exhibitions of loyalty.

Personal loyalty must be displayed. It is of little value if it does not yield personal dividends in the here and now, however selfless the devotee may claim to be. Madhavrao Scindia was a genuinely popular leader, whose young life was cruelly cut short in a plane crash in September 2001. As the scion of the royal Scindia family, he commanded a huge following in the city of Gwalior, south of Delhi, the seat of the dynasty. His funeral at the city palace drew a vast crowd of mourners. But many of them promptly forgot their sorrow the moment they saw the television cameras. Journalist Sankarshan Thakur sent this report:

> It was an utterly corrupted moment. To one side was the mournful approach of Scindia's cortege, the ornate palanquin containing his remains being slow-marched by a three-services guard to funeral drumbeats and lachrymal bagpipes. To the other were these raucous hordes lunging at the barricades, whistling, jeering, jostling, trying every trick they could to get the cameras to focus on them. They were even ready to scream 'Madhavrao Amar Rahen' (Long live Madhavrao) if only the cameramen would oblige.[20]

Strong political leaders expect fervent devotees. Discerning citizens who evaluate performance on merit are welcomed in theory, but cold-shouldered in practice. Followers look out for a strong leader to 'hitch' their devotion to. They will use every opportunity (including the presence of television cameras) to project their devotion. Both leader and follower are guided by considerations of personal gain. The projection of authority and the display of servility are two sides of the same coin of power.

Political leaders consciously cultivate an image that reinforces the aura of power and authority around them. Sometimes this tendency takes particularly ludicrous forms, such as the new-found interest in the breeding of horses by a backward class leader such as Laloo Prasad Yadav, who made his wife the chief minister of Bihar when he had to resign that job himself on charges of corruption, but is now a minister in New Delhi. The behaviour is an unconscious throwback to the traditions of the Kshatriya warrior caste, where the ruler's strength was projected by certain well-identified lifestyle traits. Democratic accountability was not one of them. A ruler was expected to have the physical strength to enforce his authority. Today, personal armies still enjoy political patronage, but are not the norm. However, many political leaders maintain a stable of 'strong-men', capable of taking the law into their own hands to implement their mentor's directives. The armed machinery of the state is also much in demand as a visible accessory of power. Politicians set great store by the number of uniformed and armed men allocated to guard them. Any move by the government to reduce the number of security personnel elicits howls of protest, even if the reality of threat is non-existent. The motivating model is that of the benevolent autocrat, generous to his followers, but strong enough to 'deal' with his opponents. Cartoonists may lampoon the politics of a politician, but any personal comment which derogates from the self-image of a 'powerful' leader, is deeply resented. Indian politicians do not like to be laughed at. They do not like to be profiled awkwardly. In an unusual but understandable pact, the media rarely focuses on the personal lives of public persons. Comments on political corruption are incessant; but the reporting of personal matters, including deviant sexual behaviour, are considered inimical to the universally accepted code of deference to the powerful who, after all, are entitled to certain 'privacies' in the exercise of power. The contrast with America is striking: in the United States, where democracy is genuinely entrenched, sexual scandals are constantly in the news; in India, where the practice of democracy still leaves much to be desired, such matters are considered akin to hitting below the belt.

Given the Indian fascination with power, elections fulfilled a deep psychological need to participate in the power game, to see who was in, and who would be out. Many foreigners are surprised by the intense involvement of the ordinary Indian in politics, making India 'the world's largest producer of politicians, elections and democratic political parties. It produces more in this regard than the rest of the world combined.'[21] People discuss politics in buses and trains and roadside tea stalls and in their homes, and are deeply involved in the equations of power: who wields it, who will wield it, who once wielded it, who may wield it, and who can never wield it. The play of politics, with its betrayal and intrigue and calculation and conspiracy, holds the common person in thrall. People may protest the incessant intrigue and manoeuvring, but they find the rise and fall of individuals on the barometer of power is of far greater interest than the reasoned evaluation of issues and causes.

Indeed, in spite of the traditional loyalties by which it is sustained, power is an overriding *secular* goal for Indians. For instance, caste ties can as easily be invoked or overlooked in its pursuit. Candidates assert their caste identities to win elections. But castes are often willing to overlook their mutual exclusiveness to form alliances that can win power. In his book, *Mistaken Modernity*, the sociologist Dipankar Gupta gives several instances to show how caste alliances 'appear to emanate from secular and political factors and do not spring fully-formed from primordial loyalties . . . If a particular combination of castes does not deliver, or has run out of steam, a new combination is immediately formed', he writes. 'Alliances such as the KHAM (Kshatriya, Harijan, Ahir, Muslim) or AJGAR (Ahir, Jat, Gujar and Rajput) defy the logic of the traditional caste system'. Similarly, the 'All India Kurmi Sabha is made up of disparate castes such as the Ayodhyas, Dhanuks, Mahatos, Kurmis, and Koeris. These castes do not intermarry, and in many cases there would be a problem of interdining as well.'[22] The cementing hold of power, and the ability it imparts to persevere in an insular internal world while pursuing the secular rewards that may accrue by cooperating in the external, has ample precedents in the pre-republican period too. Gupta cites one such, the Oudh peasant movement of the 1920s. In that struggle, 'the Kurmis, Ahirs, Pasis, Brahmins and Muslims came together against landlordism, but throughout their struggle, they ate in separate kitchens'.[23]

Parliamentary democracy of the British variety was a plant alien to Indian soil. It came out of different traditions, and had matured as part of a distinct historical experience. India was fortunate to have in Jawaharlal Nehru a genuinely committed democrat at the helm for over a decade and a half in the crucial period just after Independence. The members of the Constituent Assembly, most of them well-to-do Anglophiles in thrall to the greatest Anglophile of them all, Jawaharlal Nehru, quite genuinely believed that the gothic façade of Westminster would merge easily with the red sandstone of Delhi's Sansad Bhavan. But, 'it soon became evident that there was a massive contradiction between the rhetoric of Indian public discourse and the reality of political practice . . .'[24] The democratic experiment did not collapse prematurely—as happened in most other former colonies—because of a unique process of adjustment: the opposed traditions quickly carved out a complementary playing field, where neither could prevail fully, but both could survive.

The alien graft both grew on, and was stunted by, the sap of the old. It survived because there was a high degree of tolerance among the people for its evolutionary distortions. Indians did not expect to elect angels. They showed understanding of the compulsions that led to electoral malpractices. They were forgiving of ethical deviations. Instances abound of corrupt politicians, caught beyond a shadow of doubt with their hands in the till, comfortably re-elected in the very next election. The case of a leading politician from Himachal Pradesh, Sukh Ram, is instructive. Sukh Ram was Minister of Telecommunications in the central government in the mid 1990s, when he was accused of involvement in a telecom equipment purchase scam. The Central Bureau of Investigation (CBI) raided his houses in Mandi in Himachal Pradesh, and in Delhi. Wads of currency tumbled out from under beds, plastic bags and suitcases. Charges were framed against him and the Congress Party, to which he belonged, promptly expelled him. But Sukh Ram was not fazed. He quickly floated a regional party, the Himachal Vikas Congress (HVC), and won the February 1998 assembly elections from Mandi with a huge margin, winning 64.63 per cent of the vote against the 16.79 per cent secured by his nearest rival. That was not all. Since the two main parties, Congress and the Bharatiya Janata Party (BJP), could not secure a majority on their own, the HVC became king-maker. Sukh Ram was wooed by both. The BJP, which had stalled Parliament for days to protest the telecom scandal, now welcomed him with open arms. In the BJP government that was subsequently formed, Sukh Ram was the de facto deputy chief minister.[25]

The incident is instructive because the behaviour it shows is the norm, not the exception. Sukh Ram never admitted that he had done anything wrong. He was a professional politician, who had come up the greasy pole, from legislator in the state assembly to state minister to member of Parliament and, finally, cabinet minister in the central government. He knew the mechanics of the focused pursuit of power and was dismissive of the opportunistic morality of his critics. The Congress Party behaved entirely along expected lines both when it expelled him on 'moral' grounds, but also when it wooed him when he could make a crucial difference to the power equation. The BJP invoked moral indignation to crucify him in New Delhi, and took recourse to traditional pragmatism when he was crucial in winning power in Simla. The voters of Mandi couldn't care less about his alleged corruption. To them he was a patron, who had put Mandi on the telecom map of India, creating employment and boosting local incomes.

It is often believed that the pervasive poverty and illiteracy of India allows politicians to get away with such unscrupulous behaviour. This is not true. Educated Indians behave in exactly the same ways in the pursuit of power as their poor or illiterate compatriots, with one important difference: among the educated there is a great expression of moral outrage. But this indignation—for Indians rarely let an opportunity pass where they can assert their inherent morality or condemn the lack of it in others—does not lead to any resolve, at the personal level, and especially at personal cost, to change the old value system. Both well-to-do and poor Indians value the services of an effective patron over that of a principled politician. Patrons are expected to take care of their followers. So long as they can deliver, their lack of moral credentials is of little consequence, and that is why the Indian political system tolerates such a high number of politicians with criminal backgrounds. Vir Sanghvi, the editor of the *Hindustan Times*, once wrote with obvious exasperation: 'If a serial killer stood for elections to the US Senate he would lose. If a sex-crazed rapist tried to make it to the House of Commons, he would lose his deposit. In most successful democracies voters are discerning enough to not vote for crooks, dacoits and murderers. Our problem is this: we vote for them, time and time again.'[26]

Sanghvi rightly attributes this proclivity to a 'crisis of character that runs across all sections of society. It may be tempting to blame the poor or to curse the politician', he says. 'But they are not the problem. We are.'[27] The word 'crisis' seems to indicate that such behaviour is a recent phenomenon, a malaise that has suddenly manifested itself. But the real crisis lies in a failure to fully accept that Indians are predisposed to act in certain ways. Little can be achieved by merely bemoaning the symptoms of the crisis if the underlying reality is not analysed, accepted and then dealt with. In a country where resources are scarce, and opportunities for upward mobility are limited, political power opens the gates to both. The resources of the state, which is the single largest source of patronage, are very highly prized. Success in politics holds the most effective key to such resources. Politicians vie for them; people aspire to them. In this happy condominium, traditional attitudes towards power, status and hierarchy have only been reinforced in the functioning of the world's largest democracy.

The truth then is that democracy has survived in India not because Indians are democratic, but because democracy has proved to be the most effective instrument for the cherished pursuit of power. A people stifling in the pressure cooker of a hierarchically sealed society embraced the *machinery of democratic politics* for the promise it held of upward mobility within the inherited framework of an undemocratic society. The hierarchical frame of mind did not give way to a new egalitarianism; democracy was attractive for its unprecedented ability to provide legitimacy to hierarchies, both old and new. No other institution could provide such a nationwide canvas for the interplay of existing notions of power, status and hierarchy. Democracy did not adopt India. Indians usurped democracy because it could be moulded to fit earlier structures without threatening them. It caught the popular imagination not for the new values it symbolized, but for the possibilities it opened up for the consolidation of the old. The miracle of India is that the practice of democracy has flourished within its boundaries for over five decades in the *absence* of a democratic temperament.

However, the very survival of democracy has nevertheless led to certain consequences which could hardly have been visualized when the first ballot boxes were set up in 1951. The foremost of these is the gradual but genuine political empowerment of the weakest and poorest sections of society. 'Democracy has a way of putting ideas in the heads of the lower classes and the proliferating demands for spoils threaten to catch up with the operators of the machine.'[28] When the great democratic experiment began, the vast masses of the poor were reconciled to be quiescent vote banks, manipulated by the upper castes and the already entrenched elites. But, after fifty years and dozens of elections, the weakest have realized that power can flow in their direction too from the ballot box, and this has emboldened them to work for their own interests. This is no mean achievement, so long as we remember that the questioning of old hierarchies has not led to a change in the old value system. For instance, political parties and groupings that represent the interests of the Dalits and aggressively question the caste structure, remain exceptionally sensitive to the *principle* of hierarchy, effortlessly falling in step with traditional behavioural patterns. They do condemn a system which had kept them at the lowest rung of the social ladder, but—as the record of the Bahujan Samaj Party in Uttar Pradesh (UP) shows—subscribe to the societal consensus on the primacy of ends over means, and the need to project 'status' as an adjunct of power. When Mayawati, the Dalit chief minister of UP, celebrated her 47th birthday in January 2003, the *Times of India* wrote in its lead editorial:

Over one lakh laddoos. Sixty quintals of flowers. A birthday cake the size of a mini-bus. A return gift for every party worker. A city painted in blue. A giant pandal made in fine glass, apparently inspired by the sets of the great Bollywood classic, Mughal-e-Azam. On Wednesday, old imperial Lucknow woke up to the mother of all birthday parties. So what if it cost the state several crore rupees. So what if it did not sit well with the idea of democracy. It was a spectacle that more than matched the occasion, the 47th birthday of Behenji Mayawati, self-styled leader of the dispossessed and political leader of more than 100 million people. For weeks on end, the entire might of the UP state, such as it is given the empty coffers, was harnessed to the cause of Behenji's birthday bash. From bureaucrats to party leaders, the who's who of UP's power elite was mobilized to raise every necessary rupee for the enormous extravaganza.[29]

But to the credit of the *Times*, it put the event in perspective, by writing further:

> Let's be clear. It wouldn't do to merely take the high moral ground . . . Nor would it be fair to say Behenji was doing anything excep-tional. If fact, she was only emulating an increasingly dominant political idiom where the state is but a surrogate for the self, and politics an extension of the personal. The Lucknow show might have been grander; but it was, in essence, no different from any of the dozens of such celebrations that routinely take place in Lutyens's Delhi—a case perhaps of a medieval monarchical idiom over-powering the ersatz spirit of India's shell democracy. It would be too easy to single out Behenji, when she is merely the latest symbol of an all-round crisis of values.

The 'crisis of values', a favourite cliché of the Indian media, is in fact a pointer to the values Indians subscribe to. The real triumph of Indian democracy is not that it has succeeded in bringing about a qualitative change in such values, but that it has effected a *shift in power* towards hitherto excluded constituencies, thereby creating new vested interests in the continuation of the institution. The fact that Mayawati, a Dalit whose people have been discriminated against for thousands of years, could celebrate her birthday as the chief minister of India's most populous state is a tribute to the empowerment bestowed by democracy. The manner in which she celebrated it is proof of the culture of democracy in India, a culture that is universal in its grasp.

The increase in the number of stakeholders in the institution has given a new edge to competitive politics. Paradoxically, it has bred, too, the virtues of accommodation and moderation. The avenues for upward mobility, and the pursuit of power and pelf which democracy enables and legitimizes, would close if the institution itself collapsed. Indians do not like the disorder—and unpredictability—of system-less situations. They are past masters in the art of compromise, in stepping back from the precipice, in forging a modus vivendi that obviates the need to choose between extremes, and in finding solutions that accommodate conflicting interests. Such an approach has the sanction of classical notions of statecraft. For instance, according to the *Digvijaya* theory of the *Ramayana*, 'vanquished kings were reinstated in their kingdoms as a matter of principle'. The working of democracy in India, with its constant need to forge a viable coalition of interests representing varying classes, castes and regional loyalties, has given these inclinations the urgency of necessity. Pranab Bardhan in his seminal work, *The Political Economy of Development in India*, acknowledges the 'subtle and resilient mechanism for conflict management and transactional negotiations' in Indian democracy. 'The democratic machine of Indian politics', he writes, 'with its well-defined network of distribution of spoils in exchange of support, its highly centralized organization responsive to pressure from important interest groups at different levels in the political system, its institutionalized procedures of transaction which lend it a degree of legitimacy as well as moderation, and its way of absorbing dissent and co-opting leaders of the subordinate classes, has impressed many a political scientist.'[30] Bardhan was concerned that progressive political empowerment would increase the number of knives in a finite cake, and affect the 'ability of the system to compromise and muddle through'. He need not have worried. The amoral approach to politics, the expedient use of ideologies, and the lure of power and patronage have continued to exercise the democratic energies of the Indian people away from self-destruction, and towards co-operation and compromise. Stephen P. Cohen pays tribute to this propensity when he says that Indians have a special genius for political accommodation and management, that is noticeably absent in many other parts of the world, such as the Balkans and much of Africa and the Middle East.[31]

Democratic India has important lessons for political scientists. The foremost of these is that there are no universal laws to explain the success of democratic institutions. Democracy can take root not because of the intrinsic strength of the ideas it represents, but because of certain 'strengths' in the character and ways of thinking of the people to whom it is being transplanted. Such 'strengths' need not necessarily be congruent with the democratic idea. But however antithetical they are, they should, in the crucial early years, be tolerant or supportive of the working of the democratic machinery. This gives time for the democratic idea to take root, and demonstrate its advantages, especially to the weakest sections of the people. Indians provided this critical gestation period, not because they were democratic by temperament, as they would like the world to believe, but because their centuries-old undemocratic instincts were strong enough not to view the new implant as a fatal intrusion. In societies where indigenous traditions are not so strong, democracy can be summarily rejected as an unacceptably strong threat. The paradox is that there could be greater chances of democracy failing in societies where civilizational opposition to it is weak, out of fear that it could completely destroy existing structures and hierarchies. In India, with its complex and ancient culture, and entrenched ways of thinking and behaving, democracy did not provoke the production of so many antibodies. The transplant grew stronger, almost by default; it followed no conventional patterns; in some respects it shrivelled even as it grew stronger. The most important thing is that it grew in conformity with the ethos of the people, their values and their social structures. Each year of survival increased the chances of a more equal interaction, and a more resilient and less artificial synthesis, between the opposed traditions. By not dying prematurely, it began, ever so gradually, to change the texture of the soil in which it was implanted. Certainly, its roots could have grown deeper. But very few can doubt that they have spread much more widely than could have been predicted in 1947. In the last general elections in April–May 2004, 5,398 candidates from 220 political parties contested 543 parliamentary constituencies. Sonia Gandhi confounded political pundits by leading the Congress Party to victory. 380 million people, representing about 56 per cent of the 675 million registered voters, exercised their preference using 1.25 million electronic voting machines in 700,000 polling booths across the country, the highest in Ladakh at an altitude of 5,180 metres, 20 miles from the nearest road! Undoubtedly, Indian elections are the 'largest organized single political activity ever in human history'.[32] Democracy in India has finally found a lasting home because of what the Indian people are, and not because of what they should have been, or presume themselves to be.

Chapter Three

WEALTH
The Myth of Other-Worldliness

Gastion Bastion Road in New Delhi extends north-west from Ajmeri Gate. It is known universally as GB Road, although its new name—meant to repudiate colonial memories—is Swami Shraddhanand Marg. The spacious boulevards and expansive greens of Lutyens's Delhi are not too far, but GB Road is much more a part of the old city—overcrowded, dirty and noisy. A flourishing whole-sale market for tiles and sanitaryware is located on it. The road also boasts the largest number of brothels in the city.

If on an afternoon you are at GB Road to buy something for your bathroom, you will witness something quite incredible. The merchants who sell ceramics and linoleum and bathroom fittings have their shops on the ground floor. In between the shops are stairs that lead to the bordellos above. Heavily painted women sit under the light of naked bulbs on the landings. A gaggle of men ogle from below. Pimps negotiate busily, amidst a cacophony of catcalls, lewd comments and raucous laughter. Women openly solicit from windows, balconies and terraces. In the shops, traders begin the day by lighting an incense stick in front of Lakshmi—the goddess of wealth—and continue to sell tiles and taps, as if oblivious to what is going on outside.

I once asked a shop owner how he could so calmly concentrate on his business in such a milieu. He was an elderly man. A large garlanded photograph of his late father was on the wall behind him. His son, a young man in his twenties, sat nearby, totting up figures on an electronic calculator. 'My *dhanda* (business) is my *dharma*', said the old man. 'It does not matter what is going on outside. Once

I am in my shop, I do *dhanda*. So long as I make money, I fulfil my *dharma*. Those outside must be fulfilling theirs.'

The often (and unfairly) maligned trader best represents a universal Indian trait: the ability to single-mindedly pursue material benefit in the most adverse and improbable situations. Foreigners, taken up by the great spiritual legacy of India, have noticed but nevertheless underestimated this ability. Indians have deliberately promoted an other-worldly image. They quite enjoy being seen as perched above the gross pursuits of the materialistic world. The image is a myth. Indians have always had a down-to-earth relish for the materialistic world. Far from being disdainful of the temptations of money and wealth, they have consistently valued these goals. Given the right opportunities they can emerge as among the most resilient and focused commercial operators of the new millennium.

It is important to understand first of all that there is no ideological reason, no unshakable philosophical premise, which would make Hindus reject the real world for the spiritual. In Hindu metaphysics 'all things are "substantial" (*dhatu*). The only difference is that some are subtle (*sukshma*), some gross (*sthula*). Contrary to the notion that Indians are "spiritual", they are really "material minded". They are materialists, believers in substance: there is a continuity, a constant flow of substance from context to context, from non-self to self—in eating, breathing, sex, sensation, perception, thought, art or religious experience.'[1] Hindu metaphysics analyses the world for its enduring attributes; since nothing of this world can be permanent or can endure infinitely, it must be 'unreal', that which by its very nature is destined to perish. The 'real' must be able to outlive the ephemeral; it should transcend transience; it must be devoid of finite attributes, beyond the constraints of birth and death, indestructible, self-sustaining, and beyond definition. This concept of the Ultimate is however a theoretical construct, valid at the level of hypothesis, but spectacularly irrelevant in practice. For instance, Hindu metaphysics may postulate that the Absolute is attributeless, but Hindus, without questioning the loftiness of such a concept, have proceeded to extravagantly humanize their gods. They rejoice at their births, laugh at their childhood pranks, follow their dalliances, celebrate their marriages, participate in their enmities, and worship their progeny.

There is, moreover, nothing world-denying in the practice of the Hindu religion. Professional priests expect to be rewarded in cash or kind, preferably both. When they perform a ceremony, they are fed sumptuously, and many folk tales satirize the Brahmin's gluttony. The traditional Hindu concept of heaven is very 'this-worldly', replete with houris and the best comforts and embellishments money can buy. Rituals prescribe that the physical needs of even the gods must be looked after through periodic oblations. Hindu gods are not ascetics, shying away from the mundane pursuits of this world. Almost universally they are physically appealing, and enthusiastic participants in the affairs of mortals. Goddesses are invariably beautiful in a very earthy sense, with full breasts and high and pointed nipples. 'Hindus were incapable of loving or worshipping any woman, divine or human, unless she not only had beautiful features but also ample feminine charms. Besides, she had to be gorgeous with splendid dresses and ornaments. Her jewellery had to jingle as much in fighting, as it did in sexual intercourse . . . '[2]

The Hindu devotee prays to achieve rewards in this world. He is willing to give material gifts to the Almighty to achieve these, and if one divinity is less willing to oblige, there are many others to choose from. No divinity in the entire galaxy of Hinduism has ever proscribed an offering in cash or kind. On the contrary, in some of the most important temples, priests aggressively egg on worshippers to contribute generously at the altar. The famous Tirupathi temple in Andhra Pradesh has an annual income of over US $100 million. Every day thousands of devotees donate cash and gold, and for those unable to make a personal visit, the temple Trust enables donations through a website. Devotees may believe in the afterlife, and the transience of the finite world, but their outlook in prayer is very pragmatically rooted in the realities of the present world. The villagers in M.N. Srinivas's *The Remembered Village* in Mysore give commonsensical evidence of this:

When one deity failed a devotee he approached another in much the same way as when one patron failed him, a client approached another . . . To put it crudely, devotees expected to benefit from propitiating deities, and the benefits sought were health, wealth,

children, good crops, victory over rivals, and a sense of security
...While the theologian conceived of god as immanent, ineffable etc.,
the villager dealt with him as he dealt with his powerful patron or his
Trader, Smith, Barber, Washerman or Potter. He wanted benefits
and favours from the deities he propitiated . . . while the villagers
cited supernatural events and happenings as evidence of the
handiwork of god, they were not a credulous lot. They were *shrewd,
commonsensical and hard headed*, and this trait of theirs was seen
repeatedly and in a wide variety of contexts.[3] (emphasis mine)

The most important deities in an average Hindu's life are Lakshmi
and Ganesha. Lakshmi, the wife of Vishnu and the mother of Kama,
the god of desire, is the goddess of fame, good fortune, wealth and
prosperity. She is an ubiquitous presence in homes across the
country, in cities and villages alike. On Deepavali, the festival of
lights, which is one of the most important festivals of India, every
Hindu prays to her to bring wealth and prosperity. Many devotees
keep their doors and windows open the whole night so that she
can enter the home unobstructed. Expectedly, she is of special
importance for traders and those in business. Her portrait adorns
shops, offices and business establishments, and her blessings are
sought to keep the account books in the black. Devotees praise her as
one worshipped by the entire universe, a beacon of light illuminating
the world. Some lines in the *aarti* (invocation) to her are notable for
their candour:

> *Jis ghar mein tum rahti, tahen sab sadguna aata,*
> *Sab sambhav ho jaata, man nahin ghabrata;*
> *Tum bin yagya na hote, barat na ho paata,*
> *Khan paan ka vaibhav, sab tumse aata.*
> (In the home you inhabit, virtues come automatically,
> All becomes feasible, the mind is free of worry;
> Without you no yagya, no fast can be performed,
> You impart the grandeur to a person's style of living.)

No important event can begin for a traditional Hindu without
seeking the blessings of Ganesha, the beloved elephant-headed deity,

who is the god of material wealth, and especially of commercial success. The son of Shiva and his consort Parvati, Ganesha's appeal transcends sectarian divisions. He is worshipped not only by all Hindus, but also by Buddhists and Jains. Ganesha is also the patron deity of writers, for he assisted the sage Vyasa in completing the *Mahabharata*. But while students seek his benediction just before an exam, or before beginning their first lesson in writing, he is essentially and most widely worshipped as the remover of all obstacles to worldly success. No other Hindu icon is found so pervasively at the entrance of shops, restaurants, offices and homes as an omen of good fortune. Ganesha's portly figure, with its ample and well-fed stomach, has nothing to do with the self-denying asceticism often associated with Indian spirituality. Nor is Lakshmi, one of the most important manifestations of female power in the Hindu pantheon, an emaciated recluse. She is beauty personified, emerging from a sea of milk, holding a lotus in her hand, radiant in complexion, the harbinger of plenty, bountiful in showering her followers with gold, horses and cattle, and all the worldly riches they desire.

Hinduism provides explicit philosophical sanction for the pursuit of material gain. In the world view of the Hindu, *artha*, or the acquisition of wealth, is included among the four *purusharthas*, or fundamental goals of life. The other three are *dharma*, the obedience to the *shastras*, *kama*, the pursuit of desire, and *moksha*, the path to salvation. Hinduism is a practical religion. It espouses a balanced life, in which the demands of this world are given their due, and a follower is expected to respond to them effectively. A normal life has four broad stages: the early years, *brahmacharya*, are most profitably devoted to the acquisition of knowledge; the next phase is that of the *grihast*, the householder, who must pursue a livelihood and experience the joys of physical pleasure; *vanprastha* is the intermediate stage, when the responsibilities of a householder cease, and a person prepares to gracefully withdraw from a direct involvement in the daily vicissitudes of life; and, finally, the final years are meant to be devoted to the afterlife, the bliss of *moksha*. At no point does Hinduism advocate a reversal of this linear process. An individual could choose to renounce the world very early in life. That would be a personal choice, and may win respect in some quarters. However, it is not considered in any way to be superior to a robust engagement with the dividends the world can yield. In fact, the texts specifically state that if a person pursues *dharma*, *artha* and *kama* in a harmonious manner, giving each its due, and not excluding any, *moksha* could be a natural consequence.

In such a holistic approach, a person who neglects *artha* would be in transgression of the ideal code of conduct. Hinduism gives materialism philosophical validity, not by inference but by specific inclusion. Indeed, Hinduism must be the only religion that expressly includes the fulfilment of physical desires, and the pursuit of prosperity, among the supreme aims of life. Vatsyayana, who authored the *Kama Sutra* in the early years of the Christian era, made the perfectly valid point that if *kama* is included among the four purusharthas of a successful life, it would not do to be just any kind of lover: a person must be an *accomplished* lover. The same logic would apply to the art of making money. In fact, Vatsyayana himself gives *artha* priority over *kama*, and, for practical reasons, even over *dharma*. When *dharma*, *artha* and *kama* come together, he says, then *dharma* is more important than *artha*, and *artha* takes precedence over *kama*. But *artha*, he adds, should always be the first priority for a king because the livelihood of men is dependent on it alone.[4]

Kautilya in the *Arthashastra* echoes the same sentiment: '[Some teachers say that] the three objectives of human endeavour [*dharma*, *artha* and *kama*] are interdependent and should be pursued equally. Excessive importance given to any one brings harm not only to that objective but to others as well. Kautilya, however, says: *artha* (sound economics) is the most important; for, *dharma* and *kama* are both dependent on it.'[5] The estimation of relative importance is not based on some transcendental criteria. The logic is remarkably utilitarian, shorn of the pretensions that might be expected in a society where the Brahmins and the scriptures had such a dominating role. For those unimpressed by this pragmatism, the argument is convincingly elaborated: 'without *artha*, *dharma* cannot be practised, nor *karma* obtained, without which sons cannot be born to worship gods and ancestors, and thus *moksha* itself is in jeopardy.'[6] Material well-being was never seen as an obstacle to *moksha*; on the contrary, only a person with a livelihood could be expected to properly devote himself to the pursuit of salvation.

Hinduism's social sanction to the acquisition of wealth differs dramatically from the Biblical injunction that a rich man will find it next to impossible to enter the portals of heaven. A popular invocation, sung by Hindus almost universally on religious occasions, asks the Almighty to let joy and wealth enter the home—*sukh sampatti ghar aaye*. Hindu society may have relegated *banias* to a position below the Kshatriyas and the Brahmins, but Hindus have little respect or compassion for the indigent. The king, says the *Arthashastra*, 'shall be ever active in the management of the economy. The root of wealth is [economic] activity and lack of it [brings] material distress. In the absence of [fruitful economic] activity, both current prosperity and future growth will be destroyed. A king can achieve the desired objectives and abundance of riches by undertaking [productive] economic activity.'[7] Such precepts are not found in the *Arthashastra* alone. The *Shanti Parva* of the *Mahabharata* emphasizes that it is the duty of the king to extend all assistance to the trader and the businessman. Abdul Kalam, the President of India, in his inaugural speech in 2002, quoted from the *Thirukkural* written two thousand years ago: '*Pini imai Selvam Vilaivinbam Emam Aniyemba Nattirkiv vainthu*: Important elements constituting a nation are: being disease free; *wealth*; *high productivity*; harmonious living and strong defense' (emphases mine). The *Thirukkural*, authored by Thiruvalluvar, consists of 1,330 verses dealing with the familiar themes of *dharma*, *artha* and *kama*: virtue, wealth and love. The book is refreshingly secular in tone, and largely sceptical about other-worldly matters. People in the south still consider it to be the very repository of wisdom. In the north the *Ramayana* is probably the most widely revered text, and it offers this nugget of advice: '*dhanam arjaya kakuthstha dhanamulam idam jagat, antaran nabhijamn nirdhanasya mrtasya ca*: Acquire wealth. The world has for its roots wealth. There is no difference between a poor man and a dead one.'

The Sanskrit *Ramayana* is dated to about 500 years before Christ. More than a thousand years earlier, the flourishing Indus Valley Civilization had a system of weights not found anywhere else in the ancient world. Scholars consider this evidence of a very 'considerable merchant class, through whom a commercial arithmetic developed'.[8] The Aryans came to India around 1500 BC. They overran the Indus Valley cities, but were benign to the emergence of their own merchant class. We know that in Vedic society traders travelled to foreign shores for business; the textile industry was particularly well developed; trade guilds flourished; moneylenders (*vardushikas*) were well established; commercial rates of interest (*vriddhi*) were prevalent; and investors (*prayojokas*) competed with each other for profit. It is interesting that although usury was common, moneylending 'did not incur the reprobation of Hindu moralists, as it did that of medieval Christianity and Islam'.[9]

The foundations of Indian tradition were, therefore, most enlightened in accepting the place of worldly wealth in the desired scheme of things. A.L. Basham, who has written perhaps the most comprehensive study of ancient India, sums it up well:

> It has often been said that ancient society was not an acquisitive one. Admittedly the brahmans, who claimed moral and spiritual leadership, set themselves ideals of dignified austerity, but these ideals were not always followed in practice . . . In most early Indian literature the world is viewed from the angle of the well-to-do. Poverty, it is more than once said, is living death . . . From the time of the Rig Veda, which contains many prayers for riches, worldly wealth was looked upon as morally desirable for the ordinary man, and indeed essential to a full and civilized life. The ascetic who voluntarily abandoned his wealth performed an act of renunciation, which entitled him to the utmost respect—(but) the ascetic's life was not that of an ordinary man, and the theoretical classification of the four stages of life gave ample scope in the second stage to the householder, who was indeed encouraged to build up the family fortunes, and to spend part of them at least on the pleasure of the senses. Thus the ideals of ancient India, while not perhaps the same as those of the West, by no means excluded money-making. India had not only a class of luxury-loving and pleasure-seeking dilettanti, but also one of wealth-seeking merchants and prosperous craftsmen, who, if less respected than the brahmans and warriors, had an honourable place in society.[10]

In later times, foreign observers such as Xuan Xang, Marco Polo and Abul Fazl consistently remarked on the worldly instincts of Indians. Obviously, the banias were more openly money-minded, but a healthy respect for moneymaking continued to pervade other sections of society too. Marco Polo, who visited India in the thirteenth century, claims that the 'Abraimans', by which he means the Brahmins, 'are the best merchants in the world'. It is not known what they sold to him to provoke this fulsome praise, but most Hindus would not be surprised by the compliment. 'No Pradakshina Without Dakshina: No circumambulation of the deity without paying money' is a demand that any Indian will immediately associate with a priest. Today, when the prescriptive frame of caste is loosening, and many Brahmins are doing very well in business and management, it is tempting to speculate that their success is only a continuation of the commercial acumen of their more traditional predecessors. In the holy city of Pushkar in Rajasthan, the hereditary priests of the Savitri Devi temple have gone to court to compel the guardians of the nearby Brahma temple to share the offerings received from devotees. Their argument is that Brahma, the creator of the world, had 'divorced' his wife Savitri because she did not arrive in time to participate in his *yagna* (ritual sacrifice) to create the world. As such—so lawyers were arguing in the local court in the year 2001—the Creator should be made to pay alimony to the Goddess. This attempt to marry mythology to alimony in the quest to raise income must surely have very few parallels elsewhere in the world.

In traditional societies, ingenuity operates mostly within the realm of social acceptance. The Brahmins in Pushkar knew that their aspiration to maximise their income would not erode their spiritual legitimacy in the eyes of the common man. Indeed, they would only be doing what is expected of them, and what everybody else would like to do. Hundreds of years ago a group of Buddhist monks built for themselves the wondrous Ajanta caves in central India, to escape the greed and materialism of Brahminical Hinduism. In one of the caves, a huge luminous statue of the Buddha stands serenely. At its base, in one of the stone feet of the Master, a hollow—as old as the statue itself—has been carved out. When I once asked why, I was told that it was to collect the monetary offerings of devotees! Certain traditions—and expectations—don't change, and while Buddhists in India may be more restrained in such matters, the Hindus are very much what they always were. For instance, in the famous temple of Jagannath at Puri in western India, one of the four main pilgrimage destinations for Hindus, the Pandas—temple priests—are battling the Archaeological Survey of India (ASI) to keep their own little 'hollow' full. The ASI wishes to strip the temple of its mutilating white plaster and re-expose the original—and beautiful—stone architecture of the temple. The Pandas are protesting that the architectural rediscovery would distract devotees—and adversely affect their earnings.

Entrepreneurship in the service of material gain is an irrepressible Indian trait. The very poor may have been deprived of the opportunity to practise it, but recent experience shows that all that is needed is the opportunity. A seasoned administrator, who has spent a great deal of his career in the countryside, once told me that a landless labourer, if allocated a piece of land as part of the land redistribution schemes of the government, becomes overnight a most resilient 'capitalist'. He defends his acquisition with unexpected tenacity, pre-empts predators, and although not always successful, uses every manipulative and persuasive skill in the book to hold on to and increase the productivity of his property. Undoubtedly, the essential Indian acceptance of hierarchy and inequity has worked against the fullest expression of entrepreneurial talent. But those who have beaten the system—and more are doing so now—have shown that the consistent social sanction given to wealth and material prosperity has not been in vain. One example, outside the mainstream business world, that comes to mind is that of the intermediate farmers who benefited from the 'green revolution' of the 1960s. These robust rural entrepreneurs took full advantage of government subsidies on power, fertilizers and fuel, made judicious use of credit schemes, and profited from the absence of taxation on agricultural wealth and income to emerge as a powerful class of 'bullock capitalists' in a remarkably short period of time.

Adversity has honed the entrepreneurial talents of Indians. The pursuit of prosperity had ideological legitimacy, but the trading class—much as in Confucian China, where the merchant was placed even below the peasant—had to prosper under the shadow of social inferiority. A rigidly hierarchical and feudal dispensation coveted the fruits of business acumen, but refused to publicly acknowledge it for fear of affecting the ordained social hierarchy. Even so, those outside the fossilized feudal elite and above the helplessly destitute always displayed an uncanny ability for economic survival against the greatest odds. For instance, the Indian capitalist class actually *grew* in strength under British rule in the years 1914 to 1947. This cannot be simplistically explained away as the collusion of a comprador bourgeoisie with the colonial power. In many areas, such as textiles, Indian capitalists were *competing* with the ruling foreign power. The first Indian cotton mill was set up in Calcutta in 1818, and the first textile mill in 1854. Indian entrepreneurs rose from the bazaar, consolidating their financial position through the traditional vocations of moneylending and trade. The most spectacular successes were achieved by the Marwaris who, sensing economic opportunity, migrated in the nineteenth century from their villages in Rajasthan to Calcutta, specializing as brokers and agents to the British. Many amassed great wealth in highly speculative forward trading during the First World War. Others made their fortunes in trading. During the interwar years of British rule, Indian entrepreneurs controlled 70 per cent of the domestic market and 80 per cent of deposits in the organized banking sector. Their commercial aspirations required considerable political adroitness because the independence movement set them against British rule, while their business interests were hit by anarchy or political extremism. A prolonged period of political disturbance could affect business, but supporting the freedom struggle could win important economic concessions. A fine example of the ability to negotiate this ideological minefield is the Resolution passed in 1942 by the Post-War Economic Development Committee of the Federation of Chambers of Commerce and Industry, which resolved to pursue 'whatever is sound and feasible in the socialist movement—*without capitalism surrendering any of its essential features*'[11] (emphasis mine).

India guaranteed only the survival of the fittest; the opportunities were few, the level playing fields fewer, and the people seeking the same breakthroughs many. For every success story there were hundreds who failed, and thousands waiting to compete. Luck was important, but in a world harsh to losers the winning formula was a mix of much more: an ability to anticipate opportunity, resilience, flexibility of tactic, a canniness to judge human needs, and a talent to make the circumstances fit the need. There is an Indian expression and, like others, quite impossible to translate adequately: *jugaad*. People are encouraged to use *jugaad* when faced with a blank wall, or a difficult problem. *Jugaad* is creative improvisation, a tool to somehow find a solution, ingenuity, a refusal to accept defeat, initiative, quick thinking, cunning, resolve, and all of the above.

Indians have an instinct for *jugaad*, and its manifestations—in the most unlikely of situations—can take you aback. If you miss your early morning Shatabdi train from New Delhi to Chandigarh, a man will approach you seconds after the train pulls away. He will commiserate, but ask you not to worry. He will offer to arrange a taxi right up to Chandigarh, at the most reasonable rate, and invite you to join him for a cup of tea while the arrangements are being made. He stands every day on the railway platform, waiting for those who miss the train.

In the central Indian town of Aurangabad, Nand Kishore Kagliwal, who left his father's small textile shop and struggled successfully to set up a flourishing business in the sale of plants and seeds, narrated to me, as we sat sipping a fine single malt on his manicured lawns, his first lesson in entrepreneurship. As a young man he once drove to Chowpatty in Bombay for a stroll along the sea. Bombay was less crowded then, and it was not difficult to find a parking place on the beach. When he returned he found that one wheel had sunk in the soft sand. In spite of his best efforts he could not get the car moving. A small boy watching the proceedings agreed to help for a fee of five rupees. In desperation, Kagliwal agreed. The boy produced a wooden board and wedged it under the wheel. Gripping the hard surface, the car easily pulled out. A very grateful Kagliwal happily paid him. 'How did you have the wooden board so handy?' he asked. Folding the five-rupee note in his pocket, the lad said matter-of-factly: 'There are others who make the same mistake.'

In India, a lost opportunity is an unforgivable waste. And improvisation is the mother of survival. An Indian car mechanic, having learnt on the job and without formal training, will find a way to repair any car, even if he is unaware of the make or cannot pronounce its name. A leaking radiator will be plugged, with the right compound if available, or with chewing gum if necessary. If a standard part is not available, it will be fashioned. An English traveller recorded in 1614: 'The truth is that the natives of that monarchy (the Mughals) are the best apes for imitation in the world, so full of ingenuity that they will make any new thing by pattern how hard so ever it seems to be done.'[12] The ingenuity can go beyond mimicry. In Punjab rustic farmers have improvised their own locomotive, colloquially called the Maruta. It is assembled from assorted junk—tyres, pumps, wooden planks and cannibalized parts. It has no registration, no insurance, a single gear and a fixed speed, but it moves. In Saurashtra the *chhakda*, a locally devised three-wheeled motorcycle rickshaw, provides a transportation lifeline to 6,000 villages. The contraption, which puts together a Bullet motorcycle, the wheels of a Fiat car and a diesel pump used to draw water, can carry up to 30 passengers and run for 35 km on a litre of diesel. Only recently recognized by authorities as legal, the 'vehicle' has now interested buyers in East Africa and Bangladesh. In Amreli, a drought-prone district in Gujarat, a farmer with only a Class Five education has devised a motorcycle tractor that can plough, weed and sow at much less than the cost of maintaining bullocks.[13] In the slums of the metropolises, those without television antennae make do quite well with the rim of a bicycle wheel. Technology is moulded to suit need, in effortless sync with the ebb and flow of daily life. In relatively well-to-do rural homes, and in *dhabas* that line the highways, especially in the north, lassi (buttermilk) is churned in vast quantities by using a modified washing machine. A machine is seen as a means to an end, not an end in itself. It is looked at in terms of the *uses* it can be put to, and not 'underutilized' by restricting its functions to the manufacturer's manual. The engine of a tractor, for instance, helps plough a field; it become a means of transport when attached to a trailer; and it provides the 'home service' of a farm implement when hooked to a grain thresher.

A scarcity economy and shortage of capital have made Indians inventive about improvising on inputs and reducing costs. In the

Indian economic lexicon, nothing is entirely valueless, and everything is potentially of value. Indians do not take easily to the Western culture of throwing things away. They are uncomfortable with disposables, because they instinctively see things in terms of possible use, not of fixed periods of usage. Educated Indians will routinely reuse gift wrappers, preserve aluminium foil, recycle wedding gifts and diligently peel off unmarked stamps from letters. A million *kabadiwallahs* (peddlers of junk) make a living from finding something of value in trash. They are willing to buy or sell any junk, from newspapers to empty bottles. Their business premise is simple: everything has the capacity of being recycled, because everyone is looking to minimize costs. Thus the neighbourhood grocer keeps paper bags made out of trashed newspapers, the poor look to make a bargain on the throwaways of the rich, and used plastic bags are recycled by plastic manufacturers. It is estimated that 60 per cent of India's plastic waste is recycled, compared to 10 per cent in China and 12 per cent in Japan.

Indians have had little option but to be street-smart about making money. Indeed, the street is the biggest employer in the country. India has a veritable army of 'footpath businessmen': small shopkeepers, tea stall owners, dhabawallahs, artisans, kabadiwallahs and rickshaw pullers. It is estimated that ten million men and women work as street hawkers and vendors, and more than sixty million people are directly dependent on this trade. The organized sector of the economy—private, public and corporate—employs only 3 per cent of the workforce. The overwhelming majority—almost nine out of ten people—are self-employed, squeezing out an income in conditions of work that can hardly be imagined by a businessman in the developed world. In Europe, 90 per cent of the working population work in the formal sector; they are productive in controlled and predictable environments where the safety net is visible. By contrast, the 'footpath businessmen' of India work on a razor's edge: every day is a new challenge, and almost no coordinate can be taken for granted. In spite of this, almost 60 per cent of India's gross savings comes from the unorganized sector. Business is, indeed, the livelihood of a great many of the poor.

The phenomenal growth of Small Scale Industries (SSI) is further proof of this grass-roots entrepreneurial energy. It had always been the official policy to provide financial and fiscal incentives to small-scale enterprises. The decades after 1947, when overall industrial growth was low but consistent, provided a generally enabling environment for such ventures. In 1969, the nationalization of banks by Indira Gandhi facilitated the availability of capital. Ancillarization and sub-contracting by larger firms helped too. But asphyxiating regulatory controls, and the depredations of a shamelessly extortionist bureaucracy, would have stumped all but the most committed entrepreneur. It is a tribute to the talent and grit of the Indian pioneers that they not only survived but flourished. Between 1966 and 1978, almost half of all factories that started production were in the small-scale sector; by the mid 1970s, the SSI had grown to within striking range of contributing almost half of the country's total industrial production. The point to note is that the profitability of these small ventures was often higher than that of the organized corporate sector. Nothing—not the government's 'socialist' commitments, nor the absence often of basic infrastructure, nor the miles of red tape—could keep these tenacious capitalists down. Today, the SSI sector employs 80 per cent of factory workers, accounts for 50 per cent of the value added by the manufacturing sector, and about one-third of all exports. Certain significant areas of export income, such as garments and jewellery, are almost entirely its monopoly.

There are roughly 2.5 million small-scale businesses in India. It has been estimated that cumulatively they pay something like a billion dollars a year in bribes. The extortion is an inconvenience, but there is no startling moral issue involved in the transaction. The payments are calculated as part of fixed costs; often they are a cost-effective way to buy immunity from wrongdoing. Those accepting bribes consider the additional income a legitimate perk of the job. Businessmen survive because they are concerned with the final result, not the morality of the means. Predators proliferate because they know this. In fact, those who take graft and those who pay it are both entrepreneurs, bound by the same principle that nothing should distract from the opportunity to make money.

Corruption is, of course, not unique to India. What is unique is the level of its acceptance, and the 'creative' ways in which it is sustained.

Indians do not subscribe to antiseptic definitions of rectitude, as are common in, for example, the Scandinavian countries. Their understanding of right and wrong is related far more to efficacy than to absolute notions of morality. An act is right if it yields the desired end; it is wrong if it does not. To pay *chai pani* costs to an official flunkey is right if it smoothens the way to the desired goal. The payment of baksheesh is a matter of the right investment, not morality. No invocation to Lakshmi emphasizes the importance of making money only by conventionally legitimate ways. The goddess represents wealth and prosperity; she is worshipped for these, not for sermons. Dilip Singh Judeo, a minister in the central government, was caught on videotape in November 2003 accepting bundles of cash from a man who claimed to represent an Australian mining company. The minister maintained the whole thing was a fabrication, but this taped statement has the ring of truth to it: '*Paisa khuda to nahin, par khuda ki kasam, khuda se kam bhi nahin* (Money isn't God but, by God, it's no less than God)', says the minister, and most Indians would (at least privately) agree with him. For all the condemnation that corruption publicly provokes, Indians are ambivalent about the practice. They consider it bad if they have to bribe when they don't want to; they consider it good if a bribe gets them what they want. In this sense, corruption is like litmus paper: it takes on the colour of the specific experience. The immorality associated with it is subsumed by an ingrained inclination to be worldly-wise. The world is not inherently fair; it does not guarantee a level playing field. In such a situation, success is the consequence of a well-understood transaction: give to the world what is unavoidable, in order to get from it what you want; and take from it what it can give, in order to obtain for yourself what you desire.

For this reason, business in India has rarely been hostage to morality. The half a million street vendors of Delhi pay about 100 million dollars a year by way of bribes. Captains of industry routinely indulge in creative accounting, inflating costs to take loans from easily manipulated lending institutions, and finding ways of not repaying them on time. Non-performing assets today total more than US $14 billion, which is equivalent to 3 per cent of the country's GDP. Indian chartered accountants are in demand worldwide for their ability to 'mould' balance sheets suitably. More than half of the top 1,500 companies in India pay no taxes. The over-invoicing of imports and the under-invoicing of exports is usual practice for many. The annual flight of capital from the country through this mechanism is estimated to be anywhere between one to three billion dollars. The unaccounted money of Indians in tax havens is estimated to be over 100 billion dollars. And within the country, black money accounts for as much as 40 per cent of the economy.

How much of this 'ethical deficit'—to use former Prime Minister Vajpayee's expression—is a result of the system, and how much an inherent aspect of character, is what concerns us here. Undoubtedly, a bloated bureaucracy and archaic rules and regulations encourage corruption. But these cannot explain why more and more instances are reported of parents happily conspiring with their children to buy leaked question papers for school exams. In Mumbai a question paper for a university exam sells for Rs 50,000; in Patna the going price in an engineering college is Rs 200,000. Reputed schools in the capital are said to charge the same amount for admissions. In a recently revealed scam, the Chairman of the Public Service Commission of the state of Punjab is alleged to have pocketed as much as Rs 250 million to recruit as many as 3,500 doctors, engineers, police officers, teachers and revenue officials, all totally unqualified for their jobs. Anything and everything is for sale. If you need forged government stamped papers you could buy them from Abdul Karim Telgi who—so it was discovered in 2003—was making millions of dollars every month doing precisely that in collusion with some of the country's top cops and politicians. The job of a trained teacher in a government school in Delhi can be bought; so can that of a police inspector in Bangalore, or a peon in Chandigarh. There are fixed rates for government transfers: 'lucrative' assignments command competitive bids. In Lucknow upper-caste Brahmins and Thakurs queue up to buy false Other Backward Caste and Scheduled Caste certificates in order to take advantage of affirmative action to which they are not entitled.

The public sector of government is culpable, but not only. Educated middle class citizens steal 50 per cent of the electricity in Delhi. A great many industrial units steal power, or pay for much less than they consume. Doctoral theses are available for sale on a website, and academicians with influence can 'arrange' for the theses of their favourite students to be sent only to the right examiners. In the holy city of Hardwar on the banks of the river Ganga, the mahants who head the religious ashrams are linked to the local land mafia, and involved in land-grab activities. Animal organs are sold on the Har Ki Pauri, right along the sacred ghats. When a minister sought to check on this, angry shopkeepers assaulted him. Mahatma Gandhi, who led India to independence, disapproved of the consumption of alcohol. Gujarat, his home state, is officially dry. However, Porbandar, the city where the Mahatma was born, has become the bootlegging capital of the province and even young children are used to transport illicit spirits. In Uttar Pradesh and Bihar, one-third of the teachers in government schools pocket their salaries while never attending school. The Noida toll bridge in Delhi is running at a loss because well-to-do families, out on joy rides in swanky cars, cruise along the eight-lane expressway without paying the toll. When they reach the toll plaza, they say they took the road by mistake because the signs were confusing. They are then permitted to turn round and cruise happily back to Delhi.[14] In Kochi, in the lush southern state of Kerala, a quack exposed for selling a 'miracle' drug for AIDS continues to market his spurious formulation, and makes so much money that he is at the top of the state's list of income tax payers. His plush mansion in the heart of the city is called Virus.

These are snapshots, but they reveal a larger picture. The Berlin-based organization, Transparency International, in its annual survey of global corruption, has placed India for several years in a row near the bottom of a list of 102 countries, leading the *Times of India* to wonder whether 'there is something in the subcontinental soil which makes it particularly hospitable to the growth of graft'. Such international indictments trigger anguished editorials, but do not really surprise or shock Indians. Two thousand years ago, the *Arthashastra* was matter-of-fact in stating that detecting whether a government official is stealing public money or not is as difficult as ascertaining when a fish is drinking water. Spectacular malfeasance, especially in politics, always provokes a great deal of moral outrage, and there has been no dearth of scams of this kind to keep indignation simmering. But in the daily business of life, Indians are willing to live with an ethical deficit quite easily. Their priority is survival, not salvation.

Survival is the imperative of the present; salvation the promise of the future, desirable, but negotiable once survival is ensured. In a cut-throat world, the immediate task is to get on with the job, to reach a desired goal, to finesse an obstacle. The premium is on pragmatism and agility, the capacity to seize an opportunity when it comes, and to profit when possible. What matters is not fixity of principle but clarity of purpose. When an entrepreneur in the state of Karnataka comes across an unyielding official, he uses a splendidly evocative phrase to coax him to bend the rules: 'Swalpa adjust madi: Please, adjust a little.' This hybrid of Kannada, the local language, and English is both a plea, and a refusal to admit defeat; it is a request for flexibility and a call for compromise; it is an euphemism for the offer of a bribe but equally a statement of purpose. The focus is on the solution, on the task at hand, and on the need to break an 'unproductive' impasse in the absence of multiple choices. Ideological distinctions, or fine moral categories, or anything else which distracts from the main business at hand, have no real value. A popular joke illustrates this attitude well. A eunuch once went to a shop to buy vegetables. Later, someone asked: 'Was that a man or a woman?' The shopkeeper, busy with his customers, replied laconically: 'Sabzi lene aaya tha, leke chali gayi: He came to buy vegetables; having bought, she left.'

If this Indian attitude—this irrepressible energy to somehow get ahead, to survive in the most difficult circumstances, to be clear about personal objectives, and to work for a desired end irrespective of the means—nurtures corruption, it is also the nursery of resourcefulness and enterprise. Businessmen who have no qualms about paying a bribe, can be startlingly honest if their trade depends on it. For instance, in Gujarat diamond merchants routinely entrust millions of dollars worth of diamonds to the Angadias, traditional specialists in providing door-to-door courier service to the towns of Surat, Ahmedabad and Mumbai. There are no receipts or records of transfer. The system runs entirely on trust. Similarly, among the Marwaris, a loan can still be obtained merely on the understanding that it will be repaid on demand and reciprocated if needed. No other paperwork is considered necessary. During the cricket World Cup in 2003, over one billion US dollars was spent on betting in India, the highest figure among participating nations. Since betting is illegal in India, there was no way of enforcing settlements, but bets were honoured. The resort to honesty in such examples is not about morality; it is as utilitarian as the acceptance of corruption. Indeed, for every example of corruption, there are countless others that illustrate a far more important truth: Indians are simply better at pursuing material gain than pondering moral deficits.

Every morning, 5,000 entrepreneurs in Mumbai wake up at the crack of dawn to complete with clockwork precision an operation that would leave management gurus in the West stupefied. They are known as the *dabbawallahs*. Their job is to deliver 150,000 lunch boxes to offices in Mumbai. The 'tiffins' are collected from homes, processed though a human network, sorted and delivered, and returned home the same day. No computer system tracks this movement. The boxes are colour-coded and numbered so that even illiterate *dabbawallahs* make no mistake about addresses. Only one error occurs in eight million transactions, which has led Forbes Global to give the enterprise a Six Sigma rating, an efficiency level of 99.999999. The cost to the customer, at about US $3 per month, is affordable. The annual turnover of US $20 million is minuscule when compared to the scale of the operation, but sufficient to ensure a return of around US $100 for each employee, a sufficient monetary incentive by Indian standards of living.

In general, Indians respond with remarkable alacrity and efficiency to monetary incentive. During the Revolt of 1857, merchants in Delhi swore loyalty to the last Mughal king, but risked their lives to smuggle vital supplies to British troops on the Ridge outside the city. It was a high-risk high-return venture: discovery meant certain death at the hands of the Indian rebels, but the beleaguered British contingent was prepared to pay a high premium on the goods. The lethargy and laziness of which the British accused the natives was a colonial myth perpetuated by the British. Indians droop if deprived of the opportunities for upward mobility and material gain, and these were scarce—except for the very few—during British rule. They revive and blossom if the *opportunity presents itself and the monetary rewards are clear*. In 1946, in Kaira district in Gujarat a socially progressive Congress leadership encouraged farmers to fight the stranglehold of middlemen in the milk trade. The Kaira District Cooperative Milk Producers Union Ltd was formed. The colonial government refused to deal with the cooperative, but capitulated after a crippling fifteen-day strike. Cynics questioned the ability of rustic farmers to deal with sophisticated dairy equipment and to market products like butter and cheese for discriminating urban consumers. They were wrong. The cooperative, and its popular brand name, Amul, soon established a nationwide presence. Today, 173 milk producers' cooperatives and twenty-two federations supply pasteurized, packaged and branded milk to more than a thousand cities across the country. Eleven million farmers earn more from what they produce. The country's milk production has trebled in less than three decades, and India has become the largest producer of milk in the world.

That people outside the traditional commercial loop are capable of such robust enterprise is noteworthy. The Marwaris, and other trading groups like the Bhatias, the Jains, the Parsees, and the Khojas, have had generations of business experience. Their commercial ventures were cushioned by an effective community support system, a network of commercial contacts, and access to credit and banking facilities.[15] But the farmers in Gujarat who triggered India's white revolution were mostly illiterate and part of a subsistence economy, with no exposure to modern concepts of marketing. Similarly, the seven women who started the production of Lijjat papadams in Bombay in 1959 on borrowed capital of Rs 80 (less than US $2 at today's prices), had not gone to management school. They were semi-literate, and came from low-income male-dominated families. On the first day of business they produced just four packets of papadams. Today, their company has a turnover of over US $60 million, employing 40,000 women, with sixty branches countrywide. In the early 1970s, Ela Bhatt, a lawyer and labour union leader, motivated women workers in the ruthless unorganized sectors of the economy —rag pickers, hawkers, construction workers, slum-dwelling weavers—to form the Self-Employed Women's Association (SEWA).

What began as a political statement soon became a flourishing economic enterprise. Today, SEWA has seventy-one cooperatives and over 70,000 members. Among other successful business projects, it runs a micro-finance bank, to which its poorly educated but commercially savvy members have taken like fish to water. They have quickly learnt to optimize savings, negotiate loans (often using their jewellery as collateral, which the bank allows), make effective investments and tackle exploitative moneylenders and middlemen.

A talent for commerce is not the monopoly of Indians. But they appear to have a flair for converting opportunity to commercial advantage in the most unexpected ways. Udupi, a small town tucked away in coastal Karnataka, is the birthplace of the thirteenth-century Hindu saint-philosopher Madhavacharya. The town has a famous Krishna temple, and is regarded as one of the seven centres of pilgrimage for Hindus. However, today Udupi is even more famous in India as a culinary brand name. When residents of Udupi migrated to Mumbai for a living they opened restaurants, serving the delicious meals given to pilgrims in their home city—crisp crêpe-like dosas, hot steamed idlis and vegetable-filled utthapams. The new restaurateurs were short on capital and business experience, but worked hard to give their clients good, clean food at reasonable prices. Soon enough, restaurants and hotels named after Udupi began to crop up all over India, and in cities as far-flung as Los Angeles, Tokyo and Johannesburg. Madhavacharya had devoted his life to defining the ultimate nature of divinity. His descendants did quite well for themselves by giving so many satisfied customers more literal food for thought.

The state of Bihar in north-eastern India does not provide the most salubrious climate for economic enterprise. More than 55 per cent of its people live below the poverty line, which means that they do not have money for two meals a day. It has the lowest per capita income in the country, and the general impression of the state is one of economic stagnation, administrative apathy and corruption. Most people believe that Biharis are not interested in changing their fate; they do not have the capacity for hard work, and lack the drive to escape their humiliating impoverishment. However, such stereotypes are untrue. Even Bihar has not been able to douse the economic ingenuity of its people if the right opportunity presents itself. The people of Katisarai in Nalanda district, some hundred kilometres from the state capital Patna, are a case in point. They have worked very hard for the last several years to capitalize on the one economic hope they had: the production of traditional ayurvedic medicines. Natural herbs are available in the nearby hills of Rajgir and the adjoining districts. These are painstakingly collected and processed into indigenous medicines that have by now takers not only in India but also in the neighbouring countries of Bangladesh, Nepal and Pakistan. In what appears to be a cottage industry, over eighty units manufacture drugs for diseases like diabetes, leucoderma and other chronic ailments. The medicines are mostly sent by mail order, to the benefit of local post offices. The entrepreneurs advertise their products resourcefully. Their offices are equipped with computers and fax machines, and their investment-to-profit ratio would be a management guru's envy.

Not too far away, in the extremist Naxalite-infested Chhotanagpur area of the state of Jharkhand (until recently a part of Bihar), some tribal farmers, belonging to the poorest and most exploited section of society, have shown the same capacity for enterprise. Helped by a project of the World Bank, they have multiplied their income several-fold by growing flowers—gladioli, gerberas, marigolds and tuberoses —for sale. Cooperative farming was not known in these parts, nor did these marginal agricultural workers have any experience of organized economic activity. But when they saw the opportunity, they have been willing to pool together the only asset they had—their meagre land holdings—and have been remarkably receptive to training and technical advice.

Indians rely on their inherent feel for enterprise. They are not resistant to formal business education, but many—especially the elderly in the traditional trading communities—still consider it an expensive indulgence. Largely unaware of the natural commercial talents of the 'natives', British firms recruited business executives from upper-crust families, who were educated in elitist public schools, dressed well and spoke good English. For these Calcutta boxwallahs, business was an incidental accessory to the clubhouse, and the grimy dealer who actually sold the goods an avoidable intrusion. But while the dealer may not have had the right accent, he was good at making money. Soon after the British left, the social equations began to change. The boxwallah, unable to stay afloat in the commercial torrent of the marketplace, began to fade into the sepia tones of the silver framed photographs on his mantelpiece. The dealer stepped out of his godown to self-confidently take in the world at his own level. V.S. Naipaul, during his travels in India at the end of the 1980s, talks of how the traditional dealers, often the envy of the Western-educated boxwallahs, are intrinsically talented at making money, working from early morning till late at night in their small shops, judiciously using their profits to expand their business, and showing off their money in their garishly done up houses.[16]

When Venugopal Dhoot set up Videocon International in 1984, he withdrew his younger brother from an MBA course and sent him to work at his colour TV factory. Videocon is today ranked among the top three TV brands in India, with a turnover of over US $6 billion. Dhoot had prepared himself for Videocon by working in the family business of cotton and sugar. He was willing to take the risks to push the business towards new horizons. Many of his contemporaries, from bigger business families, preferred to persist in the old grooves, making easy money through the unchallenged monopolies and lack of competition of the licence-raj era. They were critical of the socialist rhetoric in private, but deferential to the bureaucrat-politician in public. There was money to be made in the crevices of the outmoded regime of government controls, and working the system required its own brand of enterprise and agility. The economy may not have been doing particularly well in the socialist era, but Indian businessmen were hardly immobile during that period. Many of them were rather like trapeze artists, clinging to the government where it proved profitable, but ready to grasp new commercial opportunities when they were available.

The real opportunity came in 1991, when the then Prime Minister, Narasimha Rao, ably guided by his erudite Finance Minister, Dr Manmohan Singh, announced a series of economic reforms to dismantle state controls and prepare Indians to participate more vibrantly in the global economy. The reforms were but a beginning, but they signalled a decisive break from the dogmas of the past. The philosophy of socialism, which sought to curb private initiative for the ostensible purpose of a larger public good, was clearly not in sync with the Indian psyche. The discordance had nothing to do with the intrinsic merits or demerits of the doctrine, or the objective reasons for its application in a country with the largest numbers of the absolutely poor in the world. The truth is that Indians have an inherent suspicion of collective altruism, and are not willing to dilute their exuberant commitment to personal profit, even if the larger public good dictates otherwise. Any system ignoring these inherent biases was bound to fail. Vested interests used the infrastructure of socialism for personal gain. Politicians fattened on its lack of transparency. Bureaucrats revelled in the power—and money—it yielded. Businessmen learnt quickly to work it to their advantage. The poor occasionally benefited, and were grateful for the crumbs rhetoric could deliver. But nobody really believed that socialism could work in India—least of all some of its most vocal supporters.

Of course, socialism had failed in other countries too. But in India, where half the population in 1947 lived below the poverty line, the need for a policy that legitimized the intervention of the state in favour of the poor seemed to be self-evident. Jawaharlal Nehru was convinced of the moral imperative to orient policy for the benefit of the downtrodden. His socialism was the counterpart of Mahatma Gandhi's strong emotional identification with the poor. The idealism of these founding fathers was genuine. But whereas Nehru believed socialism was the answer, Gandhiji did not. He was born a bania, 'conditioned by birth to follow the ethic of the Porbandar bazaar-entrepreneur'.[17] He did not hold capitalists in disdain, as the patrician Nehru was wont to do, even though the Congress Party was running on the 'donations' of such capitalists in Nehru's own lifetime. Gandhi felt deeply for the poor, but never questioned the raison d'être of the rich. He was aware of their utility, and understanding of their motivations. His mistake was to try and motivate them to *voluntarily* forsake some of their wealth for the benefit of the poor. This they would never do, and as a man of the masses Gandhi should have known that, were he not blinded by the intensity of his own idealism. It is ironical—but entirely in keeping with the Indian reality—that the messiah of the poorest of the poor died in the Delhi home of the Birlas, one of the richest business families in India. This did not dilute his identification with the poor, but it recognized the legitimacy of wealth, and reflected the instincts of the people far more accurately than the idealistic socialist vision of Nehru.

Indians could never quite comprehend the personal austerity of Gandhi. They respected him for it, but more as a person from earth might look up to the powers of someone from another planet. As we have seen, Indians revel in the fruits of the material world. Notwithstanding pervasive poverty, their tradition is to welcome material gratification, not denigrate it. Gandhi's imperviousness to the temptations of the material world left them awed, but unconverted. They admired his ability to restrict his wants, but were not prepared to emulate him. His ashrams were a place of curiosity, not of inspiration. He was revered because he could renounce the lure of power and pelf, something Indians did not expect anyone to do. He was looked up to as a Mahatma because in his denial and sacrifice he was so *different*, so unlike everyone else. Even conventional saints, the sadhus and babas who proliferate in India, are porous to earthly munificence. I once accompanied the then President of India to Puttaparthi, the seat of Sathya Sai Baba, who has one of the largest followings in India. The swanky red Mercedes used by the saint dwarfed the presidential limousine. Most Indians do not consider such display to be wrong or antithetical to spirituality. Gandhiji did, and did so inflexibly, which is why his brand of self-denial failed so dramatically. No sooner had he died, and even during his lifetime, than his followers betrayed his spartan code of living. They wore the homespun *khadi* that he wore, and paid copious amounts of lip service to his ideals, but took to the opportunities of the good life effortlessly.

Mahatma Gandhi's triumph was the independence of India. His failure was the subsequent rejection of Gandhism. The personal austerity that Gandhi propagated found very few takers, for the same reason that socialism found very few believers. Both went against the grain of the way Indians are. Nehru's personal faith in socialism spawned a vast and unproductive hypocrisy. During his years as prime minister (1947-64), and for more than two decades after that, socialism became an article of faith to be breached in practice and praised in theory. Even in 1991 when the new economic policies were introduced, they were proclaimed in quasi-socialist terms. But the change in the mood of the nation was transparent, and Gurcharan Das caught this well in his book *India Unbound*. The year 1991 removed the stigma supposedly associated with the pursuit of wealth. It buried the need for hypocrisy about the aspiration to become rich. Most importantly, it made policies congruent with the temperament of the people. People could now do openly—and with greater effectiveness—what they had tried to do surreptitiously under Nehruvian socialism: find ways to make money for themselves. Economic liberalization removed the self-imposed veil on Indian motivations. For long the professed bias of state policy was for the poor of India. No longer. Material wants were now suddenly severed from any notion of guilt. In a sense, it was the collective exorcism from the nation's psyche of the 'repressive and life-denying nature of Gandhi's idealism',[18] an exultant escape from his emphasis on austerity, and a smug—and more confident—return to tradition.

The lush growth of consumerism that sprouted from the groundbreaking decisions of 1991 was entirely in keeping with Indian inclinations. Gandhi's children showed little diffidence in their desire for the most expensive cars, the latest consumer gadgets, designer clothes and accessories, and five-star living. Not everybody could afford them, but everybody wanted them. The market understood this well. Enterprising firms opened up to offer the right loan for the right product from the right source. The credit card industry mushroomed. In 1995 alone MasterCard grew by 106 per cent in India, the highest growth rate in the Asia-Pacific region. Visa grew by an unprecedented 94 per cent and American Express by 135 per cent. Consumer giants spent millions of dollars on advertising. The explosion of satellite television beamed the objects of desire into people's homes in a manner inconceivable but a few years previously. If people in small-town India could not afford the designer clothes they saw on television, their irrepressible—and not very discriminating—wants sustained one of the largest markets of fake labels. The targets of this consumerist overdrive were celebrating, not protesting. The popular Pepsi ad simply stated: '*It's my life.*' The mother in a hair oil ad proclaimed: '*Zamana badal gaya hai*: The times have changed.' Any earlier notion of limiting wants was happily countered by the chorus of a popular song: '*Meri marzi*: It's my sweet will.' If some doubts about this heady hedonism still lingered in the minds of a few of the older generation—especially those who could not afford the new luxuries—the young were in no such quandary. In one survey, 75 per cent of the children said they wanted to own the products advertised on television. A leading magazine that did a cover story on the 'Age of the Super Brats' concluded: 'In an upwardly mobile world, where grown-ups chase power, ambition and money, with money predominating, children are increasingly deciding how the cash is spent and on what—leading to a war whose only Hiroshima is a Toblerone, a Barbie or a Baskin Robbins.'[19]

In discussing the impact of 1991, we have to be careful not to confuse an 'ought' with an 'is'. Given the numbers of the poor in India, state policy *ought* to have retained its bias for the poor, and effectively implemented policies that attacked poverty and curbed the conspicuous consumption of the rich. But such an *ought* ran squarely against the entrenched Indian *is*, the proclivity to pursue personal well-being with little thought of any other social priority. The options, in terms of policy formulation, were thus very narrow. Socialism, or even a broad welfare state, was doomed to failure. And only that kind of capitalism could succeed that was socially insensitive. An active concern for the deprived and the suffering is not a prominent feature of the Indian personality.

The rich in India have always lived a life quite oblivious to the ocean of poverty around them. Noam Chomsky observed during a visit to India in 1996 that the Indian elite had a lifestyle more opulent than anything he had seen even in America.[20] In one of the poorest countries of the world, the aspiration for affluence, as an insular goal unto itself, is universal; the poor are deprived but not different from the rich in this regard. They too want to be rich, and will gamble to succeed if the opportunity exists. The organized lottery market in India totals a staggering $7 billion—roughly 2 per cent of the country's GDP. Not everybody can win, but once the poor manage to clamber on to the middle class wagon or higher, they display exactly the same insensitivity to those they have left behind. Though identified with larger social groupings—kin, caste or community— Indians are generally incredibly self-obsessed, wrapped up in their personal world of loss and gain to the exclusion of anything else. It is accepted that people are born to their own destiny, and suffer or prosper in accordance with their previous karmas. Life is a continuing saga, and the possibility of redemption from want and hunger that the poor seek can await their next rebirth, with no need for human intervention. Hierarchy is an integral feature of society, with near-divine sanction. Those below are ordained to be deprived, and those at the top are entitled to what they have. If the opportunity arises to break out of a preordained fate, it must be seized *against* the opposition of others, through *individual* effort, and for *personal* gain, not that of the community. Given such a world view, 1991 only further 'deepened the tendency which the wealthy Indian had to ignore the sufferings of the poor'.[21] But it also triggered a spurt of entrepreneurial energy that could have the consequence—ultimately —of doing more for the poor than all the well-intentioned activities of the state. In short, 1991 nudged India onto the only economic paradigm that is congruent with the character of its people: the top-to-down percolation model of growth, where a growth in the size of the pie contributes to a possible impact on inequity, and any attempt to curb or mould economic activity primarily in deference to the concerns of equity is unworkable.

The new entrepreneurs that 1991 spawned showed what Indians can do if allowed to pursue their natural talent for making money. Many of them were first-generation entrepreneurs, and most did not belong to the traditional trading classes—further proof, if any is needed, of the commercial acumen of Indians as a people. The pioneers were risk takers. They had a sense of vision, a belief in themselves, and were exceptionally nimble in seizing the right business opportunity. They began with rags and ended with riches. Subhash Chandra, who never attended college, was the son of a small-town cottonseed trader. In 1992 he decided to ride the new wave of entertainment television in India by setting up the country's first Hindi-language satellite channel, Zee TV. He didn't have the US $5 million required to bid for the Star TV transponder. He won the bid nevertheless, and then showed a chutzpah in raising money that left stalwart competitors like Nusli Wadia of Bombay Dyeing and the Jains of Times TV stumped. Today, he is India's first self-made media mogul, often called the Murdoch of Asia, with a net worth of 2.5 billion dollars.

Sunil Mittal was born the son of a parliamentarian. With no business background, he set up a small firm selling bicycles in 1970. Today, his company, Bharti Enterprises, has become one of India's leading private telecom service operators, controlling 20 per cent of the mobile communication market with sales of US $300 million. C.K. Ranganathan started off in 1983 with the equivalent of US $300 in his pocket, and faith in the shampoo he produced. Post-1991 his business proliferated into several new brands, taking on multi-national giants like Hindustan Lever. Ranganathan's father was a mathematics teacher; his mother was a housewife who wanted to set up a children's school. When he began production in a small boarding room, his only real asset was an idea: how to tap the vast and largely untapped rural market by selling shampoo in sachets priced as low as Re 1. Today Cavin Kare, his company, has a turnover of over US $40 million. (Ranganathan was undoubtedly inspired by Karsanbhai Patel, corporate India's favourite case study, who started off in 1969 making detergents in his backyard and retailing them on his bicycle; by the 1980s he had made Nirma one of the world's largest-selling detergent powders.) Naresh Goyal began his career in 1969 as an employee of Lebanon International Airlines. Subsequently, he worked for the Jordanian and Philippine national carriers. But when India introduced its Open Skies policy in 1991, he launched his own airline. Jet Airways commenced operations in 1993 with four leased Boeing aircraft. Today it has emerged as the country's leading private domestic airline, with a fleet of thirty planes operating more than 195 daily flights to thirty-nine destinations across India. In less than a decade its gross revenue has grown from US $43 million to close to $500 million.

These are just a few examples to give a flavour of the energy and buoyancy waiting for the right opportunity in India. For every well-known name, there are thousands of anonymous entrepreneurs lying in wait to seize the big time. The most spectacular results can, of course, be seen in the information technology sector; outside infotech, the pharmaceutical sector has seen a proliferation of young entrepreneurs, with remarkable results. Sushil Suri, not yet 40, has made Morepen Laboratories a global concern in the field of health care. Cipla, Dr Reddy's Labs, Wockhardt and Ranbaxy are other pharma firms making a worldwide impact. India has emerged with the world's fourth-largest pharmaceutical industry in terms of volume, and pharmaceutical exports have topped $2 billion. The export of auto-components grew five times in 2003, and with fifteen of the world's largest automobile manufacturers now buying components from India, is expected to top $15 billion in a couple of years. In the turbulent arena of finance, innovators like Uday Kotak have shown an ingenuity and instinct to stay ahead of obstacles that must have few parallels anywhere. The yen to explore new horizons by those with no hereditary business background can be seen across the spectrum. Anjan Chatterjee, who left a secure job at the age of 27 to set up his own successful advertising agency, soon moved on to create a flourishing chain of speciality restaurants in Mumbai, Kolkata, Pune, Bangalore, Chennai, Hyderabad and Delhi. Many old business houses, buffeted by the uncertainties unleashed by 1991, are now reinventing themselves on the strength of the commercial savviness of the younger generation. Kumar Mangalam Birla, 36, now, was 27 when his father died. On taking over, the young scion of the Birla family questioned conventional economic wisdom by withdrawing from a series of investments planned by his father. He then launched a clutch of acquisitions and alliances in the new high-potential sectors of software and insurance, leading his group on a growth trajectory that has made him among the richest men in India. Abhishek Dalmia, of the Dalmia group, has acquired a swash-buckling reputation as a shrewd corporate trader; Satish Reddy has steered Dr Reddy's Labs into a formulations giant; Analjit Singh, the youngest son of Bhai Mohan Singh of Ranbaxy, has joined the billionaires' club with the success of Max India; Harshavardhan Neotia has given to the old family firm of Ambuja Cements a new profit graph; Sameer Modi, of the troubled Modi group, has set a new track record with his company, Modicare. The fourth-generation entrepreneurs of the giant Murugappa group of Chennai (founded in 1884) have quietly allowed professionals to run their empire; and the owners of Dabur, the ayurvedic conglomerate, called in international consultants to help loosen family control.

Such examples of commercial success, of innovation, drive, vision, determination, adaptability and adventure are anchored in the fundamental Indian openness to, and talent for, acquiring material wealth. For every success story there are, of course, dozens of failures. Traditional Indian firms have their strengths, but also their weaknesses, and of these perhaps the most debilitating are a lack of teamwork and a weakness to pursue quick profit. These reflect ingrained ways of thinking and planning, as does the distrust of anyone outside the family, which inhibits the adoption of modern practices of management. But such weaknesses are more than compensated for by the *desire to succeed*, which is probably more intense in India given the omnipresent fear of poverty, the cut-throat competition for each opportunity, and the asphyxiating hold of hierarchy. If success demands a change in management practices, Indian entrepreneurs are likely to adopt them faster than expected. If money is a likely consequence, they can be confident risk takers, willing to break away from the constraints of the past. More than anything else, they empathize with improbable success stories—the rags-to-riches syndrome—that stand the system on its head.

Dhirubhai Ambani, perhaps India's most celebrated rags-to-riches entrepreneur, was born the son of a poor schoolmaster, and began his career as a petrol pump attendant in Yemen in the late 1940s. While he was in Aden, Yemeni officials found that the country's currency, the silver rial, was becoming scarce in the market. They soon discovered that Ambani was melting the silver coins and selling them as ingots to bullion dealers in London. When reminded of this much later in life, Ambani said with disarming sincerity: 'I don't believe in not taking opportunities.' Back in India, Dhirubhai's first trading office was so small it could not accommodate more than four people. When he died in July 2002, his business empire was worth over US $12 billion, and included the world's largest greenfield oil refinery. Interestingly, Ambani was also instrumental in triggering an investors' revolution. After his fast-growing group went public in 1978, millions of middle class investors junked their veneer of financial caution and happily took to the buying and selling of scrips.

The Bombay Stock Exchange lists more than 6,000 companies—second only to the New York Stock Exchange—and in the heady early years when the stock market offered a real opportunity for the first time for ordinary investors to make money, it was not surprising to see salaried workers, with no prior knowledge of the stock market, visiting stockbrokers during their lunch breaks.

Indians envy the manner in which wealth pole-vaults people over prescriptive barriers, and admire the way it insulates them from the unproductive claims of morality. Above all, they understand the incentives that fuel entrepreneurial drive. Dhirubhai Ambani was a successful entrepreneur, not a moralist. He played the licence-raj to his benefit, and cultivated political patronage to milk the command economy. This aspect of his meteoric rise was known to people, and commented upon, but Indians respect him nevertheless for the unprecedented wealth he created and the returns he guaranteed to the ordinary investor. The rough and tumble of Dhirubhai's life, its fantastic success and its canny pragmatism, its carpet-bagging odour and its smell of the bazaar, is a metaphor for the aspirations of the Indian entrepreneur. It is the ability to pursue opportunity and profit, which he so flamboyantly exhibited, which have yielded dividends in the challenging economic environment of India, and created wealth across the world. Across Africa, Indians are known as traders, and in many countries they enjoy an image as hard-nosed profiteers. In the United States they have emerged as the richest immigrant ethnic minority. In Antwerp they have overtaken Jews in the world's most famous diamond bourse; their share in the $26 billion diamond business has grown from 25 per cent in the past to 65 per cent today, while that of the Jews has fallen from 70 per cent to about 25 per cent.[22] In the UK, poor migrants from Gujarat have managed in one generation to establish a near monopoly over the brisk corner shop trade, giving rise to the saying: 'Give an Indian a corner and he'll set up a shop.' Success stories illustrating this entrepreneurial energy abound. Ghulam Noon was born in a housing complex on Mohammad Ali Road in Mumbai, the son of a small sweet shop owner. He went to the UK almost penniless in 1964, but is today the uncrowned king of the curry and frozen food trade. The Queen knighted him in 2002. Reuben Singh, whose parents came to England

in the early 1970s, was 17 and still in school when he started his first
venture—a women's accessories company—with only £500 as
capital. Today Reuben runs a business empire of 14 companies,
worth over £330 million, and has been listed in the Guinness Book
of World Records as the world's youngest self-made millionaire. In a
recent interview, Singh articulated the heritage of his forefathers well
when he candidly confessed his passion for the four 'Cs': companies,
cars, clothes and cash.

If Indians really are such pragmatic materialists, what then is the
role of spirituality in their lives? In answering this question the first
thing to understand is that in India affirmation of one attribute never
fully denies another. This is not a country of simple blacks and
whites. Shades of grey streak the most vivid contrasts. It would be
wrong therefore to infer that since Indians are material minded they
are not spiritual. Religion plays an important role in their lives and,
according to the latest survey by the Census of India, there are 2.4
million places of worship in the country, as against only 1.5 million
schools and half that number of hospitals. What is important,
however, is to understand how the spiritual tradition impacts on the
personality of the people, what strengths it gives them, what weaknesses it fosters, and how it is sustained in parallel with the resilient
materialism we have portrayed.

Hinduism has no organized church, no one god, no paramount
religious text, no codified moral laws and no single manual of
prescribed ritual. The predominant emphasis is on personal salvation,
a journey in which the individual is essentially alone with his karma
and his god. The absence of one universally-followed form of religious
worship does not, as we shall discuss later, necessarily contribute to a
liberal temperament. But it does create a peculiar mood of hope in
which the individual never ceases to believe that, as a consequence of
his *personal* and *private* compact with the Almighty, his destiny could
one day change. The mood is not easy to scientifically define or pin-
point. Usually it is heavily camouflaged, concealed beneath the
seemingly endless and mandatory demands of kith, kin, caste and
community, and the constraints of poverty. But somewhere, even in
the most dire straits, a Hindu will nurture a feeling that something
suddenly can miraculously intervene to change the contours of his life.

It is quite common to find this motto written on trucks: '*Milega muqaddar*: I shall find my destiny.' A sense that, out of the blue, a personal god can smile, a guru's blessings can work, a religious donation can fructify or a ritual prove efficacious never leaves a Hindu. Hinduism sets no ceilings on divine intervention. Anything is possible. People believe that one day the wheel of fortune will turn the right way, and religion can help it in that direction. '*Kismet ka karvat lena*', the turn of fate, or '*Bhagya ka badalna*', a turnaround in luck, are not only common Indian phrases but also articles of faith. Astrologers proliferate, and are much in demand. In fact, as Nirad Chaudhuri concludes in his inimitable way 'in a Hindu, faith in his horoscope was far stronger than his faith in any god or goddess or even God.'[23] A very well-known—and often-quoted—Sanskrit *shloka*, or saying, expresses the notion that a woman's character and a man's fortune can never be predicted. (*Triya charitram purushya bhagyam, daivo na janati kuto manushya*). Good fortune, like suddenly finding a hidden pot of gold, is a possibility that can never be denied. *Sab bhagwan ki leela hai*: the world is but an aspect of god's cosmic play, in which anything can happen, playfully and effortlessly, as a joyous expression of divine whim. Hindu mythology is full of stories of huts turning into palaces, and base metal turning to gold. I recall my elders often saying: '*Na jane kis bhesh mein mil jaaye bhagwan*: You never know in what form you will run into God.'

Naturally, such an attitude tolerates a great deal of superstition and ritualism. There is no rationale to what may please a personal deity, or invoke a dormant benediction. The offering of a lock of hair, a donation, a pilgrimage, a penance, a vow, a fast, an amulet, an oblation, the repetition of a particular Sanskrit chant, the feeding of monkeys or cows—anything may work to alter the apparently unalterable framework of our lives. This irrepressible faith gives to Hindus an optimism that refuses ever to fully deflate. In the direst of situations they have an emotional identification with every rags-to-riches story, and this identification is personal: if it can happen to others, it can happen to me. In this sense, Hindus do not labour under the ponderous certainties of Christianity or Islam, where human redemption is predictable in measurable ways. Hinduism, as practised, is full of the mysterious possibilities of a tropical jungle.

Hindu metaphysics constitutes a truly magnificent structure of thought. But most Hindus have no inclination for the intricacies of philosophy. They know little about the six schools of Hindu thought, and even less about the thinkers who defined them. Their pre-occupation is with the ritual of religion, and the rewards it can confer, and in this pursuit they can be, within the framework of their religion, remarkably eclectic. At the Sri Bhagwati Sai Sansthan Mandir at Panvel, not far from Mumbai, a dog is worshipped as the reincarnation of Sai Baba of Shirdi. When Sai Sri Pandu Baba (as the dog has been christened) left for his heavenly abode in 1997, he was bathed in waters from India's holiest rivers, and buried in a *samadhi* (grave) lined with sandalwood, to the chanting of Vedic hymns. Needless to say, the priests at the temple have found a successor to the Pandu Baba in the form of another dog, and the crowd of worshippers has not lessened. In a village near Lucknow, the grave of an English captain who died during the 1857 Revolt is widely worshipped. The Gora Baba is known to fulfil every wish of his followers, and being an Englishman he is especially pleased when offered liquor, cigarettes and meat. A prayer is incomplete without the ritual lighting of a cigarette, which is then offered along with an incense stick.

The Vedas recognize thirty-three gods, the Puranas 330 million. The Hindu has, therefore, no dearth of divinities to keep him busy. So long as they can fulfil his desires he has very little interest in understanding the epistemological nature of reality. However, certain concepts derived from philosophy, do have a significant influence in his life. Two of these, *maya* and *karma*, need special mention. All Indian schools of philosophy accept *maya-vad*, the theory of *maya*, in one form or another. In lay terms, *maya* is the magical power that creates the illusion that the world is real. The phenomenal world is actually a deception. People caught in *maya-jal*, the snares of the illusory world, think it is real. In reality, nothing exists except the ultimate being, Brahman. The rest is appearance, the result of ignorance, fleeting and impermanent, as unreal as a dream. *Karma*, as commonly understood, simply implies that a man's destiny is linked to his deeds in a previous birth; good deeds bring good consequences, and bad ones bad. Death only kills the physical body. The soul, which is imperishable, continues its cycle of rebirths, changing bodies as people change clothes, until finally it merges with the Absolute.

This is a simplistic rendering of concepts that have provoked tomes of analysis by metaphysicians. But our concern is with how ordinary Indians understood them, and how they impact on our everyday lives. The belief that the world is in essence unreal, a victim of maya, does not inhibit Hindus from the full-blooded pursuit of material possessions. But in periods of adversity, when losses occur, or prosperity appears to be out of reach, the doctrine gives to failure the cushioning of philosophical acceptance. No defeat can be that great if viewed as the transient setback of an illusory world. In terms of a familiar metaphor in Hindu philosophy, the world appears to be a snake when it is actually just a rope; it cannot—indeed should not—affect you because it is not what it is made out to be. This dual appreciation of reality, in which the world both *is* and *is not*, provides the perfect peg on which to hang the burden of setback. It does not bar the pursuit of worldly assets (and it is significant that in one sense *maya* means wealth), but when things are not going well, it *devalues* the full impact of failure. If a person is a winner, he is a successful practitioner in the world of *maya*; if he is a loser, he can console himself that his loss did not, ab initio, have any real value.

The theory of *karma* also operates to insulate a person from the impact of setbacks. The travails of life are ephemeral when seen in the context of the long journey of the soul towards salvation. In such a journey, the impact of transient adversity is diminished because it acquires a larger backdrop. The sense of personal responsibility is reduced. Defeat becomes easier to accept, for there is always the scapegoat of deeds in a previous life beyond our control. The principle that we are responsible for our actions, and for their consequences—which is the enlightened bedrock of the theory—is simplistically interpreted to mean that for what goes wrong today we cannot be blamed, and for what may accrue in something as remote as a future reincarnation, we need not be too concerned. The important point is that even death cannot obliterate the possibility of another round. There is always reason, therefore, not to lose hope.

No failure is final. No event takes place in isolation. The causal chain is interconnected. The ups and downs of life are part of a cosmic drama, whose final act no one has seen and none can predict. The successful could reap the consequences of their evil actions tomorrow. The defeated could have another court of appeal, beyond the control of human manipulation. The cosmic wheel is structured to take a full circle. Human misfortune is a speck on the vast canvas of time (*kala*). Destiny could change in later life, or in the next birth, or the one thereafter.

Spirituality thus serves Indians well in weathering periods of adversity. This is not an uncommon consequence of all religious faith, but the Hindu spiritual safety net is in many ways especially built to create reasons for solace in the bleakest of situations. The Hindu has chosen selectively from his spiritual legacy—faith in a personal deity, the devaluation of the phenomenal world when needed, and the juxtaposition of a larger canvas to suffering and setback—to create a protective cocoon around him. Certainly, the hope and resilience he displays is not warranted by the circumstances in which he and most of his compatriots are. But his religious beliefs provide the psychological ballast to stay afloat in the roughest of waters.

Few Indians are consciously aware of the strength that spirituality gives them. To believe in certain ways is a reflex for them. They rarely question or analyse their natural—and often cheerful—stoicism, in which religious faith and worldly-mindeness blend effortlessly. In some respects, spirituality is a defence mechanism. It serves to disarm the hostile invader (and India has had more than her share of these over the centuries), encouraging him to conclude that the conquered are harmless pacifists absorbed in the rewards of the afterworld. It also masks the formidable entrepreneurial and commercial skills lurking below the spiritual surface. Foreigners are often misled, because Hindus appear to be 'other-worldly'. *In reality they are not so much other-worldly as they are oblivious to anything in the world that is not of direct interest to them.* A pious Hindu will take a dip in the holy waters of the Ganga seemingly totally unaffected by the filth and garbage on and around the bathing ghat. His concern is the religious ritual, and the rewards it could yield; anything outside this personal zone of priority remains perpetually out of focus. The practice of religion sanctions this self-centredness: a Hindu will be obsessed with the ritual purity of his person, but seem not to notice the filth around him. When Mahatma Gandhi visited the famous Kashi Vishvanath temple in Varanasi, he was 'deeply pained' by what he saw. In his *Autobiography*, he describes the approach through a narrow and filthy lane, swarming with flies, the loud voices of shop-keepers and pilgrims, the rotten and stinking flowers inside the temple. Nothing much has changed in the decades since then. I visited the Jagannath temple at Puri in the first year of the new millennium. The main approach to the temple was flooded. An overpowering stench of sewage pervaded the place. Huge cockroaches could be seen on the ornate garlands around the deities. There were swarms of flies on the *prasad*, the consecrated food meant for devotees. Stray dogs, some with open sores, were everywhere. None of this deterred or distracted devotees from their prayers.

This self-obsession, in which the obvious discordance of the surroundings makes no dent, is not a sign of spiritual transcendence, as it sometimes appears to be, but of a callous insularity. A Hindu is effectively impervious to his surroundings, and indeed to the very visible pain and suffering around him, because anything outside his own narrow ken of interest matters little to him. Islam and Christianity display more visible connections between the individual and the community. In Islam there is the Friday congregational gathering, and in Christianity the visit to the church on Sundays. There is no such institutional counterpart in Hinduism, and almost no emphasis on a need for the individual to contribute to his community within the arena of spiritual search and fulfilment. The emphasis on the self as the centrepiece of the spiritual endeavour tends to stunt the individual's concern for the community. This insensitivity to the external environment, coterminous often with the most overt preoccupation with spiritual pursuits, has become so much a part of life that it is mostly not even noticeable to the educated Hindu. But it can come across as a startling revelation to the foreign observer. A.M. Rosenthal wrote perceptively in 1957: 'An individual-to-individual callousness, despite India's belief in her own spiritualism, was always part of India. No miracle has taken place.

This callousness is still so strong in the country that it is the greatest danger for a foreigner living in India, for it is a frighteningly easy thing to find it creeping into one's soul.'[24]

Materialism and spirituality coexist in India in ways, I suspect, that strengthen the former without eroding the hold of religion. An Indian entrepreneur is fortified by an inner world of personal faith opaque to the outsider. He is able to better withstand mishap and distress because of certain specific and unique concepts that form part of his religious beliefs. He sustains a sense of hope in the future even in affliction. He believes that the rags-to-riches story can happen to him, and is convinced that divine intervention can play a role. He is not constrained by a given set of ethics since Hinduism, while not espousing amoralism, does not have a single or unambiguous ethical centre, and accepts a moral relativism that refuses to be straitjacketed by simplistic notions of right and wrong. And his ability to be focused about goals, even at the cost of the larger good of the community, is strengthened by the individualism inherent in the practice of his religion. Spirituality, writes Ashis Nandy, is 'hardly the overwhelming aspect of Indianness'; yet 'there remains an irreducible element of spiritual concerns which informs the toughest materialism in India.'[25] Together they create an alchemy that reinforces both. An Indian is inherently an entrepreneur and willingly a devotee, and the one is the seamless extension of the other. The perceptive Scottish journalist James Cameron, who lived and travelled in India before and after 1947, captured this rather well when he wrote:

> I like the evening in India, the one magic moment when the Sun balances on the rim of the world, and the hush descends, and ten thousand civil servants drift home on a river of bicycles, *brooding on Lord Krishna and the cost of living*[26] (emphasis mine).

Chapter Four

TECHNOLOGY
Success in the Shadows of the Past

The recent emergence of India as a power to reckon with in information technology prompts the question: do Indians have some special talent in this field? What is it that makes an increasing number of citizens of the world's most illiterate country so successful where computers and their software are concerned? Could there be something about Indian culture and society that has made the software industry grow in India by around 50 per cent a year for the last several years? Indian software exports are projected to top US $50 billion—more than the entire value of the country's exports today—by the year 2010. Is it sheer coincidence that the co-founder of Sun Microsystems, Vinod Khosla, the designer of the Pentium chip, Vinod Dham, and the creator of Hotmail, Sabeer Bhatia, are all Indians? How has it come to be that a significant number of NASA scientists, Microsoft employees, IBM workers, and Intel scientists are Indians? Do 40 per cent of the largest 500 companies in the world have back processing offices in India only because it is cheaper, or because India is, as Bill Gates says, incredibly rich in technical talent? What is responsible for the fact that Indians are behind four out of ten Silicon Valley start-ups? Why has General Electric opened its biggest research centre in Bangalore, a city most Westerners would not have heard of just a few years ago? And why does the same city now produce the chip for every phone designed by Nokia?

The very visible phenomenon of India's providing the brainpower for some of the largest and most familiar of international corporations deserves serious scrutiny for what it reveals of the Indian personality. Are Indians 'naturally' good at number crunching? Is versatility at the keyboard rooted in some aspect of India's heritage? Is it an inherent talent, or has it been cultivated in recent years? What is the role of the cultural milieu in nurturing this proclivity? To what extent are entrenched ways of thinking, and of responding, a contributing factor? What traits impede greater success, and which ones facilitate it? Has the new technology diluted the hold of tradition on those who practise it? These are questions that need to be explored, for a great many expectations now ride on the proficiency of Indians in this sector. Can the IT 'revolution' do for India what the textile industry did for Britain in the nineteenth century, or what oil has done for the Middle East more recently? Any claims about 'inherent qualities' need to be evaluated cautiously, especially since India's profile as an IT power is still very new. My aim, therefore, is to explore tentatively, to examine a few elements that seem significant, and to lay out the grounds for a debate whose conclusions for the moment must be kept open.

In its broadest definition, information technology is a term that encompasses all forms of technology used to effectively create, acquire, store, process, analyse and distribute information. It involves the creation and management of data, including its dissemination through a network that includes both telephony and computer technology. Proficiency in mathematics and engineering, preferably—but not necessarily—specialist training in computer sciences, are assets. Given these activities, and the skills they require, do Indians have some special edge in this field?

There is little doubt that an ancient tradition of excellence in mathematics existed in India. Scholars have reason to believe that the Indus Valley Civilization, which flourished 2,500 years before Christ, used a system of weights and measures based on an awareness of the decimal system. It is clear too that the cities of this civilization could not have been built without knowledge of simple geometry. In later times, mathematics emerged as India's single greatest contribution to the world of science. The term *ganita*, meaning the science of calculation, occurs with great frequency in Vedic literature. As far back as possibly 500 BC, the *Jyotisha Vedanga*, a manual of astrology, was using sophisticated methods of calculation to fix the position of the new and full moon and other astronomical inferences.

A group of sixteen *sutras* or word formulae were widely used in Vedic times to solve arithmetic and algebraic problems. These ancient techniques, lauded for their simplicity and flexibility, have been all but forgotten, but attempts are now being made to resurrect it for regular study under the rubric of 'Vedic Mathematics'. It is interesting that the use of mathematics was evident in aspects of daily life, such as the construction, in accordance with exact specifications, of sacrificial altars used in Vedic ritual. It would appear that Vedic Hindus considered certain numbers, such as 3 and 7, sacred, and used them in increasingly sophisticated permutations. In general, there is evidence of a preoccupation with numeration as part of religious ritual, and this can be seen even today in the chanting of the Sahasranam, the thousand names of Vishnu, or the Laksharchana, offerings made to the deity a hundred thousand times. In a learned article on Vedic Mathematics, the late Bibhutibhusan Dutta wrote:

> Vedic Hindus developed the terminology of numeration to a high degree of perfection. The highest terminology the ancient Greeks knew was 'myriad' which denoted 104 and which came into use only about the fourth century BC. The Romans had to remain content with a 'mille' (103). But centuries before them the Hindus had numerated up to parardha (104) which they could easily express without ambiguity or cumbrousness. The whole system is highly scientific and is very remarkable for its precision.[1]

In the medieval period, Hindu astronomers and mathematicians, of whom the most famous were Aryabhata I (fifth century), Brahmagupta (sixth century), Mahavira (ninth century) and Bhaskara (twelfth century), made groundbreaking contributions to the development and elaboration of mathematical concepts, unknown to the West until the Renaissance or even later. Aryabhata I, for instance, had calculated that the earth revolves around the sun about a thousand years before Galileo was persecuted for the same claim. It is well known too that the concept of the zero, called the *shunya*, and the decimal system, originated in India, and reached the West through the Arabs, who for long called mathematics *Hindsat*, the 'science of India'. The Syrian astronomer-monk Severus Sebokht wrote with awe in the seventh century of the rational system of mathematics of the Hindus, 'and of their method of calculation which no words can praise strongly enough.' A.L. Basham writes that the 'unknown man' who devised the decimal system 'was from the world's point of view, after the Buddha, the most important son of India. His achievement, though easily taken for granted, was the work of an analytical mind of the first order, and he deserves much more honour than he has so far received.'[2] It is not unreasonable to infer that a part of this rich mathematical legacy would have percolated to the skill banks of ordinary people, particularly since the study of mathematics was linked to fields such as astrology. It is likely too that the educational curriculum gave some degree of importance to a basic proficiency in mathematics. Over the centuries, a bias in favour of competence in mathematics may have been internalized at the level of the population at large. This would have been particularly noticeable to foreigners, who could make comparisons with their own peoples. For instance, J. Fryer, a traveller from Europe in the seventeenth century, had this to say about Indians: 'Arithmetic being the most profitable science is the best understood by them, *to which they have a Natural propensity*, and will in a trice without the help of pen or Ink cast up the difficultest sums, and never pause upon it'[3] (emphasis mine).

Some Western scholars believe that 'Indians have an intuitive insight into the behaviour of numbers, and their arrangement into patterns and series.'[4] Of course, it is difficult to substantiate such a remark scientifically, though P.V. Indiresan, former director of the Indian Institute of Technology in Chennai, seems to agree. Indiresan says that in exploring a paradigm, Indians 'do not proceed the way Westerners do, step by step. Instead of applying deductive logic through painstaking scholarship to extend the paradigm to its breaking point, *they look for inspiration through inductive logic*.'[5] Such an approach seeks instinctively, and often at the cost of scientific rigour, to discover the underlying principle behind the mere accumulation of facts, and mirrors 'the unified field awareness of traditional Indian thought processes'.[6] An Indian will try and resolve a problem by looking beyond the minutiae to the bigger picture, which could reveal the basic *interconnectedness of things*, for his perceptions have been moulded by a world view which sees a unifying causal reason behind all phenomena. He will seek to identify cause-and-effect as a matter of reflex, look for a pattern in the mosaic of facts, and view data not only for its individual elements but as part of a network. Often the connection, the pattern and the network will come to him by intuition or inspiration.

A receptivity to the interconnectedness of things comes naturally to an Indian. His metaphysics tells him that even at the level of the smallest atom matter is part of an indivisible whole; his society informs him that an individual is part of a network of kith, kin and caste; his religion proclaims that nothing is random, and birth and death and everything in between are part of a causal link. Does this perspective, in tandem with a flair for mathematics, give Indians an advantage in a discipline dealing with the networking and infra-structure of information? Perhaps. But it is tempting to dwell on certain traits that could perhaps have a bearing on the manner in which Indians deal with information. For instance, Indians tradi-tionally have a mania for classification. While accepting the ultimate unity of both matter and spirit, they proceed to break it down into finite categories in a manner that has few parallels anywhere. Everything is meticulously—even relentlessly—classified. Matter is segregated into five gross elements: earth, fire, water, air and ether (*akasha*). A person's nature is broken down to three constituent elements (*gunas*): *sattva*, *rajas* and *tamas*. Flavours are subdivided into six kinds: salty, sweet, sour, sweet-sour, bitter and spicy. There are nine kinds of emotions: wonder (*adbhuta*), terror (*bhaya*), disgust (*bibhatsa*), humour (*hasya*), pathos (*karuna*), anger (*rudra*), love (*shringara*), heroism (*vira*) and peace (*shanta*). Human health depends on three kinds of humours: phlegm (*kaff*), gall (*pitta*) and wind (*vayu*). Women are of four basic types: *padmini* (lotus-like), *sankhini* (conch-like), *hastini* (elephant-like) and *chitrini* (varie-gated). Men too are of four essential categories: *anukula* (sincere and devoted), *dakshina* (one who distributes his affections equally), *satha* (cruel) and *dhrishta* (shameless). There are sixty-four ways to make love, and men are categorized as hares, bullocks and stallions, and women as gazelles, mares and elephants in accordance with penis length and vaginal depth. Life has four principal goals: *dharma*, *artha*, *kama* and *moksha*. People belong to four castes: *brahmin*, *kshatriya*, *vaishya* and *shudra*. The human journey goes through four phases: *brahmacharya* (the age of learning), *grihast* (the life of a householder), *vanaprastha* (an intermediate period of gradual withdrawal from the world) and *sanyasa* (renunciation).

Many more examples can be given, and each of these would provide an intricate tapestry of further classifications and sub-classifications. The essential point is that the Hindu seems to have a profound inclination to differentiate the world around him. He cannot resist the impulse to segment, to break down empirical phenomena into constituent units, to arrange into compartments what may appear to be a seamless whole. Such an exercise pre-supposes the ability to continually structure a link between a sum and its parts, and to build a maze of sub-categories without losing the reference point of the whole. The phenomenal world consists of discrete elements, each defined by a specific paradigm; every paradigm has its own elements; each element has an assigned characteristic; horizontal and vertical linkages join the elements; taken together, the paradigm and its elements form a network; each network is linked to another; all networks ultimately merge into the indivisible One. The Hindu is, therefore, not fazed by the sheer accretion of data or the elusiveness of a paradigm; like a beaver collecting pieces of wood, he proceeds to deconstruct both, examining the possible components, reducing them to comprehensible smaller units, linking these to each other, and playing around with the parts while aware of the need for a unifying principle.

Is there a correlation between how a civilization structures its collective wisdom and the way its people think and behave? Is it a coincidence that mathematics was the most significant contribution of Indian science? Is it just happenstance that for centuries Indians seem to have been comfortable with *structuring* information? Is it only fortuitous that Indians have been conditioned to conceptualize and understand the 'networked' nature of things?

How is it, for instance, that India had built one of the world's most extensive databases—and a perfectly workable system to access it for mass applications—more than three thousand years ago? The *Bhrigu Samhita*, a treatise on astrology first written in Vedic times, compiles at least 500,000 horoscopes, and claims to have an infinite number of records of people and the events in their lives. On the basis of this database, 45 million horoscopes can be permuted. Advanced statistical methods determine the rules and principles to work the compilation. Sophisticated mathematical calculations are an intrinsic part of the exercise. Clearly the treatise was not written by one person or in one generation. According to lore, the sage Bhrigu was concerned that notwithstanding their knowledge of the Vedas and the Puranas, economic prosperity eluded Brahmins. He therefore embarked on a long penance to propitiate the goddess of wealth and good fortune, Lakshmi. The goddess was pleased by his devotions. She appeared before him in a dream and advised him to initiate the science of Vedic astrology, which would provide Brahmins with a respectable source of income. What Bhrigu began was nurtured and expanded upon by succeeding generations of disciples.

The issue here is not the merits or demerits of the science of astrology. What is relevant for our purposes is the sheer scope and magnitude of the database underpinning the astrological exercise. Equally significant is the dispersal of this data throughout India. The original *Bhrigu Samhita* is no longer extant, but it has been copied on palm leaf and bark and paper, and carefully preserved by thousands of astrologers who have added to the corpus over the centuries.

The *Bhrigu* is not the only example of extensive and functioning databanks that greatly predate the advent of modern information management. The *pandas* of the northern pilgrimage towns of Rishikesh and Haridwar on the river Ganga maintain what is arguably the most extensive corpus of genealogies anywhere in the world. A pilgrim has only to give his family name and the hometown of his ancestors for these traditional archivists to pull out records tracing the family's lineage for several generations. Obviously, the records are neither complete or accurate in every instance. The population has grown so phenomenally in the last few decades that it would be impossible to keep track of every family history. But by all accounts the database is still extraordinarily extensive and systematically catalogued.

The influence of such traditions on India's success in computing is of course debatable, but these examples are nevertheless suggestive. However, we are on much surer ground when we link success in the knowledge industries to other aspects of Indian culture. Like other major agrarian civilizations, whether in China or in Europe, traditional Indian society looked down upon manual work, and considered the opportunity for higher studies a measure of hierarchical superiority. In the traditional caste system, menial and manual work was consigned to those on the lowest rung of society. In fact, according to the 'sacred' law texts, the Shudras—the lowest caste— were forbidden even to inadvertently listen to the recitation of the Vedas. If they did, hot oil could be poured into their ears; if they attempted to chant a *shloka* their tongues could be cut out; and if they committed the offence of reading the Vedas, their eyes could be gouged out. The sociologist André Béteille writes:

> The caste system gave a distinctive, not to say unique character to work practices and norms in India. Not only was work elaborately differentiated and graded, but the gradation was sustained by ideas of purity and pollution that had deep roots in religious belief and practice. Elsewhere, the lowest types of work may be considered degrading or demeaning, in India they were treated as ritually defiling. Nowhere in the world was the idea of work as a source of defilement, even permanent and hereditary defilement, carried to such extremes as in India. The stigma of pollution that was attached to such work as scavenging, tanning and flaying cast a shadow over many, if not most kinds of manual and menial work. Oil pressing, distilling, laundering, fishing and even ploughing the land were all considered as tainted in varying degrees.[8]

The Brahmins, at the top of the hierarchy, had social sanction to pursue knowledge as their principle vocation. The others sought to maintain their hierarchical superiority by the degree to which they could distance themselves from manual work. The feudal gentry were insulated by landed wealth. For those not so blessed, the pursuit of higher education was the most effective bulwark against the 'degrading' compulsions of manual labour. Until recently, it was not uncommon, especially in South India, for offices to display nameplates with every educational degree acquired by the individual— starting from school—mentioned in proud detail; every such degree provided further proof of the individual's place above those consigned to menial work. In North India it is still common to reprimand a child: study or else you'll cut grass (*ghas katoge*); the prospect of manual work invoked as a threat. Education was valued because it could widen the distance from the labouring multitudes. Avenues in the past were limited, including mostly the legal profession, teaching and a babu's job in government. But an explosion of new opportunities, particularly in the hitherto unfamiliar area of technical education, took place after Independence.

The person who deserves the greatest credit for this development was Jawaharlal Nehru, India's first Prime Minister. Nehru, with his Westernized education and belief in socialism, was impatient to get rid of the 'dead wood' of tradition as he promoted the 'new man' or the 'modern man', the 'man in the era of science', the 'industrial man' and so on. He presented a vision of an industrialized India, rational and scientific in outlook, and modernized in the Western sense of the term. To him science and technology were instruments to build a new nation, and indeed a new kind of Indian, and he set out to create the infrastructure of scientific and technical education to provide increasing numbers of Indians with the opportunity to train as doctors, engineers and scientists. In a nation where the majority of the people were illiterate, the overwhelming need, of course, was not so much for higher technical learning as for primary education. Article 45 of the Constitution adopted by newly independent India in 1950 provided for free and compulsory education for all children until the age of fourteen. The first five-year developmental Plan (1951-56) allocated 56 per cent of the education budget to primary education. However, the middle and upper classes were less animated by the provisions for basic education, which was already available to them, and more excited by the opportunities for higher education, which could provide new avenues for upward mobility, away from the world of hierarchically inferior manual labour. It was pressure from these influential classes that led to a most remarkable growth in institutions of higher learning, as the expense of primary and secondary education.

In the first two decades after 1947, the budget allocated for technical education was consistently higher than that for secondary education. While in the first Five Year Plan 5 per cent of the overall educational budget was allocated for secondary education, 14 per cent was earmarked for technical education. The second Plan (1956-61) allocated 18 per cent to technical education, and the third (1961-66) 21 per cent. In the following five years (1966-69), technical education had the lion's share, equivalent to one quarter of the education budget. In the same period, funds for higher education increased dramatically, reaching the same level as those for elementary education. The resultant educational edifice, in which the foundations were relatively neglected while building the super-structure, effectively reflects the nature of Indian society. Today India has the largest number of out-of-school children in the world *and* one of the world's largest reservoirs of trained and skilled manpower. The enormity of such a contradiction could arguably only be sustained in India, for only an Indian can so unperturbedly accept the inevitability of social disparities, and pursue personal interest so unconcernedly at the cost of the larger good of the community.

Ironically, however, it is precisely this that has contributed in such great measure to India's emergence as a possible global power in technology. Given the scarcity of resources, and other competing priorities, it may not have been possible—even if the will was there—to eradicate illiteracy *and* invest so consistently in institutions of higher education. Unlike China, India did not make a choice dictated by considerations of equity and equal opportunity. Thus, while the campaign against illiteracy languished and suffered the consequences of official apathy, some of the world's leading technical institutes were established as part of an enviable infrastructure of higher education. China's literacy rates are significantly higher than India's, but India sends six times more students to universities and other institutions of higher education than China. 25 per cent of all males and 45 per cent of all women remain illiterate in India, but the seven Indian Institutes of Technology (IITs), at Mumbai, Delhi, Kanpur, Kharagpur, Chennai, Guwahati and (now) Roorkee, produce world-ranking engineers and scientists. In addition, there are seventeen Regional Engineering Colleges, and a network of diploma-level polytechnics across the country. Overall, India has over a thousand engineering colleges, and an equal number of institutes provide the

Master of Computer Application degree. The country's 291 universities and around 12,000 colleges produce two million degree holders a year. Of these 120,000 are engineering graduates, and the figure approaches a million if the products of polytechnics are also taken into account.

The country with the largest number of people in the world who cannot read and write nevertheless produces an army of technically proficient graduates. This may appear to be a paradox, but it is not an enigma, because it is the transparent consequence of the way India's social heritage has moulded its people. The choices before a developing nation are not infinite. Within the framework of possibilities, people in different societies will make different choices. In some cases, like in China, the political system has been coercive enough to enforce a levelling of hierarchies. In India it was not. Democracies are not very effective in imposing their will, especially when the self-interests of the privileged have deep-rooted authority. In such societies, policies that contravene tradition are likely to remain for much longer as statements of good intent only. For instance, for all the lip service paid to it by officialdom, vocational education has never really taken off in India. A government scheme for the vocationalization of secondary education was finally drafted as late as 1998, but it still awaits proper implementation. The concept of vocational education has proved much too reminiscent of the anathemas associated with manual labour. The demand was always for a higher degree, which could conform to the traditional notions of hierarchical eminence. A degree in a higher technical discipline was particularly coveted. In the past, professional Brahmins enhanced their scarcity value by monopolizing the study of the ancient texts. Indian graduates in technology had a similar scarcity value. In the field of knowledge they were the new Brahmins, assured of unquestioning respect and social approval for acquiring a kind of knowledge that—as in the structures of the past—remained inaccessible to most Indians.

Rigidly stratified societies generate intense pressures for upward mobility. When these pressures collide with opportunity, the release is explosive. The ferment of middle class India is testimony to this. The surge of ambition and aspiration to move up the scale, to avail of openings hitherto denied, and to forge a future beyond the possibilities of the past, had been growing since 1947. But the opportunities multiplied many times after the economic reforms of 1991, and the advent of information technology. Computer firms began to sprout overnight, and multinationals began to body shop in India's technically trained human bazaar. For once, the government was quick on its feet, and invested in computer schools and training institutions, and in introducing and upgrading IT-related courses. Sensing the financial opportunities, private training institutes began to proliferate. At the turn of the millennium, the great Indian technology El Dorado seemed to be finally at hand.

A factor of critical importance is that Indians are willing to work very hard to reach this El Dorado. For every place in a technology institute there are thousands of aspirants. In 2003, over 200,000 students sat for the combined entrance exams for admission to the IITs; only 2,000, or less than 1 per cent, were selected. This kind of competition could be daunting; it could lead to resignation, an acceptance of the improbability of success, a withdrawal from the competition. Not so in India. On the contrary, competition has only accentuated the desire to succeed. Parents begin to groom their children from an early age. Families with modest budgets spend extravagant sums on private tuition. Children prepare for entrance exams with single-minded determination. Sixteen-year-old Shatrunjay Verma, came first out of *two million candidates* who sat for the school-leaving exam in Uttar Pradesh in 2003; since his village, Bagula Nagla, did not have electricity he used a kerosene oil lamp to study and cycled ten km daily to school. The effort seems to be in inverse proportion to the prescriptive immobility of the past. Those who make it do so against the fiercest odds; their grounding in the basics is usually very sound; and their enthusiasm for the new discipline, and the opportunities it presents, seemingly limitless.

Much of this enthusiasm has to do with the prospect of money. We have already discussed how, contrary to conventional stereotypes, Indians respond to the incentive of money. While it must remain debatable whether they have some particular talent for IT, there can be no doubting their desire for material rewards. As a career prospect, IT came with the promise of greater financial reward than

the traditional professions. It offered dozens of stories of entrepreneurs who began with thousands and ended up with millions. The
success of people like Narayana Murthy of Infosys, or Azim Premji
of Wipro Technologies, became part of folklore, known to every
aspiring young computer scientist. Murthy qualified for the IIT
Kharagpur in 1962 but could not join because his father, a government servant earning Rs 500 a month, could not spare Rs 150 a
month for a hostel. He joined the local engineering college in Mysore,
and later did a degree in management. After a couple of nondescript
jobs, he and six other computer engineers set up Infosys in 1981 with
a capital of Rs 10,000—equivalent to US $1,000 at the then rate of
exchange. In 2000 Infosys had a market capitalization value of
around $40 billion. Benefiting from stock options, a hundred of its
managers were worth over a million dollars, and as many as 400
employees had made over $200,000. Azim Premji ran a prosperous
hydrogenated fats company until his foray into IT made him at one
time, according to the *Forbes* ranking, the third richest man in the
world, three places above the Sultan of Brunei.

The value of IT shares has fallen since then, but the glamour has
not faded. There may be more personal computers in New York
than the whole of India, but over 500 portals are being launched in
the country every month. Often to the surprise of family and friends,
members of conservative middle class families continue to give
up stable jobs and blow up their savings to become dotcom
entrepreneurs. Many of them fail, but without dissuading new
entrants, and for valid reasons. A pack of new IT entrepreneurs, with
no inherited wealth, have for the last several years dominated the list
(in rupee terms) of Indian billionaires. The monetary windfalls of
successful Indians in Silicon Valley are no less inspiring. Sabeer
Bhatia sold Hotmail to Microsoft for $400 million in 1998. Vinod
Khosla, who founded Sun Microsystems, is worth over a billion.
Hemant Kanakia got $450 million from Ericsson for his Torrent
Network Technologies. Indians who are millionaires many times
over on the strength of their achievements in the IT sector, stud
Silicon Valley.

On the tiny Mediterranean island of Cyprus, over a thousand
young Indian software professionals earn their living. They come

from all parts of India; most of them have been recruited straight from college, and are young enough not to camouflage their real feelings under the cloak of idealism worn so effortlessly by so many of their countrymen. They make a good representative sample, and I sent an e-mail asking them to put down the reasons why Indians have done well in IT. Their replies were most revealing. Almost all of them felt that Indians are inherently good at mathematics and have a special talent for the computer sciences. One of them wrote: 'If we look into the basic building blocks of computers/IT it is all 0s and 1s, and it is India which has given this world the great number 0— Indians for sure have something inherent which has helped us excel in this field.' Others spoke warmly of the excellence of the technical institutions in India. But a great many were candid about the financial incentive. A middle class family has no social security except money, wrote one. Another felt that the 'materialist young generation (in India) is ready to stretch its work limits for some big bucks.' IT ensures the best possible returns on investment, according to a third. The real incentive is the salary of an IT professional which is much higher than the amount spent by him to acquire his skills. Another listed several factors, but was emphatic about the last: 'Finally, the most important factor. Money. Everybody wants to get into IT because of easy money. As most of us don't have any real passion for any profession, money matters the most.'

Higher salaries, and the possibility of getting a job abroad—the fastest short cut to the good life—motivates young Indians more than anything else. Each success story becomes a role model for others to follow. Students who succeed in getting a good job, at a salary their parents could not dream of, in turn motivate another generation of youngsters to be a part of the dotcom boom. The reaction is not confined to the metropolises, but has percolated to small-town India, perhaps with even more intensity, because the desire to break out of the limitations of poverty is greater here. Computer schools, like the National Institute of Information Technology (NIIT) and Aptech (one of India's leading players in IT training), have effectively capitalized on these aspirations, as students from Palghat to Patiala, from Junagadh to Jalpaiguri, flock to them. Stories of how Indians have worked to harness their proficiency in technology to a share of the good life spread across the country. One of the most remarkable examples is that of Patwatoli village in Bihar, home to the backward Patwa (weaver) community. The hamlet is impoverished, and could be expected to breed Naxalites rather than engineering graduates. Yet by the year 2002, 22 boys from Patwatoli had passed the entrance exams for the IITs, and three times as many were looking forward to entering other engineering institutes. The boys came from poor families. They lacked the money to buy books, or join expensive preparation classes. But they had a role model in Jeetendra Prasad, who qualified from Patwatoli for the IIT in 1991, and left for New Jersey in 1997 to join PricewaterhouseCoopers. His story created a dream, and the children of poor weavers in the boondocks of Bihar were willing to chase it. They earned money to buy books by giving tuition during the day, and studied all night for the exams. As more students succeeded, the community set up a support infrastructure, creating 'home centres' where students could live together to study. The investment was finely tuned to the dividends it could yield. Krishna, a near-illiterate weaver, whose son Munna qualified for the IIT, was frank about his expectations: 'Here people say Munna will go to America after qualifying in the examinations and earn a lot of money.'[9]

The boys of Patwatoli had to struggle harder to improve their English than to perfect their maths. One of them confessed to going to sleep with a dictionary to add to his vocabulary! In general, however, a working knowledge of English has been an asset for Indians in the global IT market. Once again, this is *a classic example of the ability of Indians to convert a weakness into a strength*. The British did not propagate English in India to add to the IT skills of Indians in the new millennium. For them language was a means to consolidate their colonial rule. Lord Macaulay had stated the colonial agenda with complete clarity as far back as 1835: 'We must at present do our best to form a class of persons who may be interpreters between us and the millions we govern; a class of persons, Indian in blood and colour, but English in taste, in opinions, in morals, and in intellect.' In a country whose culture and civilization was thousands of years old this was an audacious statement of policy. But Macaulay could not, even in his wildest dreams, have predicted how successful his policy would be. Educated Indians persevered to master the alien language; they saw it as a tool for higher employment, and as a means to get closer to the rulers. Even today Webster's dictionary defines a 'baboo' as a native clerk who writes English. Of course, it was not unusual for a colonial power to succeed in moulding the attitudes and lifestyle of the native elite. But what makes India unique is the ease with which this objective was achieved, and the enduring ideological hegemony of the colonial power long after its defeat. The pursuit of English was the most visible symbol of this cultural emasculation, for it was entwined with a deep sense of racial inferiority in the presence of the white-skinned rulers. Thus, while many other subject nations made the attempt to reverse cultural colonization after independence, or at least to reassert the relevance and priority of indigenous cultural roots, Indians flocked to English-medium schools with greater vengeance after the British left, and drifted away from their cultural roots in direct proportion to the extent of their 'education'. In time, the knowledge of English became a status symbol. People were judged on the hierarchical scale by their ability to speak English with the right accent and fluency. The British aim to not only physically subjugate the natives but also to colonize their minds was a spectacular success.

This is not an indictment of English. On the contrary, there can be little doubt of the international reach of the language, and its utility as a second language or a link language. It is, however, a comment on the Indian elite, and the ease with which they have made the language meant to rule them their first language. It is a comment too on the neglect of Indian languages, many of which have languished in the shadow cast by the pursuit of English. A language is not only a utility; it is a symbol of a culture, the repository of the heritage of a people, an indispensable mark of identity. For all the success of Japanese economy, their mother tongue remains their first language; as it does for the Russians and the Chinese. To the credit of India's founding fathers, the Constituent Assembly sought to give free India a national language of its own. But the decision to make Hindi in the Devanagari script the official language of the country within fifteen years after Independence could never be implemented. The linguistic chauvinism that overwhelmed the cause of the national language was a rather convenient development for the pan-Indian English-speaking elite, whose knowledge of Hindi was minimal or inadequate. Hindi, the proponents of English argued, was being made into an unspeakably difficult language by the 'narrow-minded' experts entrusted with its development. Their demand was for a more anaemic Hindi that could be understood by *them*. Hindi was a language with centuries of evolution and a sophisticated and extensive vocabulary. It could not be crippled or retarded simply to make it more comprehensible to those who had developed a greater facility in English. The humiliation inherent in even making such a request was largely unfelt by the brown sahibs of India.

In James Joyce's *Portrait of the Artist as a Young Man*, Stephen Daedalus expresses the anguish of an Irishman at having to speak English: 'The language in which we are speaking is his (the Englishman's) before it is mine. How different are the words home, Christ, ale, master on his lips and on mine! I cannot speak or write these words without unrest of spirit. His language, so familiar and so foreign, will always be for me an acquired speech. I have not made or accepted its words. My voice holds them at bay. My soul frets in the shadow of his language.' Indians have fretted too in trying to learn English, but their souls do not appear to have been in much anguish. In fact, the enthusiasts of English have even argued that its perpetuation at the cost of a national language is in the national interest. How this could be when less than two per cent of the population speaks English at all adequately is a pertinent question. The more important consideration is whether a foreign language can ever substitute for one's own. In a letter in 1935 Yeats expostulated: '[Rabindranath] Tagore does not know English, no Indian knows English. Nobody can write English with music and style in a language not learned in childhood and ever sing the language of his thoughts.' In the mid 1960s, V.S. Naipaul in *An Area of Darkness* said much the same thing. Calling English 'the greatest incongruity of British rule', he added that a clerk in India using English in a government office is 'immediately stultified', since he can never fully grasp the nuances of the foreign language 'which limit(s) his response and makes(s) him inflexible.'[10]

It is true that some Indian novelists in English have in recent times made important conquests in the West, and won international recognition and accolades for their work. But they are less than a handful, a very, very small minority. Yet even they can be taken aback—as happened to a well-known Indian writer in English when an appreciative foreigner asked: 'Do you *also* write in English?' The foreigner assumes that an Indian, belonging to a country that has eighteen fully developed languages, must be writing in his own language. He is often genuinely perplexed when told that Indians consider English to be their language of preference.

The truth is that for most Indians English has been largely an instrument of social exclusion; the Indian elites have presided over this linguistic apartheid, while the rest of India has consisted of victims or aspirants. Such a state of affairs has fostered a deep sense of inferiority in many who, while excelling in their studies in spite of the burden of education in a foreign language, have been unable to acquire the fluency in English of their social 'superiors'. Gandhi was aware of this. 'Our love of the English language in preference to our own mother tongue', he wrote in 1944, 'has caused a deep chasm between the educated and . . . the masses . . . The result has been disastrous. We are too near our own times correctly to measure the disservice caused to India by the neglect of its own languages.'[11] Even Nehru, whose first language was English, had no doubt about the place of the foreign language: 'Some people imagine that English is likely to become the lingua franca of India. That seems to me a fantastic conception, except in respect of a handful of upper-class intelligentsia—we must not confine ourselves to English spectacles.'[12] He also had the perception to identify an even more pernicious development, which would cast its shadow long after 1947—the creation of a new elitist English-educated class in India which had little contact with the masses.[13]

The development of Hindi and the other Indian languages, as part of an overall and cogent policy backed by the requisite political will, should have been the aim in post-colonial India. That it was not is a significant pointer to the priorities that impact on Indians. Indians can be incredibly focused in pursuing the concrete benefits of this world, rather than the diffused loyalties of culture and heritage, which they take for granted. Thus, those towards the top of the social order, who knew English well, saw no reason to displace a language that provided them effortless social standing, access to the best educational institutions and the best jobs. Those below, for whom English did not come as a class inheritance, chafed at this invidious system of social exclusion, but diligently aspired to learn the language to move up the social ladder. The acceptance of hierarchy, and the consequent preoccupation with upward mobility, shut out any notion of national pride, or outrage at the transparent inequity of the process. 'No source of inequality in our society operates in as subtle and intractable a manner as language', writes the educationist Krishna Kumar. 'Competence in English has become the single most important yardstick of a person's eligibility for negotiating the opportunity structure that can be availed of in a modern economy.'[14] The 'opportunity structure' is what has mattered to Indians, a tribute as much to their undistracted pragmatism as to their insular priorities. Inequity was not new to them; the opportunities were, and they were not about to let them go by. In the popular Bollywood film *Rangeela*, the hero's impoverished sidekick boasts that he has the 'daring' to tell his girlfriend: '*Apan shaadi karenge, kholi lagayenge, aur bachche honge to English-medium school bhejenge*: We will get married, build our shack, and when we have children send them to an English-medium school.'

Linguistic shoddiness is a disfiguring scar on a nation that has few peers in the richness of its linguistic heritage. Former Prime Minister Vajpayee is reported to have once said that the British finally left India because they could not bear any more the massacre of the English language. Indian English is littered with instances of spelling errors, grammatical mistakes, pronunciation howlers and incorrect phraseology. The continued alienness of the language is brought out by constructions such as this one, prominently displayed in a photo studio in Srinagar: WELCOME TO BE BLOWN UP IN KASHMIRI DRESS. The author of that invitation could—like many others—read and write English, but knew nothing of the language. Those who think they know English take pride in their distance from their mother tongues; those who speak English inadequately claim to know it well. The result is a nation of linguistic 'half-castes', insecure in English and neglectful of their own mother tongue. But this army

summer of 2001, there was widespread fear, bordering on hysteria, of a supernatural 'monkey man', who attacked people. In acknowledgement of a technological world, 'eyewitnesses' reported that the beast appeared to have chip-controlled movements, and could fly at the press of a button.

The ability to 'compartmentalize' the mind is both a weakness and a strength. It is a weakness because the superstitions and prejudices of the past remain insulated from exposure to modern science and technology. It is a strength because the hold of tradition is not a barrier to the world of science and technology. An Indian is never faced with the choice of either-or. His feet can be planted in the irrationalities of the past even as his hands competently mould the future of technology. His association with technology is simultaneous, not sequential. He does not have to get rid of everything backward in his tradition before he enters the modern world of science. This enables adaptability even if it prevents, or delays, real modernity. The ability to adapt to two different—and often opposed worlds—can be seen dramatically in the speed with which even villagers take to the benefits of IT. Landless tribals in Madhya Pradesh are earning more by using the government-supplied Internet-connected computer to find out crop market rates and obtain caste and land certificates.[26] Farmers in Maharashtra use the PC in their villages to get information about the harvesting time for the crop, the results of crop sampling, and forecasts about the expected yield. And 'each evening in a coastal village inhabited by fisher families, the women download information on the likely wave heights in the sea nearby. This information, available on the website of the US Naval Oceanographic Office, is then broadcast throughout the villages by loudspeakers. The fishermen thus get accurate information on sea conditions before they set out on their wooden boats.'[27]

In June 2003, President George W. Bush said that he saw India as one of the leading drivers of the high-technology world. His assessment could well be right. India produces a great many cost-effective and technically qualified people, and the number is growing, whereas in the West the popularity of engineering as a career is declining. Brainbench, a global leader in online skills measurement, has ranked India second among the top ten countries in the world in terms of the concentration of certified professionals in nine categories including IT, finance and management skills. Indians' training in the basics is thorough. Their functional knowledge of English is an advantage, even if their general lack of creativity and innovation is not. But as Silicon Valley has shown, given the right environment they can be remarkably inventive. They have the ability to bridge two opposing worlds by just being themselves, part traditional, part modern. Most importantly, they have a burning desire to succeed, to partake of the good life. The aspiration to upward mobility makes them exceptionally focused and hard-working. Instinct and conditioning have taught them how to get around a problem. A German or a Japanese will work meticulously within the system. An Indian will be far more 'willing to move beyond or outside the system to find the solution to a problem'.[28] Circumstances have taught him to take the failure of the system in his stride and find a solution anyhow. Notwithstanding such talents, the future will see obstacles, such as the move by some unions in the USA and in the UK to ban outsourcing of government contracts to protect local jobs. But these can be expected not to last, for India knows that the US and British economies, and the economies of other developed countries, will gain rather than lose from offshoring, and India's case will be fought by the firms of these countries. Average wages for skilled staff in India are still only about one-sixth of wages in the United States. According to Pricewaterhouse Coopers, operating costs for outsourcing firms in India are still 37 per cent lower than in China. Indians will need to do more to move up the value chain, to improve quality standards, and expedite the overall penetration of IT in the country. But given our capacity to muddle through, and to convert weakness to strength, the future appears to be more rosy than bleak. Of the 70 global software firms with the highest certification for quality control, 48 are Indian. The leading US firm, Deloitte Consulting, has predicted that three-quarters of leading financial institutions and investment banks will allocate tasks to Third World countries, and India will be on top of the list. Global financial institutions alone are expected to invest US $350 billion in India for outsourcing projects. Technology will loom larger on the Indian horizon than ever before, and slowly but surely it will change the way Indians look at themselves, and the way the world looks at India.

Chapter Five

PAN-INDIANNESS
Violence and the Power of Accommodation

The great Lingaraja temple in the east coast city of Bhubaneswar was built in the eleventh century and is among the most striking temples in the state of Orissa. Its pinnacle soars to a height of 55 metres and can be seen for miles around, a reminder of the past that can never be erased from the Indian landscape. Pious worshippers throng the temple, which is enclosed by gates on three sides, and closed to non-Hindus. But just outside, across the road, and part of a definitely less imposing structure, is something new—one among many new symbols of a new India—that seems to have emerged almost unnoticed from the crevices of the old. It is uncaring of its lack of pedigree, confident of its right to be, and open to anyone who has the ability to pay: the Nikhar Ladies Beauty Parlour.

On the other side of the country, close to Aurangabad, is the small town of Khuldabad. Here lies the tomb of Aurangzeb, the last great Mughal emperor, who died in the eighteenth century, and ruled an empire stretching over most of India. Aurangzeb was a devout Muslim. In keeping with Islamic injunctions he lived a simple life, and had decreed that the expense on his tomb should not exceed Rs 14 and 12 annas, the amount earned from the sale of caps he sewed and the calligraphy he wrote. His *mazaar* is within a mosque, a place of pilgrimage for believers. But almost overshadowing its entrance is an incongruity: an ISD (International Subscriber Dialling) and STD (Subscriber Trunk Dialling) booth, announcing its services in eye-catching black and yellow. Notwithstanding its cheap prefab looks, the booth has the swagger of the present; assured of its functional need, indifferent to the concerns of the past. A stone's throw away a huge billboard for a popular drink shouts: 'I WANT MY THUNDER!'

A new India has emerged in the last fifty years. It does not deny the past, nor is it immune to its influence. But it is more a product of the challenges of the present, and the opportunities of the future. When Winston Churchill said that India is merely a 'geographical expression . . . no more a single country than the equator', he was being both simplistic and arrogant. But to give him the benefit of doubt, he was probably reacting, like so many of his compatriots, to the bewildering diversity of India, a nation of many languages and ethnicities, deeply divided by insular fealties. It is possible that Churchill was not interested in looking beyond the surface, for it is always useful for a colonizing power to suggest that the colonized never had an identity to begin with. But India has a civilizational unity and many British scholars could have told Churchill that. A people who have evolved in the same crucible for thousands of years are bound to develop certain unifying traits, a tapestry of common beliefs, cultural similarities, shared outlooks and an overlapping of identities. Centuries before Christ, the *Mahabharata* mentioned as many as 363 communities spread all over India. Scholars say that Indians have a very large number of genes in common; they share a very high percentage of traits and their perceived diversity is often deceptive.

Yet under this awning of unity—more bequest of history than will—the country was, until recently, a cluster of particularities. An Indian in the North and an Indian in the South could worship the same god, or celebrate the same festivals, but knew very little about each other. Their loyalty to India was not in doubt, but their knowledge of each other was. For the greater part, their identity was specific to their caste, kith, kin and region. There were few symbols other than these to reach out to each other. The notion of unity conjured from the past did not as yet have an easily identifiable pan-Indian personality. The British created all-India institutions as part of their colonizing machinery. A common system of administration and the sinews of a fledgling railway network broadened horizons, at least for some Indians. The struggle against a common subjugating power created a kind of common identity for the subjugated, but it was specific to the freedom movement and the political goal of independence. When Jawaharlal Nehru unfurled the flag of independent India at the Red Fort in Delhi on 15 August 1947, Indians were united in their hopes for the future, but were still defined by the memories of the past. They had yet to evolve a culture of the present, distinct from but not severed from the past, and pan-Indian in its scope. The creation of such a culture, accessible to the common man and responsive to his tastes and aspirations, is a development of very great importance in the years after 1947, and of defining value in the study of the modern Indian persona.

The new supranational Indian culture is influenced by elite aspirations but no longer controlled by them. It cuts across class barriers and is nonchalantly lowbrow. It does not aspire to be classical, and has evolved in response to needs, not structured concepts. To the despair of purists it has had no qualms in borrowing from the West, or for that matter from anywhere else. It has displayed an extraordinary ability to be hybrid, often at the lowest common denominator of conventional cultural aesthetics, while continuing to be unmistakably Indian. Its evolution has been haphazard but spontaneous, showing an exhilarating lack of inhibition and an enviable capacity for improvisation. It has given common symbols and icons to Indians even in the remotest parts of the country. Riding on a media and communications revolution, it has spread faster than any cultural development before. It permeates all aspects of everyday life: dress, food, art, language, employment and entertainment. It has the arrogance of the upstart, and the self-absorption of the new. Irreverent in expression, it is dismissive of critics, and has no time for apologists. What it lacks in pedigree it makes up for in confidence, for it can count on the support of the people. Its greatest strength is that—excluding perhaps the absolutely marginalized—it includes more people across India in a common language of communication in more areas of everyday life than ever before.

The new culture is still evolving. It is difficult to define exactly, but impossible to ignore in the nationwide appeal of masala dosa and tandoori chicken, the rhythms of Daler Mehndi and A.R. Rahman, the evolution of 'Hinglish', the ubiquity of salwar-kameez, the popularity of Hindi films, the audience for cable TV, the mania for cricket, and the competition for the IIT-Joint Entrance Examination—to name just a few. What has facilitated the growth of this pan-Indian culture? Certain answers are obvious, such as the reach of Indian films and the exponential growth in the popularity of television. The revolution in communications has helped, as has the huge increase in mobility. Common aspirations, and the solidarity imparted by similar constraints, have played a significant role. The gradual but definitive democratization of the social order, and the unprecedented expansion of the economy, have contributed too. Countrywide opportunities, and standard institutions and curricula, have been an important factor. The presence of the Indian state, pervasive in its rituals of power and patronage, and all-embracing in its shabbiness, cannot be ignored. Nor can the uniformity imparted by a certain culture of democratic politics, in which the smiling face of the rustic Laloo Yadav merges quite easily with the patrician portrait of Nehru. The consequence is a far more homogenized Indian than most Indians are aware of or willing to accept.

How much has changed to nurture and sustain the rise of this new culture needs to be appreciated. When my father, who in 1941 had qualified for the Indian Civil Service, was allotted the Central Provinces as his state, there was concern in the family that he was going too far away from eastern UP (Uttar Pradesh), away from his roots and the culture and people he knew. Sixty years later, in 2001, I visited the far-flung Andaman Islands, deep in the Bay of Bengal, closer to Indonesia than to India. The Commissioner at Port Blair, the headquarters of the archipelago, was a young officer of the Indian Administrative Service. A veterinary doctor before joining the IAS, he was from Tamil Nadu, had studied at Bareilly in Western UP, was looking forward to a posting in Delhi, and was delighted—so he told me—to be assigned to the Andamans. His driver was a Sikh from the Punjab; the protocol officer was a Christian from Jaipur in Rajasthan. The director of the Anthropological Museum was from Bihar, and was preparing to move to his next assignment in Shillong in the North-East. Our guide at the infamous Cellular Jail, where hundreds of freedom fighters were incarcerated for life by the British, and which is now a great tourist attraction, was from Kerala. The officer in charge of the Aquarium—another tourist favourite—was from Bengal. On our flight out of Port Blair, a young girl in her teens began to talk to my wife. It turned out that she was a Sikh; eighteen years ago her grandfather had visited the Andamans from the Punjab, fallen in love with the place, and relocated permanently here. The girl was leaving 'home' to do a degree in computers in Chennai.

Indians have become dispersed across their own land in a manner never witnessed before. The 'Madrasis'—as those from the South were labelled decades ago—are as much a fixture of New Delhi as are the Punjabis who think it is their home. Only 30 per cent of the people in Mumbai are descendents of the city's original residents. Seven million, or more than half, are from North India; and the votes of 'outsiders' determine the results of 18 of its 32 seats in the state assembly. Attempts by the Shiv Sena—the militant political party that would like Maharashtra to be only for Maharashtrians—to ethnically cleanse the state have failed because those who have come from outside have become Mumbaikars themselves. Elsewhere, in Punjab, the robust Sikh farmers cannot do without migrant labour from Bihar. There are 10,000 prosperous Sikhs in the southern coastal town of Visakhapatnam. A sizeable segment—perhaps as much as one-third—of Chennai, the capital of Tamil Nadu, speaks Telugu, not Tamil. M.K. Karunanidhi, the belligerent voice for Tamil interests, is reportedly of Andhra origin. His rival, the current chief minister, is originally from Karnataka. The great salad bowl of India is gradually emptying into a melting pot. Youngsters, whose grand-parents had rarely travelled beyond the provincial town near their village home, don't think twice about studying and working in places that even their parents have only heard about. A new cosmopolitanism has become a feature of the Indian landscape, dissolving differences and changing the way Indians define themselves.

The remarkable thing is that this phenomenal intermingling has taken place largely by default. The government spoke of the need for 'national integration', and indeed took some measures to promote it, but never took regional or subcultural parochialisms head on. As it turned out, this lack of evangelism was the best policy. 'Attempts to tinker with the lives of people in order to build homogeneous nations have almost everywhere proved counterproductive', warns the political scientist Neera Chandoke.[1] The Indian state was adept at accommodation, not confrontation. This was the outcome not so much of conscious policy as of the peculiar Indian genius to somehow *deflect* a crisis, by capitulation, deferment or compromise. In the 1950s, when people in some states wanted internal boundaries to be redrawn along linguistic lines, the central government conceded to the demand. When the project of a national language was opposed by non-Hindi-speaking states, New Delhi postponed the decision by a decade. Indians were attached to their specific cultural identities, and it would have been unwise to force the pace of change. Caste affiliations reigned supreme; regional issues garnered vociferous support; political leaders drew strength from local and state politics; and bureaucrats in 'All India Services' preferred to be allotted their home states. Between 1960 and 2001, as many as seventeen new states and Union Territories were created as a response to regional pressures, and there are, at the last count, demands for a dozen more.

What is noteworthy is that a pan-Indian identity has emerged in spite of such loyalties, almost incidentally, and as a consequence of the *lack of organized pressure*. The identity has resilience because it was not the product of a blueprint, and therefore could never be stifled by planning. The integrating factors worked independently of partisan biases, for there were no partisans behind them. The creeping homogenization did not arouse suspicion or subversion because no one person or agency could be accused of the 'crime'. For the leaders of the independence movement, the transcendental unity of India was a given. Nehru spoke emotionally of India's 'majesty of soul'; he saw her as an anthropomorphic unity, Mother India, 'a beautiful lady, very old but ever youthful . . .'[2] This romanticized faith spilled over into independent India. The political leadership, and the educated classes, took the historic unity of India for granted, but the actual integration of Indians happened *as a by-product of other goals*. At the time of Independence in 1947, the fledgling state-owned broadcasting service, All India Radio (AIR), adopted a motto, '*Bahujan Hitaya; Bahujan Sukhaya*: The happiness and welfare of the masses'. The stated goals were information, education, and entertainment—in that order. At that time AIR had only six stations and eighteen transmitters; it covered less than 3 per cent of the territory and merely 11 per cent of the people. In the next five decades AIR expanded to broadcast in twenty-four languages and 146 dialects from over 200 broadcasting centres, covering 90 per cent of the country, and reaching almost all its billion people. Information and education may have been the professed priorities, but the entertainment segment of the service, Vividh Bharati, had the most avid listeners. Commencing in 1957, it wisely relied almost wholly on popular film music. In 1967 it went commercial, and the ditties that advertised soaps and slippers between songs by Mohammad Rafi and Lata Mangeshkar provoked a great deal of amusement and curiosity. Vividh Bharati continues to broadcast for fifteen hours every day from 200 stations, reaching 97 per cent of the population.

Television was hitched to satellite technology in India in 1975 to further the cause of 'social education'. The government took great pride that the Satellite Instructional Television Experiment (SITE) was the first attempt in the world for this purpose. Colour transmission began only in 1982 when New Delhi proudly hosted the Asian Games. The next landmark was the Gulf War of 1991, whose worldwide coverage demolished the barriers against cable television. Since then the penetration of the small screen has been nothing short of spectacular. In Uttar Pradesh, for instance, only 2 million homes have toilets, but 6.4 million have television. Doordarshan, the state broadcaster, operates 23 channels, including twelve in regional languages. Rupert Murdoch's Star TV arrived in 1993 and the Zee channel in 1995. Today cable television offers seventy channels, and thanks to its hugely popular sitcoms has devoted viewers in 40 million homes. An estimated 70 million TV sets are installed in rural India. Possibly the least watched channel is Doordarshan National, whose avowed aim is the 'promotion of national integration and the inculcation of a sense of unity and fraternity'.

Radio and television have brought Indians together as never before, although that was not the expressed goal of India's high-minded leaders, for whom 'social education' and 'information' were more important priorities. History shall be witness to the fact that Indians found what they could share in common while being entertained, not while listening to the sermons of the government, whose ideologues probably looked down on such lightweight distractions as films and film music. But there is no doubt that Bollywood has been the single biggest integrating factor in the evolution of pan-Indianness. The Indian film industry is the biggest in the world. It makes almost three films a day, spends half a billion dollars in doing so, earns a billion in return, and is growing at the rate of 15 per cent a year. Every day about 15 million people throng the 13,000 movie halls in the country. Many more watch films on VCRs and DVDs at home. Hindi films dominate, but it is useful to remember that 77 per cent of the 1,013 films made in 2001 were not in Hindi. In fact, films probably have a bigger presence in the South. Two states, Tamil Nadu and Andhra Pradesh, account for almost one-third of the cinema halls in the country. Film heroes dominate politics in South India. M.G. Ramachandran, the film star who became chief minister of Tamil Nadu in 1977, was a veteran of 162 films, and had 27,000 fan clubs with a membership of 1.5 million. N.T. Rama Rao of Andhra Pradesh also proceeded from the silver screen to the office of chief minister in 1983.

Whatever their language, Indian films belong unmistakably to one genre, and cumulatively project a world in which all Indians can participate. Their largely escapist fare is inclusive by virtue of its deliberate avoidance of highbrow aesthetics. Their characters speak a language the common person can understand. Their fantasies provide a few hours of relief to the ordinary Indian besieged by the problems of everyday life. And their happy endings and songs and dances provide a kind of entertainment with which all Indians identify. Raj Kapoor as the vagabond in *Awara*, Dilip Kumar as the tragic lover in *Devdas*, and Dev Anand as the stylish *Jewel Thief*, were national icons in the 1950s and 1960s. The dialogues from the blockbuster *Sholay* (1978) could bring a knowing smile to an Indian even in the remotest corner of the nation. Aamir Khan's hairstyle in *Dil Chahta Hai* (2001) was emulated by youngsters from Kashmir to Kanyakumari at the southernmost tip of India. For their sheer reach, Indian films are the most popular secular feature of modern India. Their mass appeal and ubiquity have given Indians a common vocabulary and a means of recognizing each other in a known and much-loved framework not available to them on such a scale before.

No Indian film is complete without songs, and the songs—even more than the film itself—are an instant binding factor. A popular film song is hummed across the country, even by those who do not understand the words. It is broadcast on radio, played at weddings, sung in schools, heard on cassettes, performed on television, and used at political rallies. Early film music was more melodious but less adventurous. The music composers of that era were mostly well versed in classical Indian music. Some of the finest film music before the 1960s came from a creative adaptation of the classical *raga* to the lighter requirements of film music. But in tandem with the growing mass appeal of films, film music also began to change. R.D. Burman in the 1970s began to experiment with a new style that did not reject the classical tradition—for that would have been blasphemy for a person of his musical background—but was willing to borrow more boldly from Western orchestration and, in particular, from pop music. Purists were appalled, but the ordinary Indian seemed quite happy with the change of pace. The popular compositions of Bhappi Lahiri and the sultry voice of Usha Uthup consolidated this irreverent break with tradition. Indipop (Indian pop), fusion and remixes began to make a real impact in the 1990s. Baba Sehgal, alias Harjeet Singh Sehgal, was an electrical engineer working a 9-to-5 job until his hit *Thanda thanda pani* was released in 1992. In the same year A.R. Rahman's first film score for *Roja* made him a national sensation. Rahman, now 30, was born a Hindu and later converted to Islam. He studied at the Trinity College of Music in London, but spent his early career composing jingles to advertise Parry's sweets and Titan watches. Although he came from a traditional music background (his father, K.A. Sekar, was a well-known music director), his innovations in sound and production became hugely popular. Times FM, catering to largely metropolitan India, was launched in 1993. The popularity of the 'new music' began to pepper the compositions of established singers of *ghazal*—Urdu poetry set to music—like Jagjit Singh and Pankaj Udhas. Alisha Chinai's *Made in India* in 1994 became the first non-film album to break unit sales records. Bally Sagoo started the craze of remixes in 1994. Finally, in 1995, Daler Mehndi took the nation by storm with his album *Bolo ta ra ra ra*. For the first time the energetic beat of the *bhangra* was heard by listeners far away from the Punjab. The album sold in record numbers even in Kerala in the south, proof of its popularity throughout the country.

This is not a comprehensive account of recent developments in popular Indian music. It merely highlights some milestones in order to focus on a far more important question: why did music that revelled in its lack of classical pretensions become so popular so quickly with so many Indians? The answer is that it had mass appeal, in stark contrast to the rarified elitism of classical Indian culture. The latter was undoubtedly of great antiquity and exceptional refinement. But in an unrelentingly hierarchical society it was the preserve of the elite. Indeed, its highly developed structure of appreciation and aesthetics could only have been the product of a class of relative leisure. This class, comprising the aristocracy and old money, provided the patronage for its development. For the ordinary people the musical staple—until the arrival of film music—was folk music. India's folk tradition was united by similar themes but divided by languages and dialects and the specifics of the regions. Unlike the classical tradition which was carefully codified over centuries into a set of universal norms, the folk repertoire survived essentially on local loyalties. Popular film music was the first step in creating a non-classical non-elitist music with a nationwide audience. Even today 70 per cent of the Indian music industry's turnover comes from film music and only 3 per cent from classical and devotional music. Indipop (which now has a 20 per cent market share) combines the vibrancy of the folk tradition with the fast-paced beat of Western music influences. It has irrevocably changed the texture of film music (the veteran film singer Asha Bhonsle is now referred to as the 'Grandma Madonna of India') and contributed to giving Indians a form of musical expression that is accessible and comprehensible. In terms of music 'the North and the South have come closer today than they have been for a long time', wrote the late Sheila Dhar, a noted classical vocalist herself. 'The new Indian pop and Hindi film music have performed the signal service of providing a common meeting ground for music directors from both systems.'[3]

It took Indians several decades after 1947 to acknowledge what they really enjoyed. The classical school had for so long been the only touchstone of musical refinement that it required courage and self-confidence to shed inhibitions about the new hybrid. Perhaps it is not coincidental that the new music began to make a real impact around 1991 when, breaking from the conventional dogmas of the past, the country adopted the new economic policies. A revolution in the audio cassette industry, spearheaded by the late Gulshan Kumar in the 1980s, had already prepared the ground. In the 'socialist' era, Kumar managed to label the production unit for his cheap T-Series cassettes as a 'small-scale industry' so that he could benefit from the loans and subsidies given by the government. But the demand for his product was far from small. The music spooled out of cheap cassettes played in cars, buses, trains, parks, shops, streets and homes at decibel levels that were equally new. The elite were the last to admit that they actually enjoyed the new music. But the pretence did not last long. I remember in 1991 a party given by a leading national weekly to celebrate its fifteenth anniversary. The venue, a five-star hotel in New Delhi, was packed with the elegant and the powerful. Some traditional but nondescript music was playing in the background as drinks did the rounds. Then suddenly somebody changed the music. The beat of Malkeet Singh's *Tutak tutak tutiya* filled the room, and nobody could resist it. The neglected dance floor was suddenly alive with middle-aged connoisseurs of the arts flailing their legs and arms. But if their children had asked them the next day if they had enjoyed themselves they would probably have denied it.

This dilemma would never have existed were it not for the entrenched disdain of the elite in India for anything enjoyed by the common man. Many countries have traditions of both classical and popular music. Both coexist, and the latter mostly has a greater following than the former. This could have been the situation in India too, except that there was nothing earlier on a pan-Indian scale that could challenge the hegemony of the classical tradition. Now that there is, and ordinary Indians are emboldened to freely express their preferences, the conflict and hypocrisy is gradually fading away. That would explain why, paradoxically enough, the popularity of the new music has coincided with a *revival* of interest in classical music. Leading classical musicians have a growing following, even as they have also learnt to modify their performances to suit the less purist tastes of their younger listeners. A classical vocalist today will dispense with the lengthy slower elaboration of the *raga*, as tradition dictates, and come sooner to the fast-paced *drut*. Some classical musicians, like Shubha Mudgal, are boldly experimenting with fusion and folk music in a manner that would have rendered them artistic outcasts only a few years ago. But Mudgal sells more recordings than her peers, and has a wider following than her predecessors.

An assertive popular culture is beginning to acquire critical mass in India. The growing popularity of Hindi is a case in point. The attempt to introduce it by fiat failed; but the growing number of people who speak and read Hindi today would surprise its opponents. According to the National Readership Survey (NRS) of 2002, the country's largest-selling newspaper is the Hindi daily *Dainik Bhaskar*. So is the second largest, *Dainik Jagran*. Of the top ten dailies, four are in Hindi. Only one, the *Times of India*, is in English. The NRS claims that since 1999 the readership of newspapers has grown by about 20 per cent to reach 156 million. Hindi has the lion's share in this growth. Hindi dominates cable television too. The country's most watched 24-hour news channel, *Aaj Tak*, with over one-third of total viewership, is in Hindi. Its main competitors have also chosen the national language. Even *Star News*, which had originally thought of a programme mix of 70 per cent English and 30 per cent Hindi, is now fully in Hindi. The popularity of Hindi has nothing to do with a new-found affection for the national language nor is it a deliberate dilution of linguistic chauvinisms. It has happened gradually, on its own, and in response to market forces that see India as a commercial unity based on who reads and speaks which language most, rather than which language *should* be spoken and read the most. If more people watch a Hindi channel, advertisers will direct more of their funds to it. Programmes in other languages may have a devoted regional following but, for reasons of economic viability, cannot compete with Hindi on a countrywide basis.

The issue of language has thus been rescued from narrow loyalties, even if in the process many regional languages are languishing. A very small number of Indians speak English with ease, but a great many more have learnt to get by in it. Many Indians are not fluent in

Hindi, but a great many more understand something of it now. Hindi films are popular in Tamil Nadu. According to some estimates, Chennai, the capital of the state that came close to secession in opposing Hindi, has more private classes for learning Hindi than any other city. U.R. Ananthamurthy, the perceptive Kannada writer, argues that 'monolingualism is a European phenomenon, not Indian'.[4] Indians, especially at the level of the common man, may know one language, he points out, but can adapt to another for survival. A new lingo dubbed Hinglish, an irreverent masala of English and Hindi words, has sprouted spontaneously in the cities. The young speak it; with the success of Pepsi's slogan—*Yeh dil maange more* (This heart wants more)—the advertising industry has also come to love it; successful films have adopted it; television resounds to it; even conservative English dailies have not been able to resist its appeal. Hinglish, like Indipop, thumbs its nose at the purists. It represents a confident new comfort zone, in which people are more concerned with communication than with ideological loyalties. The divisive enthusiasts of one language versus another have largely become quiescent as functional choices have come to dominate. Sanjay Chhel, who in 1999 wrote the story of the hit film *Yes Boss*, and who is a votary of Hinglish, says bluntly: '*Jo zabaan roti kama ke nahin deti, woh apne aap mar jati hai*: A language that cannot earn a livelihood dies a natural death.'

Markets are concerned with the maximization of profit, but in the process they homogenize too, creating what Sunil Khilnani calls a 'pan-Indian domestic class of consumers'.[5] Most of urban India brushes its teeth with Colgate or Pepsodent, bathes with Lux, washes its clothes with Rin or Surf, eats Britannia biscuits, wears Bata shoes, drinks Coca-Cola, Pepsi or Thums Up, cleans a cut with Dettol, treats a cold with Vicks and drinks Horlicks for vitality. Urban India has grown dramatically. With increasing mobility and migration to towns, the country has thirty-five cities with a population of over one million. A quarter of the country is now considered urban. Of the 250 million people who live there, 25 million have instant connectivity to almost all parts of the country through mobile phones, and the number is set to increase to 100 million in five years. Less than a hundred years ago, the first automatic telephone exchange at Simla had only 700 lines. Today, there are close to 50 million telephones, and about 500,000 villages have access to a telephone facility. More Indians are now talking to each other through a network of 1.2 million public call booths—one for every 3.3 sq km—which can connect Kashmir to Kanyakumari direct, a facility unheard of only a few years ago. ISD and STD booths, aggressively advertised by private operators, are a new feature on the landscape. Although the per capita density of telephones is still low by international standards, the availability of a means of communication to any part of the country has had the psychological impact of compressing distances and demolishing barriers. The urban-rural divide is blurring too. Of the estimated 180 million readers of the print media, 48 per cent are in rural areas. And the popular sitcoms on cable television have as much of a following in village *baithaks* (homes) as in urban drawing rooms.

Nothing brings out more forcefully the emergence of a new uniformity within India than the erosion of sartorial diversity. M.V. Kamath, the veteran journalist, describes the changes he has witnessed in his own city, Mumbai:

When first I arrived in Bombay way back in 1939 . . . it represented a rich mosaic of cultures. Every community, be it Parsi, Bohri, Kutchi, Gujarati or Marwadi seemed distinct and was easily identifiable.

The Parsi gentleman wore his white trousers and long black coat and his distinctly Parsi headwear and could not possibly have been mistaken for anyone else. The Kutchi, Marwadi and Pune Brahmin each had his distinct Pagri or turban that marked him out from the rest. The women from each community too, wore their saris differently, as photographs of that period would show. Christian women of almost all ages wore skirts and were easily identified. We were, to put it mildly, different people.

Today, I challenge anyone to differentiate one community from another from the clothes they wear . . . Hindus, Muslims, Christians, Parsis, young and old, are clad in trousers and bush-shirts if they are men and in salwar-kameez if they are women.[6]

Polyester has cast its synthetic shadow over India. Western designer labels are the preserve of the rich, but the shops of small-town India are bulging with fake labels; everyone wants to wear Gucci even if some of the products are spelt with only one 'c'. There is an identifiable similarity in tastes, preferences and aspirations. Elaborate Bollywood-inspired weddings, where the social hoopla of events lasts for days, have all of upwardly mobile India in their thrall. The wedding market, worth more than a billion dollars by some estimates, has spawned an entire industry of consultants, choreographers, trousseau designers, entertainers and service providers. When in July 2003 Indian astrologers played spoilsport by decreeing that the combination of Jupiter and Leo would be inauspicious for marriages until April 2004, there was widespread consternation—not for the unfortunate couples who would have to wait, but for the recessionary impact this would have on the bridal economy. Beauty parlours were rare a few decades ago and mostly patronized by the wealthy and the Westernized. Today they are everywhere: Delhi, Mumbai and Chennai have around 5,000 each, and Kolkata is only a little behind with some 3,000. In the wake of the Miss Universe title of Sushmita Sen (1994), and the Miss World sweep in subsequent years of Aishwarya Rai, Diana Hayden and Yukta Mookhey, beauty has become a national aspiration. Young girls in small towns queue up to participate in local beauty pageants. Modelling agencies have sprouted all over rural India. By all accounts, hole-in-the-wall parlours are not an uncommon sight in the dust and concrete of the line—now fast disappearing—between rural and urban India. Dhapali, a village in Punjab's Bhatinda district, is reported to have as many as three parlours.[7] Middle-aged matrons have joined their younger wards in experimenting with facials, threading and bleaching. In 'brown' India, every woman wants to be fairer, and *Fair & Lovely* fairness cream is the leading skin cream across India. Most Indian women are not anywhere close to being liberated, but there is little doubt that a great many of them are influenced by a common idea of appearance and glamour.

A new development is the increasing number of Indians travelling for pleasure in their own country. For all its potential as a tourist destination, India attracts remarkably few foreign tourists, not more than 2.5 million, around the same number as Cyprus. But over 200 million Indians are for the first time spending money to discover their own country. The middle class Indian tourist is a recent development. Once, a holiday for most Indians meant a visit to the family home. Today a growing number of those with some disposable income want to see for themselves the hill and sea resorts, the pilgrimage sites and monuments, and the city lights they have only previously read about. This has led to a haphazard and hurriedly erected but huge infrastructure for domestic tourism. During the holiday season newspapers are full of advertisements offering tourist packages and travel incentives. Shabby hotels and boarding lodges have mushroomed at tourist spots, often in blatant violation of municipal guidelines. To cater to this all-Indian clientele, restaurants carry strikingly eclectic menus—southern idli-dosas in Himalayan resorts and northern butter chicken in the backwaters of Kerala. Indian Railways, the largest employer in the world (employing 1.6 million people), is the means for this vast human movement. Every day a million Indians travel on 11,000 trains through 7,000 stations over tracks covering almost 100,000 km. The government has now begun the implementation of a nationwide highway construction plan which will be its biggest public works project, and perhaps the largest programme of road development in any country. By the year 2007, 13,000 km of concrete expressways costing $12 billion will link the country's major towns and regions. The first phase, dubbed the Golden Quadrilateral, will connect the four metros of Delhi, Mumbai, Chennai and Kolkata. The second will join Silchar in the east to Porbandar in the west, and Srinagar in the north to Kanyakumari in the south. Interestingly, this massive cross-shaped grid, cutting across the length and breadth of the country, pays attention to a small detail that is typically Indian. The expansion joints on the new highways have been especially devised not to trap the hooves of cows. India has the largest number of cows in the world, even if a great many of them are emaciated and neglected.

Whether travelling by road, by train or by air, Indians are no longer strangers in any part of their country. This is a new experience and is changing the way they define and identify themselves. Even in the farthest outpost there is something representative of India as a whole. And however marginalized an Indian, a part of him or her is influenced by a larger, transcendent India. Perhaps the most ubiquitous element of this subcontinental continuity is the Government of India (GOI). Nothing in independent India has grown as phenomenally as the GOI. It touches lives everywhere, in small villages buried deep in the countryside, in the barren outreaches of the Himalayas, in inaccessible hamlets of the Thar desert, in the militant-infested jungles of the North-East and in the scattered islands of Nicobar. The touch is uniform—the same shabby corridors and paraphernalia of privilege and power; the same odour of corruption, paan-stained walls, musty files and sweating supplicants; the same programmes and jargon; the same spools of red tape—a huge bureaucratic adhesive that binds and trusses and sometimes helps Indians in almost every area of endeavour.

Indians are not non-violent per se. The myth of *ahimsa* or non-violence as an intrinsic part of the Indian personality, was sold by Mahatma Gandhi and conveniently bought by the nation. In actual fact, 'the only pre-modern use of *ahimsa* in a social context was by (Emperor) Ashoka in the third century BC, and then only after considerable violence.'[8] Indians are capable of remarkable and frequent violence, and newspapers routinely report instances of domestic servants battered by educated employers, of brides tortured and burnt for dowry and of unprovoked police brutality. A few examples, taken at random, bear this out. On 1 January 2001, when the world was celebrating the birth of a new millennium, the wrists of a young bride, Reeta, were slashed in a suburb of the capital and her hair torn from her scalp for not bringing in a larger dowry.[9] On Independence Day, 15 August 2001, 17-year-old Sanju Chauhan was murdered on the orders of the panchayat of Devipur in Kushinagar district of Uttar Pradesh, on the suspicion that she had had an affair and had given birth to an illegitimate child. In the same month, Vishal Sharma, 18, and Sonu Singh, 17, were hanged by their families in Muzaffarnagar in Uttar Pradesh, for daring to want an inter-caste Brahmin-Jat marriage.[10] In November of the same year, a 23-year-old shopkeeper in Delhi was almost beaten to death by three policemen for not giving them a Diwali gift.[11] On 9 February 2002, the *Times of India* reported the case of Shobha, a girl of 15 working as a domestic help in the home of a senior government official in New Delhi. The girl had been branded with a hot iron and her hands burnt in hot lentil soup for 'disobedience'. On 4 July 2003, Ponamma, a 30-year-old widow with AIDS was allegedly stoned to death by her relatives and neighbours in a village of Andhra Pradesh.[12]

The violence lurking below the surface of a supposedly non-violent India should never be underestimated. Gandhi, the man who made *ahimsa* his credo, was shot dead in cold blood by a Hindu. The body of Indira Gandhi was riddled with bullets by two of her own security guards, who were Sikhs. In the riots that followed, mobs hounded out Sikhs and burnt them alive. During communal violence both Hindus and Muslims kill without compunction. In backward Bihar, the ascendant communities of Bhumihars and Kurmis have private armies to chastise the lower castes, and—on more than one occasion—to massacre them. The practice of female foeticide is widespread, even though prenatal imaging tests to identify the sex of a child have been declared illegal. Even earlier, when this technology was not available, female infanticide was prevalent. The normal methods were to bury the child alive, immerse her head in cow's milk, or give her a fatal dose of opium. Many foreigners are shocked by the violence meted out to animals in vegetarian India. One once told me of seeing group of children tie a live rat to a rope and bludgeon it to death against a wall as sport. The cruelty against dogs, and the manner in which animals are killed in slaughterhouses, only proves the point further. A correspondent of the *New York Times*, who was visiting India in 2002 to cover a royal wedding in Jaisalmer, observed bluntly: 'No creatures on the planet live more wretched lives than Indian dogs.'[13]

But the violence that Indians exhibit in society against the hierarchically 'inferior' or vulnerable, which is easier to inflict and often has social sanction, turns into a striking form of pacifism in dealing with an *external* enemy. The Chinese visitor Xuan Xang, who travelled extensively in India in the seventh century AD, noted that 'Indians are of a light temperament . . . with regard to justice they make *even excessive concessions*.'[14] About a thousand years later, Warren Hastings, the British Governor General, noticed a similar trait: 'They are gentle and benevolent, more susceptible of gratitude for kindness shown them, *and less prompted to vengeance for wrongs inflicted than any people on the face of the earth.*'[15] (emphasis mine)

A mild and forgiving temperament must have been to the liking of the British, until Mahatma Gandhi devised a form of protest that capitalized on this very passivity. The genius of Gandhi was that he understood why his people would support his kind of political protest. Indians are not inclined towards self-annihilation. It is not their way to initiate a confrontation where the consequences of violence could be suicidal. They have a deep-seated fear of unremitting unrest, of disorder that is endemic. Their lives are structured around a highly complex and ancient social system that would be vulnerable in a context of uncontrolled upheaval. Octavio Paz, who served as Mexico's Ambassador in New Delhi in the 1960s, and later won the Nobel Prize for Literature, wrote perceptively that 'castes were invented not for change, but for *endurance*'.[16] Indians are afraid of any situation where violence may spiral out of control, threatening the very survival of the system. Gandhi's tactic of passive resistance, which allowed a militarily superior outsider to be opposed without fatally risking life and limb, or without risking the survival of the system in one cataclysmic confrontation, was entirely in tune with their temperament. Revolutionary movements like those led by Bhagat Singh, which wanted to throw out the British through violence, were over-praised but under-subscribed. They remained on the fringe, unable to dislodge a pragmatic mindset that paid homage to martyrs but considered them cannon fodder. The Indian emphasis has always been on tenacious survival, not glorious martyrdom. Resilience rather than retribution, survival rather than conquest—where the weapon becomes the 'passive, "feminine" cunning of the weak and the victimized'[17]—has been their civilizational trait.

During the struggle for independence passivity became the strength of the weak. But by its very nature it could, in a different context, also be the weakness of the strong. Historically, Indians have a very mediocre record in defending themselves against foreign invaders. Unlike the Mongols, the Turks or the European powers, Hindus have never pursued military conquest outside the extended periphery of the subcontinent. The impact of Hindu civilization is visible all over

South and South-East Asia, but it is mostly religious and cultural. Among the major civilizations, India is 'uniquely unassertive towards others',[18] and as uniquely forgiving. In 1948, while repulsing Pakistani aggression in the Valley, the Indian army could have taken all of Kashmir, but Nehru halted the Indian General Thimayya at the urging of Mountbatten. When China attacked India in 1962, the armed forces—and Nehru—were taken by surprise. During the 1965 war against Pakistan, the Indian army was victorious, but Prime Minister Lal Bahadur Shastri generously returned the strategic Haji Pir pass to the enemy. In the 1971 war, a magnanimous Mrs Gandhi handed back almost all the military gains to Pakistan. India could have become a nuclear power in 1974, but chose not to. There is no other example of a nation that has volitionally renounced its proven nuclear capability. India opted to become a nuclear power in 1998, almost a quarter of a century *after* it had demonstrated that it could. The simple truth is that Indians are not warmongers. They have never *initiated* war against another country. In victory they have been accommodating. In defeat, such as that suffered at the hands of China in 1962, they have endeavoured to be forgiving. Their military track record has been marked by a distaste for military adventurism, and lack of desire for conquest by violence. In no other recently independent country does the army have such a relatively insignificant role in the power structure. If history is a guide, and the Indian temperament an indicator, there is every reason to believe that modern India will be a responsible nuclear power, in fact more so than those who consider themselves to be above scrutiny in such matters.

But if Indians will not attack others, can they defend themselves? The answer would appear to be that the very instinct of survival that makes them cautious about violence also enables them to ultimately defeat it. How effective they are in this process is not always clear. Sometimes they are more trusting than they should be; sometimes they are less prompt in responding to violence with violence; and sometimes they are downright incompetent. Two recent cases, the war in Kargil and the hijacking of the Indian Airlines Flight IC-814, and the extraordinary elusiveness of India's longest-absconding outlaw, Veerappan, interestingly illustrate these tendencies:

In May 1999, only a few months after Prime Minister Vajpayee had journeyed in a bus from Delhi to Lahore to extend a hand of friendship to Prime Minister Nawaz Sharif, Pakistan launched a major assault on India through the remote Kargil sector of Kashmir. The invasion was a blatant stab in India's back. Indian troops proved to be sitting ducks for Pakistani infiltrators perched on vantage mountain heights. A strategic option was to allow the Indian Air Force to cross the Line of Control and destroy the staging posts and supply lines of the invaders. The option was finally rejected, at the cost of hundreds of lives of officers and soldiers. According to official statistics, 527 officers and other ranks were killed and over a thousand seriously wounded. This exhibition of restraint, in the face of the certain death of so many, must have few parallels in military history. One has only to think of the reaction in Paris or Washington, London or Beijing if a dozen body bags arrived in the capitals of those countries as a result of verified and unprovoked enemy intrusion into their territory. However, the sacrifice was not in vain. Although taken by surprise, and lacking the meticulous preparation of the Pakistani side, the Indian armed forces gave a remarkable account of themselves. By July 1999, much earlier than anticipated, the intruders had been definitively repulsed. In spite of the heavy loss of life, especially of young officers who led their troops from the front, Indian forces were ordered not to shoot the retreating Pakistanis in the back.

Indian Airlines Flight IC-814 took off from Kathmandu for New Delhi on 24 December 1999 at 4.53 p.m. Within minutes it was hijacked by five Pakistanis led by Ibrahim Athar, the brother of Maulana Masood Azhar, one of the most violent and brutal leaders of the terrorist organizations Harkat-ul-Ansar and Harkat-ul-Mujahideen. Delhi was informed of the hijacking at 4.56 p.m. At 7 p.m. the plane landed at Amritsar in Indian territory. Authorities at the airport had instructions not to let the plane take off, but it managed to do so and reached Lahore in Pakistan, where it was refuelled. At 10.30 p.m. the plane left Lahore and the pilot was asked to fly to Kabul. However, since Kabul airport did not have night-landing facilities, the plane landed at Dubai at 1.32 a.m. on 25 December. On the morning of 26 December it took off from Dubai and landed shortly thereafter at Kandahar in Taliban-ruled Afghanistan. It remained there until the evening of 31 December when the hijacking ended with the release by the Government of India of three dangerous terrorists—Mushtaq Zargar, Omar Sheikh and the notorious Masood Azhar—who were escorted to Kandahar in an Indian plane by Foreign Minister Jaswant Singh himself. The lives of all the passengers, save one, the young and newly married Rupin Katyal, whose throat had been cut, were secured. The Taliban released the hijackers, who returned to Pakistan to continue their business of killing Indians. An emboldened Maulana Azhar publicly announced his intention of recruiting half a million people to renew the jihad against India.

The episode was most revealing of the priorities of the Indian state. From the very beginning the overriding concern appeared to be the lives of the helpless hostages. The need to confront the terrorists irrespective of the cost in lives was never an imperative as, for instance, it would have been had their target been Israel or China. The result was a weak and ineffective response that allowed the terrorists to leave for Lahore even after the stroke of luck that had made them land in Amritsar. It is easy, of course, to be judgemental in hindsight, but even such a sympathetic observer as former Foreign Secretary and strategic analyst J.N. Dixit, who thought the government acted as well as it could, feels that 'some conclusions are inescapable'. He writes:

> There was a lack of coordination in terms of speed and time between the authorities at Delhi and Amritsar. The runway was not blocked immediately after the landing of the plane at Amritsar. The NSG (National Security Guard) commandos did not scramble into their action/operational mode with sufficient speed. The hijackers had enough time to take off without facing any effective Indian resistance.[19]

Throughout the crisis, the relatives of the hostages themselves held the government hostage. They were blind to any other priority except the well-being of their loved ones. To be concerned about their safety was, of course, natural. But to hysterically demonstrate outside the prime minister's residence in favour of any deal that secured their release was the other extreme. The hijackers could have been taken out, but not without violence and the probable loss of lives. The relatives, shouting slogans for the unconditional and immediate release of their kin in the full glare of the media and television crews, were unwilling to take that risk. Their demonstrative lack of restraint in demanding a resolution that eschewed life-threatening violence, even at the cost of the national interest, put the government under great pressure, and undoubtedly affected its effectiveness in dealing with the crisis. A nuclear power, with one of the largest pro- fessionally-trained armed forces in the world, was made to cut a sorry figure. On the other hand, except for the unfortunate Rupin Katyal, nobody died.

The case of Veerappan, the forest brigand who for the last quarter of a century thumbed his nose at the states of Tamil Nadu, Karnataka and Kerala, and flouted the concern of New Delhi, is a very apt example of the flabby incompetence that can often shadow passivity. The bandit and notorious ivory smuggler killed dozens of policemen, beheaded forest officials, mutilated the bodies of victims, kidnapped scores of civilians, gunned down rivals, bombed police stations, and blew up buses. All this for over two decades, and with greater impunity with each passing year. He was once arrested in 1986, but was inexplicably set free. Karnataka and Tamil Nadu set up Special Task Forces to apprehend him, but to no avail. According to some accounts, many of the personnel of the Task Forces suffered from 'forest fear'; there were instances where they fled duty; many of them were overweight and unfit for the jungle terrain. Operations to arrest Veerappan lacked coordination and were not sustained. There was speculation as to his political patrons, but the magnitude of this kind of corruption, where politicians were involved in protecting an offender of such immense notoriety, only underscored the charge of criminal ineptitude. In 2000, Veerappan sensationally abducted the famous Kannada film star Raj Kumar. Two years later he kidnapped a former Karnataka minister under the very nose of the Special Task Force camped nearby. In the midst of all this, the outlaw had the temerity to ask for amnesty and raise the possibility of an 'honourable surrender'; the state governments were said to be giving 'consideration' to such proposals. Shekhar Gupta, editor of the

Indian Express, gave voice to the feelings of many Indians when he spluttered: 'We, with the fourth largest army in the world, the largest complement of paramilitary forces ever raised by mankind, (and) police forces of four states . . . can't even catch a thug like Veerappan?'[20] Veerappan was finally killed only in late 2004, by which time he was in ailing health and losing his eyesight. Needless to say, once he was killed, practical leaders of all hues touted the 'victory' as one of the most spectacular in the history of Indian warfare, and all the previous decades of incompetence that allowed him to plunder and kill at will were forgotten.

IC-804, Veerappan, and Kargil are examples of the manner in which Indians react to violence perpetrated against them. The hijacking drama shows clearly that even in a situation where they are being held to unacceptable blackmail, Indians will seek a compromise that involves a minimum loss of life rather than unleash violence with unpredictable consequences. Veerappan's case personifies the ineffectiveness of the 'unheroic' state. The reluctance to go for the kill, even when everything would point to that necessity, is unfortunately exhibited in other contexts too, such as sport, where Indians have shown an incredible ability to accept marginalization without a perceived loss of self-respect. Kargil demonstrated that those who are not inclined to initiate violence can often be taken by surprise by the violence of those who are. Perhaps Indians trust too easily, or are unprepared for the deception of others. Sudhir Kakar gives a psychoanalyst's explanation: 'Given the experience of his mother's immediacy and utter responsiveness, an Indian generally emerges from infancy into childhood believing that the world is benign . . . Many character traits ascribed to Indians are a part of the legacy of this particular pattern of infancy: trusting friendliness with a quick readiness to form attachments, and intense, if short-lived, disappointment if friendly gestures are not reciprocated . . .'[21] Certainly, Prime Minister Vajpayee journeyed to Lahore to meet Nawaz Sharif with manifest warmth, and his subsequent sense of outrage, and that of the nation, was acute. But beyond the outrage, Kargil reinforced the ability of Indians to unite to defeat a threat. Expressions of patriotic solidarity are not uncommon to nations in situations of war, but there was a qualitative difference in the conduct of this war because of the ubiquitous presence of the media. Never before had Indians seen the daily unfolding of battle with such immediacy, and the televised coverage of bodies of dead soldiers and officers being returned to their hometowns created a new sense of unity.

In dealing with internal threats, which seek violently to question its very existence, the Indian state has shown that when pressed it can indeed defend itself. In the late 1960s and early 1970s the Maoist Naxalite movement sought the violent overthrow of the state. It was brutally quelled, especially in West Bengal where hundreds of young people were allegedly killed in faked police encounters. In the 1980s some Sikhs spearheaded a violent secessionist movement in the Punjab. They were ultimately ruthlessly put down. In Kashmir the armed forces have stalemated a long-simmering effort of Muslim groups to break away from the Union. Secessionist movements in the North-East have been similarly dealt with. It is significant that Indians have largely been indifferent to allegations of human rights violations by the police or the armed forces. This is, of course, partly because Indians are generally insensitive to the sufferings of others in any situation, but the government is also regarded by most of them as a legitimate source of power, and they are rarely motivated to question its actions. On the contrary, they are predisposed to accept its behaviour more or less unquestioningly. The apparatus of the state gives a vast number of Indians a stake in the system, and rewards them. It operates on a meticulously worked-out scale of hierarchical privileges that is effectively attuned to the Indian traits of deferring to authority and consciousness of status. A minor official in a district office and his peon have as much of a stake in this system as a minister in New Delhi and the driver who drives his car. Both have signed up to a figurative bond of allegiance to the given order of things—and their place in it—and will fight to preserve it tenaciously.

It is important to remember that the state has rarely *initiated* violence against a potential internal threat. Mostly its response has been reactive, and the first attempt has been to try and *accommodate* the danger. Experience has taught Indians the efficacy of compromise over rupture, especially in a situation where the violent exclusion of any one group could threaten the inclusion of others. The internal segmentations of society can be exclusivist, but the principle of interdependence, in which society itself is seen as an adjustment to intersecting interests, is something Indians don't forget. The *Purusasukta* hymn of the *Rig Veda* compares society to a human body: the Brahmins are the head, the Kshatriyas the arms, the Vaishyas the trunk, and the Shudras the feet. The familiar pre-occupation with hierarchy is evident but, significantly, the text categorically states that 'no part of the whole may claim exclusive importance and superiority over the others; collaboration and exchange of services are the essence of this organismic theory'.[22] When competing parts threaten the integrity of the whole, an Indian is predisposed, reflecting his historical experience, to steer matters away from the brink towards compromise. He does not think that to concede is to lose. A concession could be a gain if it could prevent the sheer loss of energy in an avoidable rupture. Louis Fischer, the biographer of Mahatma Gandhi, pointed out that on all key issues, Gandhi gave in to the views of opponents whom he could have overruled with ease.[23] By doing so, he co-opted the extremist and sanctified the mainstream.

Not surprisingly—and not only because of the punitive powers of the government—no secessionist movement has ever succeeded in India. 'I have a theory', wrote A.M. Khusro, the noted economist and political thinker who died in 2003, 'that six to seven years stand between the start of a separatist movement and its final self-dissolution . . . all separatist movements are eventually contained.'[24] Stephen Cohen echoes the sentiment: 'The key element in India's strategy is accommodation: the Indian government will accede somewhat to the demands put forth by even the most extreme separatist group once the latter acknowledges the sovereign authority of the government of India.'[25] Appeasement, the offer of incentives, prolonged negotiations, personal blandishments, the sensitive hand-ling of egos, and the hint of the iron hand under the velvet glove are all aspects of the policy of accommodation. If local sentiments are mollified by a symbolic concession, the government will make it. Few people know, for instance, that the only radio station in India that does not call itself All India Radio is Radio Kashmir in Srinagar. The polity is inclined towards adjustment and adaptation rather than inflexible rejection, and the consequence is that most separatist movements are in time assimilated, their energy diluted by what the government is willing to cede, and what it has on offer.

Some Sikhs may have wanted to opt out of the Indian Union, but the movement for Khalistan—the separatist 'nation' of the Sikh extremists—is dead, and today Sikh politicians in the Punjab, like their counterparts in other states, are happy squabbling over the spoils of office. In Assam in the 1980s the militant All Assam Students Union (AASU) blockaded the supply of oil to the rest of India, and declared those who colluded with the Government of India, such as Congressmen, to be enemies of the people. In 2002, the Congress Party was back in power with a two-thirds majority in the state assembly, and all talk of terrorism had evaporated. A seasoned politician in Kashmir once told me that the problems in the Valley would never have flared up if in the 1987 state elections New Delhi had not intervened (as critics allege) to prevent the radical opposition from coming to power. Denied access to office, its leaders became secessionist; had they been in office they would have been seduced by the Great Indian State. Those who spoke of secession in election speeches would have been ensconced in ministerial bungalows with scores of minions at their beck and call. All the coveted resources of the state would have been at hand: the discretionary use of quotas, a gas agency for a relative, a passport out of turn for a friend, the privileged admission of children to educational institutions, the issue of permits and licences, and, of course, a great deal of money for the corrupt.

In the usual Indian way of muddling through rather than tackling a problem head on, the process of co-option slowly but surely defangs and ingests a potential threat. It is facilitated by a utilitarian—and forgiving—amnesia. Caught in the concerns of the present, the ordinary person would rather move towards the opportunities of the future than dwell malignantly on the deviations of the past. Two years after Kargil, even General Pervez Musharraf, its chief perpetrator, was given a warm welcome at Agra. As always, a good indicator of the way the average Indian thinks are the mottos inscribed on trucks. Perhaps the most common of these is: '*Jiyo aur jeene do*: Live and let live.' The slogan is not merely an expression of piety. It reflects a conditioned distaste for chaos, an understanding of the practical value of reconciliation and consensus, and an aversion to the costs of unresolved hostility.

Are Indians susceptible to religious violence? The general perception is that communal tensions are on the rise in India, and recent events, such as the sectarian violence in Gujarat in 2002, and the continuing mobilization by Hindu fundamentalist groups to build the Ram temple at the site where the Babri Mosque was demolished in 1992 at Ayodhya, would appear to bear this out. However, the apocalyptic vision of an India engulfed in unending religious strife is much exaggerated if not entirely inaccurate. Hindus would like to believe that this is because they are inherently tolerant, which is not true either. The practice of Hinduism is tainted by a great degree of intolerance. The violence and bigotry traditionally inflicted by higher caste Hindus on members of their own faith, the low-caste Shudras, has no parallel in any other religion. Nor is Hinduism particularly welcoming to outside influences. It needs only to be recalled that until recently Hindus considered all foreigners to be *mleccha*, inherently unclean, and regarded those who ventured to foreign lands—as Mahatma Gandhi famously did when he left for England to study law in 1888—as having *polluted* themselves. Why then have so many faiths found a home in India, and why do I believe that religious disharmony will not be a sustained or widespread feature of India in the future?

The first reason is that Hindus are not, and have never been, insecure about their religion. The paranoia that Hinduism is under siege, and needs to aggressively reassert itself, has been sought to be whipped up only recently by fringe fundamentalist groups whose credentials to speak for all Hindus are very doubtful. Historically, Hinduism has shown a supreme complacency towards any threat to its existence. It has never felt the need to codify its practice in a single scripture, nor thought it necessary to regiment its faithful at the altar of only one god, nor created a single church for its defence and propagation. At the level of theory it allows a freedom to dissent that is not to be found in any other major religion. Hindu metaphysics and philosophy even give space to those who argue that there is no god, and Amartya Sen has pertinently pointed out that 'Sanskrit has the world's largest literature in the agnostic and atheistic tradition.'[26]

Hinduism has always existed in a remarkably self-assured way, largely immune to attack or demise because no one entity—scripture, church or god—limits its diffused omnipresence. For its believers it is more a way of life, not without its own certainties and rituals, but without the constant need to test loyalties. A Hindu does not seek to convert, nor is he willing to be easily converted. Until the recent revivalist Arya Samaj practice of *shuddhi*, whereby those of other faiths can be converted to Hinduism by undergoing a purification ceremony, Hinduism had no concept of conversion. A person was either born a Hindu, or was forever outside the pale. The representatives of two major proselytizing religions conquered India by force, first the Muslims from about the eleventh century, and then the British in the seventeenth century. Both invaders openly used their military superiority for evangelical purposes. The Hindus accepted their political supremacy, but in spite of the obvious rewards on offer, not their faith. Of course, there were conversions, but the number of those who converted, as against the vast majority that did not, was relatively small. One has only to see what happened in other countries in similar situations to appreciate the difference. For instance, as the official religions of conquering or colonizing powers, Islam and Christianity overwhelmed the people of the African continent; their success in South-East Asia and Latin America was no less spectacular. In India they failed. The Hindus were the overwhelming majority a thousand years ago, and remain so today.

It is a matter of historical record that Hindus have not been hostile to other faiths. The reason quite simply is that they were not afraid of them. The Jews lived peaceably in India before they did anywhere else. Muslim traders from the Arab countries practised their faith undisturbed in Kerala more than a thousand years ago. The Parsis came in the seventh century and the Christians in the fourth, unsupported by armies. If the Hindus had been insecure about their religion, they could have overrun them. They did not because they did not feel threatened. On the contrary, other religions have felt the need to resist the creeping encroachment of Hinduism. Jainism distinguishes itself from Hinduism, but there are eighty-seven castes and sub-castes among Digambara Jains and thirty-eight among the

Svetambara sect. Many Indian converts to Christianity still identify themselves according to the castes to which they previously belonged. The Hindu god Ram figures in the Sikh holy book, the Guru Granth Sahib, more than any other figure. Buddhism may have emerged in the fifth century BC as a protest movement against the orthodoxies of Hinduism, but Hindu theologians claimed the Buddha as one of their own, as the eighth incarnation of Vishnu. As a new faith Buddhism had the backing of Ashoka, one of the most powerful rulers in Indian history. But it could gain few converts, and ultimately found its huge following outside the country. Even organized Islam has been concerned about loss of identity in India. 'The dominant ideology of Islam in India has always been confident that it could hold its own against Hinduism in statecraft and in martial prowess; it has always feared being overwhelmed or swamped by the slow, soporific sedativity of everyday Hinduism.' [27]

If Hindus have no reason to be unconfident about their religion, they are temperamentally opposed to any prolonged instability and disorder that could be a consequence of religious violence, especially when it is amply clear that there is no practical alternative to coexistence. In a letter to state chief ministers in 1947, Nehru stated the proposition bluntly: 'We have a Muslim minority who are so large in numbers that they cannot, even if they want to, go anywhere else. They have got to live in India. That is the basic fact about which there can be no argument.' Nehru's personal commitment to a secular India was unwavering, as was that of Mahatma Gandhi, and this was undoubtedly of considerable importance in the early years after 1947 in resisting the lurch towards communal politics. But the bedrock of the secular vision was the simple truth—far more comprehensible to the average Indian than the complexities of ideology or principle—that there is no way to survive except by learning to live with each other. Muslims in India are not confined to one geographical area. They number over 120 million—about 13 per cent of the population—and live in all parts of the country. Jammu and Kashmir is the only state where they are in a majority (65 per cent), but they are a significant proportion—almost a quarter of the population—in West Bengal and Kerala, and even more (about 30 per cent) in Assam. In Uttar Pradesh they number over thirty million and in Bihar about half of that, which is still more than the entire populations of Hungary or Greece. They have a significant presence too in the states of Karnataka (11 per cent), Andhra Pradesh (8 per cent), and Tamil Nadu (5 per cent). Nowhere are they isolated or cut off from the majority community. They are part of the national fabric in inseparable ways, speaking the same language, watching the same films, eating the same food and sharing the same cultural traits.

Coexistence is an imperative, not an option in India. Indians are pragmatic enough to understand this. Unlike the Tamils in Sri Lanka or the Chinese in South-East Asia who are often accused by the majoritarian communities of unfair economic and professional dominance, Muslims pose no such threat to Hindus in India. Hindus have no reason therefore to feel intimidated by a presence which has been with them for centuries. Muslims too see no reason to invite destruction by irrationally taking on a majority that so dramatically outnumbers them. Of course, communal conflicts have occurred in the past, and will probably occur in the future, but the norm in the last five decades has not been religious violence, as is often suggested, but the peaceful and progressive integration of the two communities *in the common project of India*.

In a paper prepared in 1996 for the Rajiv Gandhi Institute for Contemporary Studies in New Delhi, two distinguished scholars from Harvard, Ashutosh Varshney and Steven Wilkinson, made an in-depth study of Hindu-Muslim riots during the period 1960-63. According to them, even in Gujarat, which has one of the worst records of communal violence, 'twenty out of thirty-three years between 1960-93 had no or very few incidents of communal violence'. Eighty per cent of all deaths due to religious violence during this period took place in just two Gujarati cities, Ahmedabad and Vadodara. Hindu-Muslim violence is neither chronic nor pervasive but town-specific, they argue, with twenty-four towns nationally accounting for 62 per cent of the total deaths and 50 per cent of the total number of incidents. Even in the states of Uttar Pradesh, Maharashtra and Gujarat, which have most of the riot-prone towns, there are 'many more towns that are peaceful'. There were a total of 554 incidents across India during 1960-93. This translates to less than eighteen incidents a year in a country of over a billion people. Given the close proximity in which Hindus and Muslims live, the historical memory of the terrible religious violence of Partition, the role of criminals and vested interests in fomenting disharmony, and the incendiary contribution of scarcity and poverty in accentuating any cause of strife, this is not a catastrophic record by any standards, especially when most of the country has remained continuously peaceful in spite of such factors.

Incidents of communal strife attract attention, and rightly so. They are condemnable, but in order not to lose objectivity it is essential that the countless incidents of religious harmony that play out unnoticed in the daily ebb and flow of life are also acknowledged. For the millions of Hindus who annually trek to the Ayyappa temple in Kerala's Sabarimalai hills, the *dargah* (tomb) of a Muslim saint on the way is a sacred site. For centuries Muslim sufis, one of the most famous of whom was Amir Khusro, have sung devotional songs on Hindu themes. Hindus take care of the Muslim shrine of Haji Malang near Mumbai. Hindu pilgrims throng to the tomb of the Muslim Khwaja Moinuddin Chishti at Ajmer. Both Hindus and Muslims are devotees of Sai Baba of Shirdi, one of India's most popular saints. In Remanda, a village in Orissa, a Muslim family leads the annual Hindu festival of the Rath Yatra. In Icchigam, a remote village in the heart of Kashmir, 900 Muslim families have built a temple not far from their mosque to provide for just eight Hindu families. In a suburb of Bombay, Jiwaji Qurban Hussein has spent the last forty years making photo frames for images of Hindu deities. 'Allah', he says, 'wants me to continue.'

These are but a few examples to illustrate that in a great many ways and in innumerable contexts Hindus and Muslims live peaceably enough together, and as a result of centuries of cohabitation have a very high degree of acceptance of each other's presence in their everyday life. Such an acceptance may not always translate into positive tolerance or unconditional intermingling, but it does facilitate pragmatic ways of interaction even across barriers of faith. When I was still in school in the 1960s, I recall the behaviour of my aunt (my father's elder brother's wife) at our ancestral home in the eastern UP district of Ghazipur. She was a simple woman, not educated beyond a few years in school, and brought up in a very conservative way. Her life revolved around reading the *Ramayana* and a great deal of religious ritual, and I vividly recall how taken up she was by notions of purity and pollution. My uncle was a leading lawyer, and many of his colleagues in the profession were Muslims. Sometimes they would come to their home, and this was always a challenge to my aunt, who was concerned about being ritually 'defiled' even by lower caste Hindus, let alone those of another faith. My uncle did not share her views but was afraid of domestic discord. The solution was found by my aunt. Muslim guests were welcome to come home provided they were entertained in the outer drawing room, which was where my uncle received his visitors in any case. They would be served with the best of vegetarian refreshments but in crockery kept outside the family kitchen and used only for this purpose.

This ability to draw lines and then find practicable ways to transcend them is an Indian characteristic. A far more active and open collaboration can be seen in the political arena. No political party with the ambition to rule can ignore the Muslims. In the most populous state, Uttar Pradesh, which sends the largest number of representatives to the national Parliament, every sixth voter is a Muslim. In the 400 constituencies of the UP state assembly, the results in a hundred are determined by how the Muslims vote. Indeed, between 1977 and 1996, over a hundred constituencies have elected Muslims to the assembly. Nationwide, Muslims have a significant density in as many as 125 parliamentary constituencies, which constitute almost a quarter of the House. All experienced politicians, both at the local level and in New Delhi, have no option, therefore, but to be sensitive to such an important electoral factor. This is especially so because the Hindu vote has never been consolidated in an anti-Muslim bloc. Only the Congress Party in the early years after 1947 was like a banyan tree for the entire electorate. Now all political parties focus on segments of the electorate, be it the backward classes, the Dalits, or regional and caste configurations. In such a political milieu, the road to power lies through collaborative structures and alliances, and the Muslims, as the nation's largest minority, cannot be ignored.

Indians value political power, and the prized resources it guarantees, far more than religious exclusiveness. The pursuit of power is a universal goal to which fundamentalists subscribe as transparently as liberals. Power unites Indians much more than religion divides them. The official website of the right-wing Hindu organization, the Bajrang Dal, clearly exhorts its followers to 'consolidate a strong Hindu vote bank' and 'capture political power, for that along with legal and military force is everything in today's world.' The stirring of religious passions has in reality a secular goal: the capture of power. But the hot-headed activists of the Bajrang Dal do not understand that political success in India depends on the creation of a non-extremist and mainstream political platform. That is why they have remained on the fringes of the political arena, while the supposedly pro-Hindu Bharatiya Janata Party (BJP) rules at New Delhi, presiding over a large centrist coalition, the National Democratic Alliance (NDA). Religious loyalties can be used to attain power in the short term, as happened in Gujarat in 2003, but they have to be curtailed to *retain* power in the long term. The country's largest and oldest political party, the Congress, has made the threat to secularism its clarion call, for that also provides it the best political weapon to finesse the pro-Hindu forces. Laloo Yadav, the colourful rustic leader of Bihar, has staunchly opposed the Sangh Parivar – the alliance of Hindu fundamentalist organisations – because his political strength comes from the alliance of the backward castes with the Muslims. Chandrababu Naidu of the Telugu Desam Party which rules Andhra Pradesh, was a member of the former BJP-led NDA government at Delhi, but resists anti-Muslim initiatives because the Muslims are an important vote bank in his state. The working of democracy in India is the most effective bulwark against religious extremism. Even when political parties invoke religion, the common man understands that the real goal is political power, and devalues the religious rhetoric accordingly. In a survey carried out by *Outlook* magazine in Delhi, Mumbai, Kolkata, Chennai, Hyderabad, Bangalore and Ahmedabad in June 2002, 64 per cent of the respondents replied in the affirmative when asked: Do you think the BJP is using Hindu fundamentalism only as a way to get votes? A year later the same magazine did a similar survey among Muslims. The bulk of the respondents (40 per cent) replied in the negative when asked: Do you consider those fighting the Babri Masjid case as true spokespersons for the Muslim community?

Indians are not so much cynical as they are worldly-wise. Even religious leaders are enamoured more by the *pratishtha* or prestige that religion can confer than by the uncertain returns of religious martyrdom. When Mahant Gyandas, a prominent religious figure from Ayodhya, arrived at Nasik to participate in the historic Kumbh Mela in August 2003, he threatened to boycott the ceremonial bath in the Godavari river if the local authorities did not immediately sanction him 'Z-plus' security cover. This category of security is the highest possible, and ensures that the government provides a posse of gun-toting and uniformed guards to accompany the VIP wherever he goes. To the saintly mahant this visible recognition of his status, and its projection among the hundreds of thousands of devotees gathered at the pilgrimage, was more important than the simple sacraments of worship, and he was honest enough to admit it.

The stable world of enduring material benefits, not the destabilizing one of perennial religious activism, is the natural choice of Indians. Not many Indians pause to think that most of the cities of the Awadh region, which are a stone's throw away from Ayodhya where the mosque was demolished, remained largely peaceful, both in the lead up to and the aftermath of that event. In Lucknow, a great number of the city's Muslims work in the *chikan/zardozi* embroidery industry owned by Hindu traders. Any religious tension that disrupts this economic engagement is unwelcome to both. In nearby Sitapur, Hindus and Muslims are partners in the lucrative carpet industry. They would rather not attack each other even when deeply divided politically. The story is repeated in the holy city of Varanasi. A sizeable number of Muslims live here, but the waters of the Ganga have rarely been bloodied by internecine warfare. The Muslims weave the exquisite Banarasi saris, the Hindus finance the trade. Together they have a stake in maintaining peace. In Gujarat, soon after the communal riots in early 2002, leading members of the business community took out large advertisements in all major national dailies expressing deep concern over the violence and emphasizing that there is no alternative to communal harmony.

'Gujarat is and will continue to remain business friendly', the ads proclaimed, adding in somewhat wobbly English that 'the trade as well as the industry has taken in its stride the current crisis and is looking to the future with confidence'.

Communal violence in Gujarat has, I believe, peaked, and this seems to have been brought out clearly in the general elections of 2004, when, contrary to the BJP's expectations, Congress won almost half the parliamentary seats in the state. The truth is that the Gujaratis are better at pursuing business than at killing each other. The social instability that the violence created is anathema to the hard-nosed entrepreneurship with which they have come to be identified, not only in Gujarat but also across the world. The incessant strife of religious hostility is simply antithetical to business. Besides, past experience clearly reveals the diminishing political returns of fundamentalist politics. The BJP did profit from Ayodhya, but not for long. In the 1993 Assembly elections it formed the government, but the issue of the building the Ram temple at Ayodhya has steadily lost its appeal for voters. The BJP failed to achieve a simple majority in the elections in Uttar Pradesh in 1996, and has since ceased to be the single largest party in the state. In a 'Mood of the Nation' survey carried out by the magazine *India Today* in August 2003, 47 per cent said that Ayodhya does not determine their voting choice. In Uttar Pradesh, that figure goes up to 51 per cent. In Ayodhya itself, although the BJP candidate has continued to win elections, his margins of victory and share of the vote have been steadily declining. The city's shopkeepers, traditionally strong supporters of the BJP, are more concerned about the declining volume of business than about the construction of the temple. Ved Prakash Gupta, a prominent local politician who left the BJP in 2002, went on record to say that the repeated agitations in favour of the temple have hit people of his community, the banias (traders). The banias have traditionally supported the BJP, but Gupta believes that *dhanda* or business is the real *dharma* of a *bania*, and religion only a personal matter best left to each individual. In an overwhelmingly Hindu country, the fact that the majority of Hindus refuse to be influenced by the construction of a temple at the acknowledged birthplace of their most revered god, when that construction is being opposed by Muslims who are known to have destroyed Hindu temples in the past, provides strong testimony of the absence of the destructive gene of religious fundamentalism.

The Muslims of India are not made in the jehadi mould either. They have grievances, some of them valid, and some that all minorities have, but then any community in India has its dissatisfactions. Asghar Ali Engineer, a well-known Indian Islamic scholar, has made precisely this point in an interview to the Pakistani magazine *Dawn*.[28] It is not Muslims alone who have problems in India, he argued. The problems of unemployment and poverty and power shortages affect all Indians. Communal riots have taken place in the past, but 'no government has ever denied constitutional rights to the Muslims. All rights that are enjoyed by the Hindus are available to the Muslims. Violence can take place anywhere. But thousands of Hindus side with the Muslims. They fight for their rights . . . ' Even when the right-wing blatantly pro-Hindu party, the Shiv Sena, came to power in the state of Maharashtra, 'Muslims continued to pray on the roadside. The Shiv Sena made a lot of hue and cry saying that the Muslims block the road, but in their five-year term they never banned the Muslim activity.'

The truth is that Muslims are not unaware of their strategic strengths and have learnt quite well to leverage for themselves in the complex democratic machinery of India. In many states they have formed a successful political alliance with the Hindu backward castes. In others they have shown an ability to protect their interests in unexpected ways. For instance, in the assembly elections in Maharashtra in 1999, they confounded political pandits by voting for the winning BJP and Shiv Sena combine rather than for parties that claimed to better represent their interests. Like their Hindu counterparts, Muslim fundamentalist groups are a vociferous fringe. The bulk of the Muslim community would rather peaceably negotiate a problem than kill their Hindu neighbours, or be killed by them. In the national opinion poll of Muslims carried out by *Outlook* (to which I referred earlier), 52 per cent of those questioned wanted a negotiated settlement of the Ayodhya dispute. The remaining 48 per cent said they would be happy to accept a judicial verdict. Not one advocated violence. It is not surprising, then, that in a country with the world's second largest Muslim population, Al Qaeda has not made inroads.

Ashutosh Varshney has argued in his book, *Ethnic Conflict and Civil Life: Hindus and Muslims in India*, that the greater the web of civic engagement between Hindus and Muslims, the lower the likelihood of religious violence. It is an obvious and convincing thesis, and there can be no argument against his recommendation of a more vibrant civic life that involves both communities. However, Indians are notoriously poor at *consciously* building civic structures. Nor can they be expected to set up new businesses, or restructure old ones, for the sake of such associations. But, whatever the quality of interactions at local levels—and they have by no means been insignificant—the real investment in the future is *the involvement of both communities in the gradual but definitive emergence of a pan-Indian identity*. The volitional participation in varying degrees of all Indians in the larger project of a new India, in response to *secular needs and pursuits*, is the best guarantee for communal harmony, for the expectations it raises cannot be fulfilled, and may indeed be thwarted, in anything but a lay framework. A medieval Muslim leadership may still believe in madrasas, where only religious learning is imparted, but such institutions are bound to be rejected by Muslims themselves if they do not equip people to take advantage of new economic opportunities.

The signs of change are there for all to see. The Darul Uloom at Deoband, a citadel of Muslim conservatism, began a one-year diploma course in computers in 1996. The course is heavily in demand. About two years ago it also started classes in English and in journalism, which are also greatly over-subscribed. It is true that Muslims remain under-represented in government, and over-represented among the poor, but many Muslims believe today that the answer to this situation is not religious obscurantism or sectarian violence, but preparing the community to participate in the opportunities of the mainstream. In Srinagar, on 17 August 2003, the queue for application forms for the newly introduced mobile phone service stretched for more than a kilometre, and the police had to be called in to control the over-enthusiastic crowd. Muzamil Jaleel of the *Indian Express* spoke to some of those standing in the line.[29]

Abdul Rashid had left his home on the outskirts of the city before dawn to beat the rush. Ishfaq, an engineering student, had fought with his parents to apply for one. Sajjad Ahmad Bhat, a marketing executive, and Rashid, a doctor, felt that a mobile was necessary for professional reasons. And Sabiha, an undergraduate, had no doubt the contraption was worth spending all her pocket money on.

Abdul, Ishfaq, Sajjad, Rashid and Sabiha—none of them older than 30—are perhaps more representative of their community than the mullahs who rail against modern technology and preach religious hatred. Similarly, however much the mahants may seek to foment religious hostility, what most Hindus really care about are the opportunities for upward mobility. The membership of the Rashtriya Swayamsevak Sangh (RSS), the militant wing of the BJP, is shrinking, even though—or perhaps because—the BJP is in power at New Delhi.[30] India is seducing its citizens from the acrimonies of the past to the prospects of a shared and more prosperous future. This vision, in which all communities participate, is the real bulwark against the effects of destabilizing religious upheaval. In 1993, the bomb blasts in Mumbai sparked off a frenzy of religious rioting. A decade later, in 2003, when the terrorists bombed again, there was relative quiet. The Shiv Sena called a *bandh* (strike) on 30 July to protest the bombings, but Muslim organizations were equally vociferous in their condemnation. When the bombs went off again on 25 August, killing 47 people and wounding many more, both Muslims and Hindus formed serpentine queues outside the JJ Hospital in Byculla to donate blood. The next day it was business as usual for the financial capital of India. Suburban trains and buses were packed, cinema houses were full, the hawkers were back, and the stock exchange in Mumbai, which had fallen on the day of the explosions, was back on its defiant bull run.

Religious tensions in India will continue to surface, sometimes ominously, but they need to be seen in perspective. Indians do have loyalties of faith; and on occasion these can be manipulated; but they are by and large a pragmatic people who want to get on with the business of life, earning more and ensuring a better future for their children, rather than be mired in self-defeating religious strife. The image of an India perpetually poised on the precipice of religious violence is simply inaccurate. The constant criticism by 'secular' political parties of the religious fundamentalism of their opponents, and the defensive response of those so accused, conjures a picture of a nation held to ransom by religious divisions. But voters have a pretty shrewd idea of the reality, and it is more than likely that the future will see progressively diminishing returns from attempts to garner political mileage from religious affiliations. There is a self-correcting mechanism to religious fundamentalism in the working of Indian democracy, and in the priorities Indians value, especially today when economic opportunities are on the increase. The great majority of Hindus and Muslims now feel that it is in their self-interest to swim away from the islands of religious exclusiveness inhabited by mullahs and mahants, towards the mainland of greater secular opportunities. This perception is of seminal importance and is creating far-reaching changes in behaviour and response.

In 1947, against the background of the massacres of Partition, many learned observers felt that Hindus and Muslims could never live together. The people of India have proved them wrong, and whatever the pessimists may say, the situation can only improve because of the emergence in the last five decades of a sense of pan-Indianness that refuses to be circumscribed by religion or region. The Indian state, in whose constitution secularism is enshrined as an article of faith, has not been beyond the temptations of tokenism towards the minority. But gradually, and in spite of 'a large apparatus of patronage run by salaried commissars',[31] identity in this new India is increasingly being defined not by notions of majority or minority, but by instances of individual success or failure. Azim Premji is admired by Indians not because he is a Muslim but because he is among the richest men in the country. Mohammed Kaif is cheered by huge Indian audiences whatever his personal faith because he is a fine cricketer. A.P.J. Abdul Kalam, the President of India, is a Muslim but he is known to Indians for the work he has done in the field of space technology. Dr Manmohan Singh, the Prime Minister of India, is a Sikh but is respected by Indians for being an honest politician and an internationally renowned economist. In an over-whelmingly Hindu India, no one has objected to a Muslim President and a Sikh Prime Minister. In a pan-Indian context 'we are all minorities', says Narayana Murthy. 'I am a Kannada-speaking man', he says about himself, 'a minority; a Brahmin—a minority; educated —a minority; English speaking—a minority.' In this mosaic of minorities, the only majority that appears to be emerging is that of Indians. In survey after survey, the largest number of Indians have said that it would be better to build a school or a hospital than a temple or a mosque at the disputed site in Ayodhya. In understanding how people have changed in tandem with the evolution of a new pan-Indian identity we need to look today at behaviour which is different from before, and often far more revealing than all the theories to the contrary. In the early years after Independence, Muslim film stars used to adopt Hindu names for their screen avatars: Yusuf Khan became Dilip Kumar, Mahajabeen Ali Bux became Meena Kumari and Mumtaz Jehan became Madhubala. Today Shah Rukh Khan, Aamir Khan and Salman Khan rule the box-office destiny of Bollywood and feel no need to appear to be anything but themselves.

Chapter Six

EPILOGUE
A Critical Equilibrium for Take-off

In 1982 Indira Gandhi was on an official visit to Moscow. During the talks at the Kremlin, President Brezhnev, who was by then in an advanced stage of senility, dozed off. He was nudged awake by Foreign Minister Gromyko. 'What is she talking about?' grunted Brezhnev. 'I can't understand a word she's saying.' In as soft a whisper as possible Gromyko explained that the Indian Prime Minister was speaking about the state of Punjab where a violent separatist movement had assumed serious proportions. 'Your Excellency, how can you allow such things to happen!' exclaimed Brezhnev. 'Look at the Soviet Union. For over sixty years we have run this huge country without any threat!' In 1983 Brezhnev died. In 1984 Mrs Gandhi was assassinated. A few years later, the Soviet Union had split into thirteen countries. Punjab is still a part of India, and the insurgency there has long fizzled out.

There is something that the Indian people have which the citizens of the former Soviet Union did not, and that is the freedom to ventilate grievances in an imperfect system which goes by the name of democracy. Neither the Indian state, nor the fledgling democracy it had committed itself to, were expected to survive in 1947. James W. Michaels, who covered the birth of the new nation, and subsequently became the editor of *Forbes*, admitted as much many years later. 'I don't want to exaggerate', he said, 'but I think most of us who were observing it then thought the country would break up, and that parts of it might revert to some kind of totalitarian rule.'[1] Decades later, the survival of India still puzzles observers. 'Does India exist? . . . If it doesn't, what's keeping Pakistan and Bangladesh apart?', asked Salman Rushdie rhetorically, as late as 1987, pointing out that in the five thousand-odd years of Indian history, there was never such an entity as a united India.[2] Responding to such comments can be wearying. Was Britain always the united Britain it is today, or was America born as the United States it has become now, or was the Soviet Union destined from the very beginning to break apart? History provides the soil on which nations grow; they either take root and flourish or shrivel and die. India has survived, and Indians are impatient with the genuine sense of marvel—often condescending—of outsiders for something they now take for granted. When Rushdie asked historian Robi Chatterjee what was the 'glue' holding India together, the professor, who taught me too, retorted that India did not need glue, that it was not going to fall apart, and that he rejected completely 'all that Balkanization stuff'. India, he declared, was 'simply here and we will remain here.'[3]

Why will India not fall apart, and why can its people expect to prosper in the years ahead? No one reason can answer these questions satisfactorily, but a combination of factors can, as I have discussed. The unexpected survival of democracy, in a people not democratic by temperament or heritage, is one factor. Democracy has given Indians an institutional framework for the exercise of political choice and the freedom to express dissent. This has acted as an indispensable safety valve in an inequitable context with great discrepancies in the distribution of power and wealth. Although the more privileged citizens saw it primarily as a means for their own advancement, democracy has, by the sheer miracle of its survival, given the weakest and the poorest a stake in the system. Even so, democracy by itself would not be enough. A nation has to generate wealth, for if it remains irremediably poor the stability of the democratic system will be jeopardized. India does, indeed, have the world's largest concentration of the poor, but it is also true that never before have more Indians been more preoccupied with the possibility of becoming richer than with the inevitability of remaining poor. While the number of the absolutely poor is falling at a greater rate than before, 'the level of affluence is steadily increasing in India. Even between 1995 and 2002, nearly 100 million people became part of the consuming and rich classes. Over the next five years, 180 million people will be moving into the consuming and very rich classes. On an average, 30-40 million people are joining the middle class every year.'4 This is a huge psychological watershed, especially for a people who take to enterprise. The socialist era, although not entirely unproductive, was antithetical to the nature of the Indian people. Its demise has unleashed new energies and new aspirations, and the confidence that they can be fulfilled

The birth of the knowledge era around the turn of the new millennium was a catalyst that came at the right time. If it had happened earlier, Indians would have been unprepared for it. If it had come later, it might have been too late to retain the faith of the army of technically qualified specialists the country was producing. In the evolution of a people and in the destiny of nations, timing is important. Assets unveiled before their time can be thoughtlessly squandered or underutilized. They can reinforce atavistic tendencies, or strengthen undesirable elites, or widen discrepancies in society to unsustainable limits. Assets released after their time lose their impact and relevance, and the ability to play a transforming role. In India, the opportunities created by the knowledge industries caught the crest: democracy had become by then an entrenched way of life; the economic reforms of 1991 had better prepared the people and the economy to harvest global opportunities; and the higher educational infrastructure, which had taken years to build, was at optimum yield.

A new India, whose people had built a pan-Indian identity on the foundations of the past, was on hand when these developments came to fruition. If the country was mired in internecine wars or debilitated by unresolved regionalisms it would have been unable to take advantage of these other factors. A critical equilibrium combining several factors has to be in place for nations of the complexity and size of India to approach the take-off stage while remaining relatively stable. Stability is a key parameter. Without it, the achievements of the past can rapidly dissolve, and the trajectory of growth be set back by decades. In countries where a vital element is missing, progress can have illusory foundations and instability could be lurking dangerously below the surface. The Soviet Union was a superpower with enviable achievements in many areas of science and technology. But it lacked a vital element: democracy. So long as the system held, it gave the illusion of stability. Once President Gorbachev began to tinker with it, it rapidly unravelled. The Soviet experience also shows that systems that have for long been undemocratic cannot be reformed partially. Carefully crafted piecemeal changes careen out of control, swept away by forces bottled up for too long. A reformer may think that he will be able to calibrate the pace of change, but the change of pace outpaces him. The result is years of instability threatening the integrity of the nation, severe damage to the economy, and hardship and anguish for much of the population.

The Indian people have muddled their way to a critical equilibrium. Along the way, not everything is as positive as it might have been. A comparison with China, similar to India in its population and the continental size of its economy, is instructive. More Chinese children go to school than Indians. China has (on average) better medical facilities, less malnutrition, and less poverty. Its agricultural yields are more than twice those of India, and its Foreign Direct Investment (at $53 billion in 2002) almost fifteen times that of India. China exports more than India; her manufacturing base is more extensive; and her rate of growth has been consistently higher. But like the former Soviet Union, China is missing a crucial factor: democracy. Recent historical experience would indicate that no country can be stable only on the basis of its economic achievements. The Chinese people will, sooner or later, ask for political freedoms, and when this happens it is difficult to predict the degree of instability that could follow. It is possible of course that the present Chinese leadership is able to make the transition to democracy without upheaval. However, the experience of the former Soviet Union does not bode well for the gradual or partial dismantling of long-entrenched totalitarian systems. The protest of 4 June 1989 in Tiananmen Square could be history, or it could be a portent for the future.

It is also pertinent to ask how far China's enviable economic achievements are in conformity with the nature of the Chinese themselves. A recent study[5] by Yasheng Huang of MIT and Tarun Khanna of Harvard Business School argues that China's export-driven manufacturing boom is mostly a result of foreign direct investment, 'which effectively serves as a substitute for domestic entrepreneurship'. Communist China has been bold with external reforms, but has placed many legal and regulatory constraints on homegrown companies. Foreign firms have been favoured over private businesses, and state-owned enterprises given primacy over individual entrepreneurship. By contrast, India's 'softer brand of socialism' let entrepreneurship blossom in many areas untouched by the heavy hand of the state. The reforms of 1991 removed any remaining barriers against private enterprise. The result is that 'not only is entrepreneurship thriving in India, entrepreneurs there have become folk heroes'. Several credible international surveys today rank Indian firms over Chinese ones in leadership and performance. The authors conclude that the two countries have followed very different strategies for development, and while India's performance overall is not better than China's, it has outperformed China in some key areas. If these successes enable India to match and even overtake China, then it will be a testimony to the value of indigenous entrepreneurship in long-term economic development, as well as a demonstration of the limits of China's FDI-dependent approach.

One economic paradigm is beyond doubt: the Indian people have political freedom to pursue what they enjoy and do best, while the Chinese do not. This difference could be significant in the long run. Sustained rewards can only be reaped when a nation's policies are appropriate to its culture. 'Homegrown entrepreneurship' is why the threat of cheap Chinese goods swamping the Indian market has not materialized. On the contrary, and much to the surprise of many analysts, Indian exports to China have boomed, growing by almost four times to over $2 billion since 1999. Moreover, macro-economic indicators should not be the only things of interest to a foreign investor. The appurtenances of democracy—a free media, an independent judiciary, the rule of law, the sanctity of property rights—are essential to a conducive corporate environment. None of these work in an entirely unblemished way in India, but each of them unquestionably exists, and is taken for granted by most Indians. Amartya Sen rightly points out that growth is helped by the friendliness of the economic climate rather than the fierceness of the political regime.[6] That is perhaps why FDI flows into India have been steadily growing. In 2001 they surged by 66 per cent, and in 2002 by an even greater margin. Some observers feel that the shortfall with

China may be exaggerated because of differences in calculation methods; India excludes reinvested foreign investor profits and the returns of foreign equity listings from its calculations, while China does not. Beyond statistics, foreign 'investors seem to be quite happily garnering profits in India'.[7] The *Global Competitiveness Report* of 2003 lists India several places above China in the business competitiveness index. And in *Forbes* magazine's list of 200 success-ful companies outside the United States with annual sales of over $ 1 billion, Indian firms have almost doubled their presence in two years, from 10 in 2001 to 18 in 2003. Khanna and Huang's prediction, that in the future Indians could benefit *both* from FDI and indigenous entrepreneurship, thus seems not unrealistic.

India's Achilles heel is the greater poverty and poorer human development of its people. The insensitivity of Indians to the deprivation around them is to a great extent responsible for this. Indeed, so great was the number of the absolutely poor in 1947 that they could have brought the system down and taken it towards a militant socialism. A violent revolution did not occur in India because the working of democracy kept the possibility of hope above the waterline of despair. Not enough was done for the weakest and the poorest, but just enough was done continuously to prevent them from losing hope. The calculus of democratic power prevented those at the lowest rung from being forgotten; yet the indifference to their condition ensured that they were more neglected than they should have been. Oscillating between such poles, Indians, as always, muddled through. The promise of distributing land to the landless was never vigorously implemented. However, as Dipankar Gupta points out, 'it is quite pointless (now) to talk of land reforms . . . The fact is that demographic expansion has taken care of larger landholdings . . . Owner cultivators are now dominating the country-side . . . in rural India today, there is hardly any noticeable instance of unrest led by the landless.'[8] Hunger was at unacceptable levels for too many Indians for too long. But the country has a significant food surplus today,[9] and while its distribution leaves much to be desired, estimates suggest that not more than 3 per cent of the total population suffers from hunger. Thanks to the acoustics of democracy, where people have ways of being heard in spite of the flawed hearing of those in power, there have been no famines in independent India, while China, notwithstanding its higher agricultural productivity, cannot claim the same.

More people in India have been rescued from absolute poverty in the last fifty years than the entire population of Europe. The job could have been done better; over 200 million people are still very poor. Significantly, however, poverty levels fell most dramatically—by 10 per cent—in the decade since the economy was liberalized in the 1990s, further proof that in India only an expansion of the economic pie, and not state-sponsored policies seeking to redistribute wealth, ultimately benefit the poor. Democracy has been slow to eradicate poverty, but it has given the poor a stake in the system in spite of the callousness—and opposition—of the privileged.

For decades now India has implemented one of the world's most developed systems of affirmative action. The Constitution of the country provides that almost a quarter (22.5 per cent) of government jobs must be reserved for those at the lowest rung of the social ladder—the Scheduled Castes and Scheduled Tribes—who also constitute the largest number of the poorest. In 1965 the percentage of Scheduled Castes and Tribes in the higher echelons of government services was 4.5 per cent; by 1995 it had risen to 22.8 per cent. The national Parliament and state legislatures also have seats reserved for Scheduled Castes and Tribes. In the Lower House of Parliament, 106 out of 544 seats are reserved, but representation is even higher because—and this is the significant point—many members of these groups now win elections from unreserved constituencies.

In August 1990 Prime Minister V.P. Singh, heading a shaky coalition government, sought to strengthen his political base by announcing that 27 per cent of all Central government jobs would be reserved additionally for the 'Other Backward Castes' (OBCs)—intermediate castes with a mostly rural background. The new reservations were denounced by the upper castes and huge demonstrations greeted the announcement. A great deal of sectarian jockeying is a feature of the process of social empowerment in India. Everybody resents what the other is getting and nobody is entirely happy. The Dalits felt that the OBCs were undeservedly eating into their quota, and even that quota was being hijacked by a 'creamy layer' within their own group. The OBCs felt that what they got was too little too late, and that the Scheduled Castes and Tribes had been the sole beneficiaries for too long. The upper castes felt that the entire policy of reservations was wrong. But in this melee of group interests, there is no doubt that there has occurred an enduring shift of real power towards the weaker sections of society. To give one example: in 1997, 621 candidates qualified for coveted civil service appointments. One-third of these had their schooling in villages or small towns; 450 came from families whose monthly income was less than $100 a month; 114 candidates had illiterate mothers; and 87 were the sons of farmers.

Transformations of this nature consolidate themselves with every generation. A first-generation partially-educated villager, who manages to get a job at the lowest rung of the government because of the policy of reservations, begins to dream big for his children. He educates them better and wants them to be employed far above his level. A finely developed sense of self-interest impels him to cling to opportunity when it comes and build on it in every possible way. I suspect this is the case with Indian women too, who are the most deprived among the poor. In a male-dominated society where feudal values have subordinated women for centuries and kept them uneducated and dependent, a 1993 law gives them a 33.3 per cent reservation in *panchayats* (elected village councils) across the country. In Japan, women occupy only about 6 per cent of seats in local bodies; even in Australia and New Zealand—to cite other examples from the Asia-Pacific region—the proportion is lower than one-third. Of course, merely because of the reservations the condition of Indian women is not better than in these countries, but the law is a classic example of how, in the working of Indian democracy, a populist measure intended for short-term political gain can initiate transformational change far beyond the intent of its planners. Women elected to the panchayats for the first time were reluctant stooges fronting for men; those who won in the next elections were less so; and the ones who win in future will want to wield power themselves. This is the way power devolves in democratic India—slowly, excruciatingly slowly, but surely and definitively. 'I won the first election simply because I was a woman', says 47-year-old Geeta Rathore, the *sarpanch* (council head) of Jamunia Tank village in Sehore district of Madhya Pradesh. 'But I won the second election in 1999 because I proved to be a good sarpanch.' Her opponent, Amar Singh, who lost the second election in an open contest, is a powerful landlord of the village. Rathore says with genuine pride that her most significant achievement is that 'every girl child in the village now goes to school and every woman has become a member of self-help groups, with her own separate bank account and income.'[10]

Change is afoot in India, not always visible or dramatic, but sufficient to keep its many marginalized peripheries engaged. Another periphery, not marginalized and quite remote from the silent gender revolution unfolding in the villages of India, is that of Indians living abroad. The Indian diaspora numbers around twenty million. It is scattered all over the world, with major concentrations in the Gulf, the United States, Britain, and Canada. The community is largely (and newly) prosperous, very image conscious, and impatient for India to change faster. Migration from India followed three broad patterns: the first wave left in the nineteenth century as impoverished labour to work in the plantations of British, French, and Dutch colonies. This was followed by a post-Second World War emigration of educated and semi-skilled Indians to the West. Finally, with the oil boom of the 1970s, unskilled and semi-skilled workers flooded the Gulf and West Asian countries. Non-Resident Indians (NRIs) were until recently derisively called 'Non-Required Indians'; a vague sense of guilt clung to them for having deserted their country; the motherland had little use for them; and they, in turn, were embarrassed by her poverty and backwardness. Culture was the umbilical cord that held the two together; but in every other way they were on independent journeys, burrowing along tunnels of their own in the elusive search for prosperity. Today, in the light that both sense at the end of the tunnel, they are rediscovering each other.

Indians have prospered abroad. Their net wealth is estimated to be around $300 billion. People of Indian origin living in the USA—close to two million at the last count—have emerged as that country's richest immigrant community, with nearly 200,000 millionaires. Thirty per cent of the doctors in the United States are of Indian origin. Next to Mexico, India in 2001 became the second biggest source of legal immigration to America; it is today the single largest source of foreign students—66,000 entered in 2002, a 50 per cent increase over the previous year. Of the 1.7 million Indians that constitute the United Kingdom's single largest ethnic minority, one million are considered 'high status' migrants. Individual prosperity has coincided with the feeling that India is—at last—turning the corner. Nothing unites Indians more than success, just as nothing brings out their natural fractiousness more than failure. The motherland and her far-flung progeny are rediscovering each other. The government has instituted an annual event in New Delhi in their honour at which high achievers are awarded by the prime minister. No longer do migrants have to be defensive about where they came from; no longer do they have to cite past greatness and ancient cultures; now they can speak of their roots in terms of present achievements and future possibilities. They appreciate the profile of India as a 'technical' power, be it in IT, automobiles, or pharma-ceuticals. The image of an India with a begging bowl was humiliating. On the contrary, when they hear that India is actually pre-paying some of its debts, has loaned $300 million to the IMF, and is *exporting* food, they are willing to open their wallets in support. Indians working abroad sent $10 billion home in 2001, the highest remittance figures in the world. In 2003, software profes-sionals in the USA contributed to the highest remittance figures in a decade. Divided loyalties are no longer the issue, common destinies are.

Unlike immigrant communities from some other countries, Indians do not blend in easily in Western cultures; they learn the new rules quickly, but unlearn their cultural particularities with great difficulty. Many foreigners don't fully realize how much India continues to be a part of Indians. Indians are good at conveying the impression that they are well integrated in their new settings. But non-resident Indians are often well-adjusted split personalities: English or American in their work environment, irrepressibly Indian in the privacy of their homes. Indians who have lived abroad for generations will continue to consider India 'home'; a desire to ultimately return to their 'roots' is a pervasive sentiment. Many

Indians abroad can speak only English, but perform religious rituals at home that have long been forgotten even in India. Acutely image conscious, they reject their country of origin when it embarrasses them, but love it demonstratively when it does them proud. Perceptions about 'home' are selective, blanking out the unsavoury and over-projecting the positive. A new phenomenon, in stark contrast to the docility and reticence of an earlier generation, is a greater aggressiveness in protesting any slur on the 'motherland'. When Congresswoman Cynthia McKinney referred to the possibility of the balkanization of India while campaigning for the Congressional primaries in Georgia in August 2002, Indians organized to support her opponent, a local judge, Denise Majette. Volunteers worked full time for Majette's campaign; fundraisers were held; she was invited as the chief guest for an Indo-American beauty pageant; an Indian motel owner 'turned his electronic billboard next to the main highway into her campaign sign'.[11] Majette won. When in July 2002 President George W. Bush failed to mention Hinduism among the religions practised in the US, Indians erupted in indignation across America, forcing press secretary Ari Fleischer to clarify that the President had equal regard for people of all faiths, and that he always included Hindus at faith-based meetings. When the *Toronto Star* (4 October 2003) published an offending image of the goddess Durga, Indians across Canada protested loudly enough for the paper to apologize, and India Cause, an organization representing Indians in North America, accepted the apology only reluctantly. Also visible is a greater readiness to stand up for individual rights. Many Indians in Britain speak privately about instances of racial discrimination; in June 2002, Manchester doctor Rajendra Chaudhary won the largest payout for alleged discrimination yet paid by the British Medical Association.

Chiranjeev Kathuria was eight months old when his parents emigrated to the USA. Today, the 38-year-old Sikh is a billionaire, planning to become the first Indian-American to enter the Senate on a Republican ticket from Illinois. Another Indian-American, 32-year-old Rhodes scholar Piyush 'Bobby' Jindal, was born six months after his parents emigrated to America in 1971. In November 2003, in elections in the southern state of Louisiana, he almost became the

country's first Indian-American governor, losing narrowly to his
veteran Democrat opponent in a race that could have swung either
way. Indian-Americans are proud of these developments. Much of
Jindal's political funding came from Indians in Louisiana and the
larger Indian-American community. Having prospered materially,
Indians hanker for status and recognition. Already, they are on the
donor lists of major British and American charities. All political
parties woo them for funds. Over a hundred Senators and
Congressmen on Capitol Hill are part of the India Caucus. All the
three major political parties in Britain have 'Friends of India'
groups. Eleven people of Indian origin sit in the House of Lords, and
four are elected members of Parliament. How Indians vote can
'swing' electoral fortunes in several British constituencies. Hindus in
Britain have recently launched an initiative called Operation Hindu
Vote to get more Hindus to vote in British elections. British Sikhs
have made a similar move through the Sikh Federation. Both these
organizations have the avowed aim of acting as pressure groups,
supporting only those candidates and political parties which best
represent their interests. Of course, the ability of Indians to organize
will always be subject to their tendency to factionalism. The new
aggression is often informed by a narrow religious chauvinism,
which divides the community even as it spurs its mobilization.
Typically, factions proliferate, and egos jostle for individual
recognition. There is the danger too that the new assertiveness could
create a conservative backlash in the indigenous community. But
Indians can be expected to be on the right side of the power balance.
For instance, throughout his campaign, Jindal took care to ascribe
his success to 'American values'. He converted to Christianity while
still a student, and won the support of powerful conservative lobbies
for his strongly anti-abortion views. Not surprisingly, although
Jindal lost the gubernatorial election, he is now the only Indian-
American in the US Congress, a seat he won with a huge majority in
November 2004.

Paradoxically, even as Indians merge more self-confidently into
other countries, they have assumed a far greater influence in the
country of their origin. They believe that India is moving closer to her
rightful place in the world, and want to be a visible part of the

journey. Forming the vanguard of the unfolding revolution of expectations, they want India to have the malls they shop in, the highways they travel, the clean water they drink, the airports they are used to, and the condos and suburban homes they live in. Post-economic reforms, India is receptive to such ideas, especially from people who can pay for them. Moreover, such ambitions have the unreserved approval of the influential middle class, which covets the affluence and lifestyle flaunted by well-to-do NRIs. Almost every-body in this class has a friend or relative abroad, and a great many travel abroad for tourism or work. This congruence of aspirations, between upwardly mobile Indians and upbeat non-resident Indians, is already a potent driving force. It will influence the vision Indians have for the future, and mould the priorities of the government. Inevitably, and not inaccurately, critics will label the vision as elitist, but this is the only model which can succeed in India.

Whether in India or abroad, Indians have one quality which has stood them in good stead: resilience. The quality is a product of centuries of experience in handling adversity. No foreigner can ever understand the extent to which an Indian is mentally prepared to accept the unacceptable. More than half of Mumbai lives in slums—one of which is the largest in Asia—in conditions which are far from civilized. Those who live here may often be overtaken by anger but rarely by self-pity. They flock to cinema halls, plan a future for their children, celebrate festivals with joy, eat savoury *pao-bhaji* and protest eviction orders spiritedly. Families living in one-room holes in overcrowded *chawls* (low-cost homes) do not think they are terribly deprived. 'These are not sad homes. These are not sad lives. There is love, laughter, hope, fixed deposits and stunning space management: many homes here pack in a washing machine, 165-litre fridge, tele-vision, music system, god, his consort and even a wall-attached dining table.'[12] In Chennai some taps produce water only on alternate days in summer.

People protest, but their threshold for tolerating 'inconvenience' is high; life must go on, and, how long, after all, can summer last? In Delhi, an uninterrupted supply of power is a luxury, reserved only for the very privileged. But people consider themselves fortunate on the nights there is only a short power cut. The next morning they wake up, ignore the garbage around them (the city generates 600,000 tonnes of filth every day, much of which is not removed), and get on with their lives. New Delhi is short of drinking water by 150 million gallons a day; 3 million of its residents live in slums; another 3.5 million live in 'unauthorized' colonies; about half of its industrial units are located in areas where they should not officially be. But the city continues to grow and prosper regardless. Seventy-five per cent of its households own a TV; 50 per cent of the people operate a bank account; and there are more cars and scooters on its streets than in all the other metros put together. For the vast majority of Indians life is a daily challenge. Even for a middle class family, very little can be taken for granted: schooling, water, electricity, medical care, higher education, housing—everything is a struggle. And yet, the miracle is that everybody seems to be getting by and, in fact, planning for more, as if nothing is wrong. Those with a fan think of buying a 'cooler'; those with a cycle dream of a scooter; those with a small car hope for a bigger one; those who have done less well live to make their children do better. In this unending cycle of rising expectations, adversity is taken in stride. The tribulations of today are tolerated for the rewards of tomorrow. The remarkable thing is the retention of hope in circumstances that should normally nurture despair. Even the destitute have an energy that refuses to accept defeat. I do not mean to attempt to romanticize poverty. The deprivations of India, and the social callousness which ignores them, are condemnable. But the Indian is the ultimate stoic. He is so prepared for the worst that when things are just bad he considers himself lucky. For so long has he been used to surviving in less than ideal circumstances that an inventive fortitude has become a part of his personality. A springy hardiness lies coiled within him. Nothing fazes him easily. The obstacles of the world are par for the course. And he deals with them with an insouciance and stoicism that is best summed up in a scrawl I once saw written on the back of a three-wheeler in Delhi. The words of wisdom, remarkable for their brevity, simply said: '*Hota hai*: It happens.'

In an interview in 2001, Gunter Grass, the German writer and Nobel laureate, said that for a European like him it was a shock to see the conditions in which people live in the slums of India's big cities. 'But then I came to admire their stubborn, or almost exemplary will to survive, work and live', he confessed. 'For generations, these people have been living in slums but it has not broken their spirit.'[13] Indeed, the real Indian rope trick is the persistence of hope in the most hopeless of circumstances. Sudhir Kakar once ascribed it to a mind that is able to transmute 'even the slightest ray of hope into a blaze of light'. The other factor is that a great many Indians have no option but to follow Nietzsche's advice and build their homes on the slopes of Mount Vesuvius. The very imminence and continuity of danger has taught them the art of survival, the much remarked upon resilience that ensures India's 'survival in spite of everything'.[14] Perhaps it is this refusal to go under, this sheer will to survive seen in a myriad amazing ways everyday, that led Robert D. Blackwill, the former US Ambassador to India, to simply say (in a farewell speech in 2003): 'Indians have great DNA.'

In the surviving, struggling, seething mass of people that constitutes India, what has changed and what has not merges and coalesces into a kaleidoscope full of the most vibrant colours and the most persistent shadows. As the images move around in an unceasing swirl of noise and dust and colour and energy, some of them stand out, as pointers to the complexity of change in India. In July 2002, in Raipur, the capital of Chhattisgarh in the heart of India, a Dalit girl threw her slipper in anger at a judge who acquitted her alleged rapist;[15] in the same month a hundred Dalit students, whose parents were forbidden to even *hear* a Sanskrit *shloka*, graduated as *priests* from the newly set up Uttar Pradesh Sanskrit Sansthan.[16] In the burning summer of 2001, dozens of debt-trapped marginal farmers in Punjab and Andhra Pradesh committed suicide; in the same year as six million farmers became credit card holders—over 20 million farmers now use credit cards to finance their agricultural operations. In Pune, a tour company, Travel Designers, specializes in agro-tourism—its clients are thousands of farmers who travel to Israel and Europe to observe new agricultural techniques. Less than a hundred kilometres out of Delhi, in the prosperous village of Tigri, residents have no idea of what the Union Budget is, and confuse Prime Minister Manmohan Singh with film director Manmohan Desai;[17] but, also on the outskirts of the capital, is the ultra-modern plant of

Moser Baer, the third largest producer of optical media products in the world. Millions of Indians are only now discovering toothpaste in a tube; but an Indian firm, Essel Propack, has become the world's largest producer of laminated tubes, supplying 'all of P&G's laminated tube requirements in the US, and 40 per cent of Unilever's.'[18] In Bihar, hundreds of government servants have not even received their salaries for months; but when the daughter of the chief minister was to be married, Hichhan Bigha, the village to which the groom belonged, was given 24-hour electricity supply, telephone connectivity, a new road and a renovated school in less than thirty days.

Indian television programmes show no kissing; censors still frown on the meeting of lips in films; and educated women employees giggle in embarrassment when asked about an automatic condom-dispensing machine—the first of its type to be installed in 2001 in a government office in New Delhi. But in Gujarat, during the festive season of the Navratras, when youngsters sway to the folk rhythms of the *garba*, chemists report a huge increase in the sale of condoms and contraceptives, and abortion clinics double their business. For months Gujarat was only associated with images of the horrific religious violence of 2002; but in 2003 another image broke out from the gloom of prejudice and anger—that of Muslims dancing the *garba* with Hindus in Ahmedabad, and refraining from cooking meat during the days of fasting in deference to their vegetarian neighbours. In a fertility clinic in Mumbai, women undergoing treatment with only a 30 to 35 per cent chance of success, still insist on a gender test if they conceive, and opt for abortion if the foetus is female. In Haryana, a state where the ratio of women to men is dismal, female foeticide is still surreptitiously advertised by slogans which announce: 'Spend Rs 1,000 today: Save Rs 100,000 [in dowry] tomorrow!' But more girls are going to school now, and those who pass out don't want to end their education—they want an employment-oriented diploma, preferably in computers. The practice of dowry is far from being eradicated; but when in May 2003 Delhi engineering student Nisha Sharma telephoned the police to complain that her husband-to-be was demanding dowry, she became an overnight celebrity. Her story made headlines in the newspapers and on television; politicians thronged her home; the former vice-president's wife came personally to convey her appreciation; a cartoon strip called *Brave Girl* was launched; and more than 1.7 million people logged on to BBC News Online in the space of 48 hours to register their support.

Indians are not an easy people to catalogue. In the welter of contradictions that define them, I have tried to highlight the traits that will most significantly influence their destiny in the twenty-first century. Public policy can only be successful if it is congruent with the behavioural patterns of a people. Policy planners need to keep this in mind, especially in India, where a great deal of planning has for too long been based on cherished but unproductive hypocrisies. As the legatees of a centuries-old system of hierarchy, Indians have a special weakness for status; power is coveted for the status it guarantees; the state is the highest repository of both status and power; and politics is the highest-yielding path to the resources of the state. For a great many people, therefore, the business of politics will remain irresistible. The bad and the ugly among them will not respond to moral exhortation since, in any case, as we have seen, to most Indians the ends are more important than the means. There is no alternative therefore to stringent and sustained electoral reform, which will enforce a system of punitive action against the corrupt and the unethical. Simultaneously, the powers and reach of the Election Commission must be strengthened. Indians respect those who exercise power effectively. They will obey laws that are implemented with firmness. When the hierarchy of power is coherent, and the chain of command clear-cut, they are amenable to discipline, and that is often why they do well abroad. Even if democracy has, improbably enough, become a way of life, the process of democracy needs to be consciously improved, for it is utopian to believe that Indians will reform themselves in this respect on their own. Moreover, since Indians do not believe in the principle of equality however much they speak of its merits, only the effective working of democracy can ensure a more rapid empowerment of the deprived against the elitist biases of the powerful.

Second, the government needs to do all it can to encourage private enterprise. Indians are born entrepreneurs. They will respond to an environment which is conducive to this talent. Public policy needs to close the perennial debate on equity versus growth. State intervention in favour of the poor is needed in India, but realism requires us to distinguish between the desirable and the feasible. Indians suspect altruism, lack concern for the deprived, and work best in their personal interests. Any attempt to curb or restrict economic activity in response to notions of equity will lead to unimplemented plans and subverted schemes. The government's efforts to redistribute the economic pie have inevitably fallen far short of targets. The only economic model that can work in India is a percolation of benefits consequent to an increase in the size of the pie. Since the poor are far too many, the pie needs to grow faster. The last ten years have seen India emerge as the fastest-growing economy among major democracies, with growth averaging over 5 per cent and touching 7 per cent in as many as four years. A growth rate of 8 per cent or more is feasible provided the process of economic reform is sustained and business is left to entrepreneurs. Obviously, the government needs to be engaged with issues of poverty alleviation, basic education, and primary health, but it would improve its ability to do so through a partnership with the corporate sector. Some corporate leaders realize that they must be more involved in such matters in their own self-interest, but they are in a minority. Unless the government devises a comprehensive scheme of *financial* incentives for the corporate sector to invest in these key sectors, the much-needed synergy between government and business in human resource development will remain over-discussed but under-subscribed.

Third, the menace of corruption must be handled by new policy initiatives. The moral relativism of Indians allows them to practise and condone corruption on a scale that has few parallels in other societies with pretensions to be called modern. Laws to handle the malaise work poorly, or not at all. Punitive provisions will find loopholes. Those assigned to keep a check will be checkmated or bought over. Convictions will be scandalously infrequent. The answer is not to waste more time on laws that are well meaning but ineffectual. India requires a different kind of remedy. Firstly, the government must drastically reduce its discretionary powers. To some extent this is already happening, but more needs to be done. Secondly, incorruptible technology must replace corruptible human beings much more rapidly. Even as IT is creating jobs and increasing revenue, it needs to be consciously harnessed to devise systems that eliminate or greatly reduce human intervention in the conduct of everyday life and the daily needs of individuals. An entire range of activities—the booking of rail tickets, allotments, payment of bills, tax calculations, the issuing of licenses, admissions to educational institutions—which normally incubate corruption, can be made transparent through the intervention of technology. The government must concentrate on enabling the Internet and computer technology to supersede human venality, and empower the ordinary person to access and monitor the availability of basic services directly. This will not be an easy task for a country the size of India. Innovation and ingenuity will be required, which the government should reward. For instance, it has been reported that an Indian team is developing the Simputer, a cheaper variation of the PC. The Simputer can run for eight hours on three small batteries, can convert text to speech in five languages, and even boasts a touch screen usable by those who cannot read or write.[19] The use of technology to tackle the scourge of corruption must become a national goal.

Fourth, India must capitalize on the talent of its people in the knowledge industries. It is projected that until the year 2050 India will enjoy the advantage of a 'demographic dividend': the population of much of the developed world will be ageing rapidly, with a consequent shortage of young and skilled manpower, while 'India, on the other hand, will have the highest number of people in the younger age group—700 million people out of 1.1 billion people are young'.[20] Of utmost importance is the need to spread computer literacy among the broader public. China may be behind India in software exports, but it has a PC concentration of 21.6 per thousand against India's 5.7. Again, while China's per capita spending on IT is $8.90, India's is roughly one-third at $2.40[21]. There is, therefore, no room for complacency. Indians need to move up the value chain. They need to become software innovators, not remain software coolies. The government needs to devise incentives to encourage the private sector to invest more in software research and development. One way of doing this is to attract Indians who have done well abroad and create the right environment for them to set up facilities in India. The fast-track development of the physical infrastructure for this industry should also become a national priority.

Fifth, India must deal with its problem of over-population with greater determination and aggression. Coercion cannot be the answer in a democracy, but given the pragmatic nature of the Indian people, there is no reason for a system of incentives and disincentives not to work. For too long policy makers have been mesmerized into passivity by the unfortunate experience of Sanjay Gandhi's coercive methods during the Emergency. Ideally, of course, the spread of education and improved health services should be the best way for people to make informed choices about the size of their families. But if India wants to be a global power, as its people clearly want, it may have to hurry the pace through other means that are persuasive but not undemocratic. Indians respond remarkably to self-interest. They react quickly to incentives. They understand what is good for them. It is necessary for the message of family planning to be purveyed more aggressively, through the fullest and most creative use of the electronic media in particular. Some politicians may be squeamish about mentioning condoms and pills on television, but it is unlikely that the population at large will object to something they know is in their interest. The articulate middle class will certainly welcome an invigorated programme; most of its members are convinced that the unwashed poor are multiplying at an alarming rate and will soon swamp them; not surprisingly, many of them were the most ardent supporters of Sanjay Gandhi's methods. In any case, a great deal has changed since 1977. Today, more Indians than ever before sense the possibility of change and, thanks to the spread of the media, are not unprepared to internalize and act upon a message that urges them to limit their family in order to increase their well-being.

India is the world's largest democracy. It is a nuclear power. Soon it is bound to join the even more exclusive club of manned flights into space. A report by Goldman Sachs in October 2003 projects that by the year 2050 India will be the third largest economy in the world, after the United States and China. Undoubtedly it will be the second largest market in the world. At present rates of growth, the burgeoning market in the country 'would be adding nearly one France every 3.5 years and one Australia every year'.[22] The twenty-first century should see the dream of every Indian—500 million of whom are not yet 35—to see their country as a major world power come true. But a potential global power must understand what makes its people tick. This book will have served its purpose if it contributes to that end.

NOTES

Chapter 1: Introduction

1. Mark Twain, *More Tramps Abroad*, London: Chatto & Windus, 1897, the revised British edition of *Following the Equator: A Journey Around the World*.
2. F. Max Müller, *India: What Can It Teach Us?*, New Delhi: Penguin Books India, 2000, p. 58.
3. 'It was India's good fortune to be a British colony', The man who once called India a functioning anarchy, John Kenneth Galbraith, in conversation with Arun Venugopal, *Outlook*, 20 August 2001, p. 46.
4. Francis Fukuyama, *Trust: The Social Virtues and the Creation of Prosperity*, New York: Free Press, 1995, pp. 33-34.
5. Ibid., p. 13.
6. Ibid., p. 26.
7. Samuel P. Huntington, *The Clash of Civilizations and the Remaking of World Order*, New York: Simon & Schuster, 1996, p. 22.
8. Ibid., p. 29
9. Henry Kissinger, *Diplomacy*, New York: Touchstone, 1995, pp. 23-24.
10. Clifford Geertz, *The Interpretation of Cultures: Selected Essays*, New York: Basic Books, 1973.

Chapter 2: Power

1. Sudhir Kakar, *The Indian Psyche: The Inner World; Shamans, Mystics and Doctors; Tales of Love, Sex and Danger*, New Delhi: Oxford University Press, 1996, p. 138.
2. Pratap Bhanu Mehta, 'How to fight corruption', *Indian Express*, 19 August 2002.
3. Kakar, *The Indian Psyche*, (see note 1 above), p. 119.
4. A.K. Ramanujan, *The Collected Essays of A.K. Ramanujan*, general editor, Vinay Dharwadker, New Delhi: Oxford University Press, 1999, pp. 46-47.
5. Pavan K. Varma, *Krishna: The Playful Divine*, New Delhi: Viking/Penguin, 1993, p. 163.
6. Ibid., p. 168.
7. Richard Lannoy, *The Speaking Tree: A Study of Indian Culture and Society*, New Delhi: Oxford University Press, 1971, p. 294.
8. Prof. F.H. Bailey, cited in Lannoy, *The Speaking Tree*, (see note 7 above), p. 294.
9. Nirad C. Chaudhuri, *The Autobiography of an Unknown Indian*, Delhi: Jaico Publishing House, 1976, sixth impression, p. 422.
10. M.N. Srinivas, *The Remembered Village*, New Delhi: Oxford University Press, 1988, fourth impression 1997, p. 266.
11. S.P. Singh, 'Badal Jr has a son, Akalis are over the moon', *Indian Express*, 6 November 2001.
12. Srinivas, *The Remembered Village*, (see note 10 above), pp. 281-83.
13. Ramanujan, *The Collected Essays*, (see note 4 above), p. 23.
14. See Kautilya, *The Arthashastra*, edited, rearranged, translated and introduced by L.N. Rangarajan, New Delhi: Penguin Books India, 1992.
15. Prakash N. Desai, 'Personality Politics: A Psychoanalytic Perspective', in *Crisis and Change in Contemporary India*, edited by Upendra Baxi and Bhikhu Parekh, New Delhi: Sage Publications in association with The Book Review Literary Trust, New Delhi, 1995, p. 253.
16. Kakar, *The Indian Psyche*, (see note 1 above), p. 128.

17. Dom Moraes, *Indira Gandhi*, Boston: Little Brown, 1980, p. 226.

18. R. Bhagwan Singh, '11 kill selves, 2 die of shock over Jaya ruling', *Asian Age*, 25 September 2001.

19. Desai, 'Personality Politics', (see note 15 above), p. 256.

20. Sankarshan Thakur, 'Farewell to Scindia with one eye to the camera', *Indian Express*, 4 October 2001.

21. Stephen P. Cohen, *India: Emerging Power*, New Delhi: Oxford University Press, 2001, p. 28.

22. Dipankar Gupta, *Mistaken Modernity: India Between Worlds*, New Delhi: HarperCollins India, 2000, p. 115.

23. Ibid., p. 118.

24. Paul R. Brass, *The Politics of India Since Independence*, Cambridge: Cambridge University Press, 1994, p. 14.

25. Vandita Mishra, 'The Sukh Ram Katha', *Indian Express*, 17 July 2002.

26. Vir Sanghvi, 'The Politicians We Deserve', *Sunday Hindustan Times*, 21 July 2002.

27. Ibid.

28. Pranab Bardhan, *The Political Economy of Development in India*, New Delhi: Oxford University Press, 1989, fourth impression 1994, p. 78.

29. 'Laddoos of Maya', *Times of India*, 16 January 2003.

30. Bardhan, *The Political Economy of Development in India*, (see note 28 above), p. 77.

31. Cohen, *India: Emerging Power*, (see note 21 above), p. 3.

32. Kanwal Sibal, 'Understanding India', *Indian Horizons*, vol. 48, no. 4, 2001 and vol. 49, no. 1, 2002 (combined issue), pp. 1-6, New Delhi: Indian Council for Cultural Relations.

Chapter 3: Wealth

1. A.K. Ramanujan, *The Collected Essays of A.K. Ramanujan*, general editor, Vinay Dharwadker, New Delhi: Oxford University Press, 1999, p. 46.

2. Nirad C. Chaudhuri, *Hinduism: A Religion to Live By*, New Delhi: Oxford University Press, 1979, p. 244.

3. M.N. Srinivas, *The Remembered Village*, New Delhi: Oxford University Press, 1988, fourth impression 1997, pp. 320-21.

4. Vatsyayana, *The Kamasutra*, edited by Mulk Raj Anand, Lance Dane, New Delhi: Published by Sanskrit Prathishthan for Arnold Heineman; Atlantic Highlands, NJ; Humanities Press, 1982, p. 69.

5. Kautilya, *The Arthashastra*, edited, rearranged, translated and introduced by L.N. Rangarajan, New Delhi: Penguin Books India, 1992, p. 145.

6. J. Duncan M. Derett, 'Social and Political Thought and Institutions', in *A Cultural History of India*, edited by A.L. Basham, New Delhi: Oxford University Press, 1997, second impression 1998, p. 139.

7. Kautilya, *The Arthashastra*, (see note 5 above), p. 149.

8. H.J.J. Winter, 'Science', in *A Cultural History of India*, edited by A.L. Basham, (see note 6 above), p. 142.

9. A.L. Basham, *The Wonder that was India: A Survey of the Culture of the Indian Sub-continent before the Coming of the Muslims*, New Delhi: Fontana Books in association with Rupa & Co., 1971, p. 223.

10. Ibid., pp. 217-18.

11. Aditya Mukherjee, Bipan Chandra, K.N. Panikkar, Mridula Mukherjee, Sucheta Mahajan, *India's Struggle for Independence*, New Delhi: Penguin Books India, 1989, p. 384.

12. Quoted in Ahsan Jan Qaisar, *The Indian Response to European Technology and Culture (AD 1498-1707)*, New Delhi: Oxford University Press, 1982, p. 17.

13. Hiralal Dave, 'No bullocks, get hitched to Santi', *Indian Express*, 9 June 2003.

14. Chandan Mitra, 'We are like this only', *Pioneer*, 9 June 2002.

15. For more information on the Marwaris, see Gurcharan Das, *India Unbound*, New Delhi: Penguin Books India, 2000, pp. 191-204.

16. V.S. Naipaul, *India: A Million Mutinies Now*, New Delhi: Rupa & Co. in association with William Heinemann, London, 1990, pp. 343-44.

17. Richard Lannoy, *The Speaking Tree: A Study of Indian Culture*

and Society, New Delhi: Oxford University Press, 1971, p. 395.

18. Ashok Celly, *Times of India*, 26 May 1996.
19. *Outlook*, 28 August 1996.
20. Quoted in *India Today*, 15 February 1996.
21. Krishna Kumar, 'Between Two Dolls', *Times of India*, 3 August 1996.
22. Dan Bilefsky, 'Indians unseat Antwerp's Jews as the biggest diamond traders', *Indian Express*, 27 May 2003.
23. Chaudhuri, *Hinduism*, (see note 2 above), p. 202.
24. A.M. Rosenthal, 'The Future in Retrospect: Mother India Thirty Years After', *Foreign Affairs*, vol. 35, no. 4, July 1957, p. 623.
25. Ashis Nandy, *The Intimate Enemy: Loss and Recovery of Self under Colonialism*, New Delhi: Oxford University Press, 1983, p. 81.
26. James Cameron, *News Chronicle*, 1957.

Chapter 4: Technology

1. Bibhutibhusan Dutta, 'Vedic Mathematics', in *The Cultural Heritage of India*, Vol. IV, edited by Priyaranjan Ray and S.N. Sen, Ramakrishna Mission, Institute of Culture, Kolkata, 2000, p. 31.
2. A.L. Basham, *The Wonder that was India: A Survey of the Culture of the Indian Sub-continent before the Coming of the Muslims*, New Delhi: Fontana Books in association with Rupa & Co., 1971, p. 498.
3. J. Fryer, quoted in Ahsan Jan Qaisar, *The Indian Response to European Technology and Culture AD 1498-1707*, New Delhi: Oxford University Press, 1998, p. 10.
4. H.J.J. Winter, 'Science', in *A Cultural History of India*, edited by A.L. Basham, New Delhi: Oxford University Press, 1997, second impression 1998, p. 154.
5. P.V. Indiresan, 'Technology: Surmounting Cultural Hurdles', in *Independent India: The First Fifty Years*, edited by Hiranmay Karlekar, New Delhi: Oxford University Press, 1998, p. 204.
6. Richard Lannoy, *The Speaking Tree: A Study of Indian Culture and Society*, New Delhi: Oxford University Press, 1971, p. 420.

7. For the full report, access wandahl@dk-online.dk
8. Andrè Bèteille, 'Secularization of Work', *Telegraph*, 6 April 2003.
9. Amarnath Tewary, 'Song of the Loom', *Outlook*, 22 July 2002, p. 66.
10. V.S. Naipaul, *An Area of Darkness*, Harmondsworth: Penguin, 1968, p. 213.
11. M.K. Gandhi, *Constructive Programme: Its meaning and place*, Ahmedabad: Navajivan Press, 1944, p.16.
12. Jawaharlal Nehru, *An Autobiography*, New Delhi: Oxford University Press, 1980, p. 446.
13. Jawaharlal Nehru, *The Discovery of India*, London: Meridian Books, 1956, pp. 413-14.
14. Krishna Kumar, *Learning from Conflict (Tracts for the Times)*, New Delhi: Sangam Books, 1996.
15. Rashmee Z. Ahmed, 'India becomes call centre superpower', *Times of India*, 8 August 2002.
16. Sudhir Kakar, *The Indian Psyche: The Inner World; Shamans, Mystics and Doctors; Tales of Love, Sex and Danger*, New Delhi: Oxford University Press, 1996, p. 38.
17. Gunnar Myrdal, *Asian Drama: An Inquiry into the Poverty of Nations*, Vol. III, London: Pelican Books, 1968, pp. 1645-46.
18. Anirudh Deshpande, *Pioneer*, 24 January 1996.
19. See Gautam Bhatia, *Punjabi Baroque and Other Memories of Architecture*, New Delhi: Penguin Books India, 1994.
20. P.V. Indiresan, quoted in Rakesh Kalshian, 'The Devil's Laboratory', *Outlook*, 23 October 2000, p. 64.
21. Sundar Sarukkai, 'The Deity in the Engine', *Outlook*, 14 July 2003.
22. 'Vastu, evil spirit and a power plant', Times News Network, *Times of India*, 19 June 2002.
23. Sagarika Ghose, 'All too quiet on the front', *Hindustan Times*, 15 August 2002.
24. Dipankar Gupta, *Mistaken Modernity: India Between Worlds*, New Delhi: HarperCollins Publishers, India, 2000, p. 11.
25. A.K. Ramanujan, *The Collected Essays of A.K. Ramanujan*, general editor, Vinay Dharwadker, New Delhi: Oxford

University Press, 1999, p. 50.

26. Soutik Biswas, 'Seeds of E-Volution', *Outlook*, 9 April 2001.

27. M.S. Swaminathan, 'Reaching the Unreached', *Times of India*, 6 September 2002.

28. Sunil Handa, 'Entrepreneurship: The Indian Mindset', in *Independent India*, edited by Hiranmay Karlekar, (see note 5 above), p. 215.

Chapter 5: Pan-Indianness

1. Neera Chandoke, 'Holding the Nation Together', *IIC Quarterly*, volume title *India: A National Culture?*, vol. 29, nos. 3-4, Winter 2002-Spring 2003, p. 93.

2. Jawaharlal Nehru, *An Autobiography*, New Delhi: Oxford University Press, 1980, p. 24.

3. Sheila Dhar, 'Music: From the traditional to the modern', *Independent India: The First Fifty Years*, edited by Hiranmay Karlekar, New Delhi: Oxford University Press, 1998, p. 387.

4. 'The educated have lost touch with their local almanac', Jnanpith award-winning Kannada writer U.R. Ananthamurthy in conversation with B.R. Srikanth, *Outlook*, 20 August 2001, p. 102.

5. Sunil Khilnani, 'Many Wrinkles in History', *Outlook*, 20 August 2001, p. 52.

6. M.V. Kamath, on indiainfo.com, 21 July 2000.

7. Sarbjit Singh, *Tribune*, 16 February 2001.

8. Leroy S. Rouner, 'Civil Loyalty and the New India', in *Crisis and Change in Contemporary India*, edited by Upendra Baxi and Bhikhu Parekh, New Delhi: Sage Publications in association with The Book Review Literary Trust, New Delhi, 1995, p. 183.

9. Amit Bhattacharya, 'Vows of Death', *Pioneer*, 8 April 2001.

10. Vijay Pushkarna, 'Courting Death', *Week*, 9 September 2001, p. 46

11. Amir Khan, 'He couldn't give a gift', *Indian Express*, 24 November 2001.

12. Ashok Das, 'Aids victim stoned to death in Andhra Pradesh', *Hindustan Times*, 11 July 2003.

13. Guy Trebay, 'Pink Elephants', *New York Times*, 10 March 2002.
14. Quoted by F. Max Müller, *India: What Can it Teach Us?*, New Delhi: Penguin Books India, 2000, p. 51.
15. Ibid., p. 56.
16. Octavio Paz, *In Light of India*, translated from the Spanish by Eliot Weinberger, New York: Harcourt Brace, 1997, p. 60.
17. Ashis Nandy, *The Intimate Enemy: Loss and Recovery of Self under Colonialism*, New Delhi: Oxford University Press, 1983, p. 111.
18. Stephen P. Cohen, *India: Emerging Power*, New Delhi: Oxford University Press, 2001, third impression, 2003, p. 8.
19. J.N. Dixit, *India and Pakistan in War and Peace*, New Delhi: Books Today, 2002, p. 30.
20. Shekhar Gupta, 'Our Macho do about nothing', *Indian Express*, 29 September 2001.
21. Sudhir Kakar, *The Indian Psyche: The Inner World; Shamans, Mystics and Doctors; Tales of Love, Sex and Danger*, New Delhi: Oxford University Press, 1996, p. 82.
22. Richard Lannoy, *The Speaking Tree: A Study of Indian Culture and Society*, New Delhi: Oxford University Press, 1971, p. 143.
23. Louis Fischer, *The Life of Mahatma Gandhi*, London: Jonathan Cape, 1951, p. 364.
24. A.M. Khusro, 'India: A Dialectic of Opposites', in *Independent India*, edited by Hiranmay Karlekar, (see note 3 above), p. 343.
25. Cohen, *India: Emerging Power*, (see note 18 above), p. 113.
26. From the Second Sir Dorab Tata Memorial Lecture on 'The Predicament of Identity' delivered by Amartya Sen in New Delhi on 26 February 2001.
27. Nandy, *The Intimate Enemy*, (see note 17 above), p. 111.
28. *Dawn*, 13 July 2003.
29. Muzamil Jameel, 'J&K now gets its healing touch', *Indian Express*, 19 August 2003.
30. Swati Chaturvedi, 'RSS membership falling', *Hindustan Times*, 21 April 2003.
31. Mukul Kesavan, *Secular Common Sense*, New Delhi: Penguin Books India, 2001, p. 19.

Chapter 6: Epilogue

1. 'Nehru was the worst disaster to ever hit India', The man who first broke the news of Gandhi's assassination, James W. Michaels, in conversation with Arun Venugopal, *Outlook*, 20 August 2001, p. 86.
2. Salman Rushdie, *Imaginary Homelands: Essays and Criticism, 1981-1991*, New Delhi: Penguin Books India in association with Granta, 1991, pp. 26-27.
3. Ibid., p. 32.
4. N.K. Singh, 'Four-fold Path to Nirvana', *Indian Express*, 14 November 2003.
5. Yasheng Huang and Tarun Khanna, 'Can India overtake China?', *Foreign Policy*, Issue 137, July-August 2003, pp. 74-81.
6. Amartya Sen speaking at a seminar on 'Development as Freedom: An Indian Perspective', organized by FICCI and the Shri Ram Centre for Industrial Relations and Human Resources, New Delhi, 30 July 2003.
7. A survey by FICCI in 2003 revealed that 62 per cent of the foreign investing companies were making profits, 9 per cent were breaking even, and 78 per cent were planning fresh investments.
8. Dipankar Gupta, *Mistaken Modernity: India Between Worlds*, New Delhi: HarperCollins India, 2000, p. 103.
9. Food grain production reached 182.7 million tonnes in 2002-03. Buffer stocks at 30 million tonnes are significantly above the target of 24 million tonnes. Agricultural exports now constitute 15 per cent of India's total exports.
10. Yogesh Vajpeyi, 'Woman on Top', *Express Magazine*, 24 June 2001.
11. Chidanand Rajghatta, 'Indian Americans help unseat US lawmaker', *Times of India*, 21 August 2002.
12. Manu Joseph, 'How Many Legs in a Square Foot?', *Outlook*, 18 August 2003, p. 58.
13. 'No gate can withstand the crush of the hungry', Gunter Grass, the 1999 Nobel laureate for literature, in conversation with

Subhoranjan Dasgupta, *Outlook*, 20 August 2001, p. 123.

14. Rushdie, *Imaginary Homelands*, (see note 2 above), p. 32.
15. 'Dalit girl hurls slipper at judge', *Hindustan Times*, 31 July 2002.
16. Amit Sharma, 'Dalit priests hit caste ceiling in Maya's UP', *Indian Express*, 10 July 2002, p. 1.
17. Lalita Panicker, 'Village India: 'Sinha Kaun? Budget Kya?'', *Times of India*, 28 February 2001.
18. Arun Shourie, 'When sky is the limit', *Indian Express*, 16 August 2003.
19. Clay Wescott, 'In Asia, the Web is Routing Power to the People', *International Herald Tribune*, 29 October 2003.
20. Singh, 'Four-fold Path to Nirvana', (see note 4 above).
21. Rajesh Kalra, 'Dragon goes Digital', *Times of India*, 5 September 2002.
22. Singh, 'Four-fold Path to Nirvana', (see note 4 above).

COPYRIGHT ACKNOWLEDGEMENTS

Grateful acknowledgement is made to the following for permission to reprint copyright material:

Oxford University Press India, New Delhi. Extracts from the following books reproduced by permission of Oxford University Press, New Delhi:

Jawaharlal Nehru, *An Autobiography*, 1980; *Independent India: The First Fifty Years*, edited by Hiranmay Karlekar, 1998; Ashis Nandy, *The Intimate Enemy: Loss and Recovery of Self under Colonialism*, 1983; Ahsan Jan Qaisar, *The Indian Response to European Technology and Culture (AD 1498-1707)*, 1982; Sudhir Kakar, *The Indian Psyche: The Inner World; Shamans, Mystics and Doctors; Tales of Love, Sex and Danger*, 1996; A.K. Ramanujan, *The Collected Essays of A.K. Ramanujan*, general editor, Vinay Dharwadker, 1999; Richard Lannoy, *The Speaking Tree: A Study of Indian Culture and Society*, 1971; M.N. Srinivas, *The Remembered Village*, 1997; Stephen P. Cohen, *India: Emerging Power*, 2003; Pranab Bardhan, *The Political Economy of Development in India*, 1994; Nirad C. Chaudhuri, *Hinduism: A Religion to Live By*, 1979; *A Cultural History of India*, edited by A.L. Basham, 1998.

Cambridge University Press, Cambridge for the quote from Paul R. Brass, *The Politics of India Since Independence*, 1994.

Jaico Publishing House, Delhi, for the quote from Nirad C. Chaudhuri, *The Autobiography of an Unknown Indian*, 1976.

Rupa & Co., New Delhi for extracts from A.L. Basham, *The Wonder that was India: A Survey of the Culture of the Indian Sub-continent before the Coming of the Muslims*, in association with Fontana Books, 1971.

Penguin Books India, New Delhi for extracts from F. Max Müller, *India: What Can it Teach Us?*, 2000; Salman Rushdie, *Imaginary Homelands: Essays and Criticism, 1981-1991*, 1991; Mukul Kesavan, *Secular Common Sense*, 2001; Gautam Bhatia, *Punjabi Baroque and Other Memories of Architecture*, 1994; Kautilya, *The Arthashastra*, edited, rearranged, translated and introduced by L.N. Rangarajan, 1992; Aditya Mukherjee, Bipan Chandra, K.N. Panikkar, Mridula Mukherjee, Sucheta Mahajan, *India's Struggle for Independence*, 1989.

HarperCollins India, New Delhi, for extracts from Dipankar Gupta, *Mistaken Modernity: India Between Worlds*, 2000.

The late Dom Moraes, for the quotation from his book *Indira Gandhi*, Boston: Little Brown, 1980.

Sagarika Ghose, for the extract from her article 'All too quiet on the front', *Hindustan Times*, 15 August 2002.

J.N. Dixit, for the quotation from his book *India and Pakistan in War and Peace*, New Delhi: Books Today, 2002.

M.V. Kamath, for the quotation from his article on indiainfo.com, 21 July 2000.

Indian Council of Cultural Relations, New Delhi, for the quote from Kanwal Sibal, 'Understanding India', *Indian Horizons*, vol. 48, no. 4, 2001 and vol. 49, no. 1, 2002 (combined issue),pp. 1-6.

Foreign Affairs, for the quotation from A.M. Rosenthal, 'The Future in Retrospect: Mother India Thirty Years After', Reprinted by permission of *Foreign Affairs*, vol. 35, no. 4, 1957. Copyright 1957 by the Council on Foreign Relations, Inc., New York.

Foreign Policy, for quotations from Yasheng Huang and Tarun Khanna, 'Can India overtake China?', *Foreign Policy*, Issue 137, July-August 2003, Carnegie Endowment for International Peace, Washington DC.

Sage Publications India Pvt Ltd, New Delhi, for the quotes from Upendra Baxi and Bhikhu Parekh, (eds.), *Crisis and Change in Contemporary India*, 1995.

Professor Andrè Bèteille, for the extract from his article 'Secularization of Work', *Telegraph*, 6 April 2003.

Professor Krishna Kumar and Sangam Books, Delhi for the extract from *Learning from Conflict (Tracts for the Times)*, 1996.

Lady Moni Forman, for the quote from James Cameron.

India International Centre, New Delhi, for the quote from Neera Chandoke, 'Holding the Nation Together', *IIC Quarterly*, volume title *India: A National Culture?*, vol. 29, nos. 3-4, Winter 2002-Spring 2003.

Navajivan Press, Ahmedabad, for the quotes from M.K. Gandhi, *Constructive Programme: Its meaning and place*, 1944.

The Ramakrishna Mission Institute of Culture, Kolkata, for an extract from Bibhutibhusan Dutta, 'Vedic Mathematics', in *The Cultural Heritage of India*, Vol. IV, edited by Priyaranjan Ray and S.N. Sen, Ramakrishna Mission, Institute of Culture, Kolkata, 2000.

Gillon Aitken Associates, London, for use of material from V.S. Naipaul, *India: A Million Mutinies Now*, 1990 and V.S. Naipaul, *An Area of Darkness*, 1968.

Outlook, New Delhi

India Today, New Delhi

Indian Express, New Delhi

Times of India, New Delhi

Hindustan Times, New Delhi

Dawn, Karachi

INDEX